FILLING THE HOLE

FILLING THE HOLE

Sobriety and Success through Mental Science and Spiritual Law

Thorne Ivy

Filling the Hole
Sobriety and Success through Mental Science and Spiritual Law
By Thorne Ivy
ISBN-13: 9780692816875
ISBN-10: 0692816879
Library of Congress Control Number: 2016920429
Printed and bound in the United States of America
First Edition 2017

In personal life stories, the names of some characters, places, activities, and other details have been insignificantly modified to safeguard the confidentiality, privacy, and autonomy of those individuals or establishments.

www.thorneivy.com

Contents

Prologue · **xi**

Introduction · **xv**

Excuse Me, Filling What Hole? · xv

Addiction and Mental Science · · · · · · · · · · · · · · · · · · · xvii

After You Get Sober, Then What? · · · · · · · · · · · · · · · · · xviii

Finding the "New Thought" Doctrine · · · · · · · · · · · · · · · · ·xix

Don't Worry, I'm Not Preaching Religion · · · · · · · · · · · · · · xx

Knowledge is Power, but Faith is Key · · · · · · · · · · · · · · xxii

A Heads-Up about Some Freaky Topics · · · · · · · · · · · · · xxiii

How to Digest this Material ·xxiv

Will this Book be a Game-Changer or Dust Collector? · · · · · · xxv

The Bottom Line · xxvi

1   My Life Part 1 The Roller Coaster · · · · · · · · · · · · · · · · · **1**

I Was Born This Way · 1

The Anxiety Surprise · 3

TM and the Maharishi · 5

Good Times: College Daze · 6

The Alcoholic Mind Develops · 7

My First Mental Science Book · 9

Career Days, Anxieties Return · · · · · · · · · · · · · · · · · · · 12

Hitting Bottom, Quitting, and Succeeding…Only for a While · · 14

The Roller Coaster is Back in Service · · · · · · · · · · · · · · · · · · · 16

Enter "The Secret" Movie and New Thought Mental Science · · 18

Surviving Life on the Roller Coaster· 20

2   My Life Part 2 The Ride Finally Ends · · · · · · · · · · · **22**

The Perfect Storm · 22

My Daily Diet: A Case of Beer and a Fistful of Antidepressants · · · · 23

Rehab Alley: My Cell Phone Saves Me · · · · · · · · · · · · · · · · 25

Combining Meditation with Mental Science · · · · · · · · · · · · · · 26

The Transformation was Happening· 27

Why Not Share this Wisdom?· 28

3   Mind in the Atom· **31**

WTF? Did You Say Atoms?· 31

The Scale of the Atomic World · 33

The Ether or Empty Space· 33

Quantum Physics Proves Mind Exists in the Atom · · · · · · · · · · 36

Mind is in Everything · 38

The Atomic Mind Summary · 39

4   Mind in the Cosmos· **41**

The Ether or Empty Space...Again· 42

The Scale of the Universe · 45

The Big Dipper Does Not Really Exist· · · · · · · · · · · · · · · · · · 46

The Cosmos Summary· 47

5   Earth's Mysteries · **49**

Atomic Mind Amasses into Life Forms· · · · · · · · · · · · · · · · · · 49

Plants Can Think · 51

The Beetles Have Arrived!· 52

Mind is in All Forms· 53

Group Consciousness · 55

Have You Ever Had a "Contact-Buzz"? · · · · · · · · · · · · · · · · · 58

Earth's Mysteries Summary · 59

6   Vibration and the Law of Attraction · · · · · · · · · · · · · **60**

You are Constantly "Googling" Your Reality · · · · · · · · · · · · · · 60

Ancient Law · 61

Everything Vibrates, Including Your Thoughts · · · · · · · · · · · · 62
Your Signature Self-Image Frequency · · · · · · · · · · · · · · · · · · 64
How the Law of Attraction Works · 65
The Law is Both the Cause and the Cure of Addiction · · · · · · · 67
Law of Attraction Summary · 69

7   **Maya, Our Dual World** · **71**
The Duality in Nature · 72
Take Heed of the Emotional Pendulum · · · · · · · · · · · · · · · · · 73
Biorhythms and Astrology Prove Our Cycles · · · · · · · · · · · · · 75
Maya Summary · 76

8   **Spirit Messages** · **78**
Why I Believe · 78
I Agree, this is Weird Stuff · 80
Abraham, Bashar, and Seth · 83
Even Oprah Believes · 88
Dead Man Talking · 90
Yogi Spirits · 92
Spirit Messages Summary · 93

9   **Mind Talents** · **95**
If It's on the Television, It Must be True · · · · · · · · · · · · · · · · · 95
Extrasensory Perception (ESP) · 97
PSI Summary · 99

10 **Healing Science** · **100**
Psychosomatic Sickness: Mind Over Body · · · · · · · · · · · · · · 100
The Placebo Effect · 103
Jonesing for a Fix is Cured Just by Anticipation · · · · · · · · · · 106
Playing Mental PAC-MAN Cured her Cancer · · · · · · · · · · · · 107
Negative Vibrations Manifest as Disease and Addiction · · · · · · 108
Watch Out for "Health Warning" TV Commercials · · · · · · · · 110
Hypnosis: More Proof of Mind-Over-Body · · · · · · · · · · · · · · 112
Deep Hypnosis Discovery · 114
Epigenetics: Mind Over DNA · 115
Healing Science Summary · 116

11 **Emotions and the Heart** ·118
    The Heart: Much More than a Blood Pump · · · · · · · · · · · · · 118
    Emotions and the Law of Attraction · · · · · · · · · · · · · · 120
    "I won't drink today…" · 121
    The Heart's Secret Brain and Emanations · · · · · · · · · · · 122
    Metallica versus Mozart · 124
    Cravings and Urges · 126
    Prayer is Mental Science; Worry is Inverted Faith · · · · · · · · · · 128
    Emotions can be Dangerous Weapons · · · · · · · · · · · · · · 130
    The Heart Summary · 131

12 **Start with Desire** · **133**
    Desire and Love are Only Frequencies · · · · · · · · · · · · · · 134
    Why Do You Really Want to Get Sober? · · · · · · · · · · · · · 135
    Emotional Cross-Training · 139
    Desire Summary · 141

13 **Meditation-The Gateway** ·143
    The Door to the Subconscious · · · · · · · · · · · · · · · · · · 143
    How It's Done · 144
    Pavlov's Dog · 147
    Putting a Kicking and Screaming Baby Down for a Nap · · · · · · 148
    Summary: · 149

14 **Argumentum…Consciousness** · · · · · · · · · · · · · · · · · **150**
    Mental Science Wrap-up · 151
    Our Five Physical Senses · 154
    When a Tree Falls in a Forest · · · · · · · · · · · · · · · · · · 155
    Mindfulness: Are You Here and Now? · · · · · · · · · · · · · · 157
    The Concept of Time · 159
    Consciousness Summary · 161

15 **Theosophical Notes** · **162**
    Addicts are Actually Very Spiritual · · · · · · · · · · · · · · · 163
    Mental Science and Spiritual Law has Many Names · · · · · · · · 164
    Faith in the Unseen · 167

Finding Spirit in a Bottle of "Spirits" 167
Spiritual Epiphanies Can Cure Instantly. 170
Summary: We are Gods 171

16 Karma and Housecleaning **173**
Cause and Effect 173
Emotional Housekeeping 175
I Met Some Real Doozies in Rehab 177
Layers on the Onion 180
All Character Defects Stem from Fear 182
Karma Summary 185

17 Meditative Programming Technique **187**
The Theory Behind the Technique 187
Level-1: Relaxation-Meditation 191
Level 2: Gratitude and Love 192
Level 3: Acknowledgement-Faith 194
Level 4: Creation and Visualization 196
Level 4a: Negative Association— A Clockwork Orange 198
Level 4b: Positive Programming—Role playing 200
Level 5: Gratitude and Love 202
Level 6: Awaken and Receive 203
Meditative Programming Summary 204

18 Enforcing the Law **205**
Maintain Your New Self-Image Constantly 205
Get Out Your Blow-up Toys 207
Mentally Live in Your New House, Before You Even Move 208
What We resist, Will Persist 210

19 Addiction Theory and Issues **212**
Getting Wasted 212
Where's My "I Survived Alcoholism" T-shirt? 213
Addiction: The Mental-Spiritual Condition 215
Who was the First Alkie in My Family Tree? 217
Is AA a Medical Cure or a Spiritual Platform? 219

Detox is the Easy Part · 221
Watch Out for the Emotional Jack-in-the-Box · · · · · · · · · · · · · 224
Addiction Summary · 225
20 One for the Road · **227**
MYOB · 228
Breaking Up with Your Lover: Booze and Drugs · · · · · · · · · · · 230
Don't Dig Up Your Seed to See If It's Growing · · · · · · · · · · · 230
Your Feelings are Your Internal Compass · · · · · · · · · · · · · · · 232
Take Action Like Actor Jim Carrey · · · · · · · · · · · · · · · · · · · 233
Forget About the Past Slips · 234
Your Screwed-Up Pleasure Threshold · · · · · · · · · · · · · · · · · 235
Diamonds, Fish Tanks, and Catching a Buzz · · · · · · · · · · · · 236
If Addiction Enters the Room, Don't Fight It, Simply Leave · · · 237
Be Prepared to Receive Your Gifts · · · · · · · · · · · · · · · · · · 239
Get High on the Mountaintop · 241
Conclusion · 241

Recommended Websites · **245**
Bibliography · **247**
About the Author · **251**

Prologue

What if there were a program that could permanently cure your drug or alcohol addiction that didn't require any sponsors, doctors, rehab or therapy? Well, there is such a program, and its unique and powerful metaphysical approach is described in this book.

This book teaches the occult mental science and spiritual laws which cause transformation from within, reprogramming your mind for sobriety, and anything else you desire—health, wealth, love, or success. If you've been looking for that epiphany to rock your world and start a new life, look no further.

The same infallible mental laws and principles that created successful millionaires, professional athletes, great artists, and other extraordinary achievers have also proved to heal and cure sickness and disease. Our behaviors and addictions and subsequent diseases were developed in accordance with these laws, and we can cure them using the same.

Almost thirty years of my life were undermined by alcohol addiction and I tried everything to quit including cognitive therapy, medications, counseling, residential rehab programs, detox centers, and hundreds of AA meetings—with absolutely no long-lasting success.

It wasn't long ago that I hit rock bottom. A typical evening would find me finishing my twenty-fourth beer for the day, lying on the sofa watching ESPN, and getting ready to order a large meat-lover's pizza for delivery. I was fifty pounds' overweight, broke, unemployed, miserable, and obviously inebriated. Not only was I depressed, but deep inside manifested an emotional-spiritual *hole*. I was physically sick, mentally inert and spiritually dead, yet at the same time I was perversely content. I was having a destructive love affair with booze, and was committed and loyal.

Fast forward a few months later and I was a new person living a new reality. I was fifty pounds lighter, clean and sober, had a great career, and was excited about life again. Most amazingly, that empty hole inside was healed and filled. Now in my second year of sobriety, my health and success story just gets better and better each day.

What happened, you ask? After all, I tried to quit countless times before. What did I do differently this time? What I did, was learn the secret Law of Attraction and the mental-spiritual laws that govern all healing, transformation, and goal manifestation. These not only cured my addiction and desire to ever drink alcohol again, they taught me how to attain other goals in life too.

This book is *not* about religion; it's not about psychology; and it's not about going to therapy or support meetings every day. This book is about using powerful metaphysical secrets of mental science and spiritual laws that will abolish the condition we call addiction permanently. You will learn that recovery is a one-time milestone, and not a lifelong struggle. With mental science practices, you quit once, and move on to your next goal in life. You were not brought into this life to be a victim of addiction so that you could be in recovery your whole life. You are here to express life, grow, and achieve. Those who live a life "in-recovery", choose to hold-on and fight their addiction, rather than to simply overcome it.

This book is *not* a life story about me or my journey, but is a course study of the principles and practices of mental science and spiritual law. The knowledge that empowered me to triumph over addiction, fill the inner hole, and achieve success can do the same for you.

AUTHORS NOTE:

If you're like me, I tend to skip the introduction and jump right into the first chapter of a book. I ask that you don't make that mistake with this book. The introduction contains crucial tips on how to read the book, what to expect, and where the subject matter stems from. Mental science is very esoteric, and addiction is complex, so a proper introduction is necessary. It will greatly help you understand the book's framework and intentions, and make for a more effectual learning experience.

Introduction

"The passage of this book to those ready for the instruction will attract the attention of such as are prepared to receive the Teaching. And, likewise, when the pupil is ready to receive the truth, then will this little book come to him, or her. Such is The Law…in its aspect of The Law of Attraction, will bring lips and ear together—pupil and book in company."

—THE KYBALION 1912

EXCUSE ME, FILLING WHAT HOLE?

I titled this book *Filling the Hole* because it was a phrase I used to describe the times when I used alcohol to fill the void within me to feel normal. I later found that I was not alone in using this phrase. It was actually commonly used by many other addicts to describe the same feeling of emptiness, isolation, and fear which manifests inside ourselves as huge pits or *holes*. Many non-addicts also feel this same emptiness, or lack of meaningfulness, but find other ways than using drugs or booze to fill it.

A fundamental premise of mental science is the fact we are all considered to be vibrational energy beings and we radiate a specific non-physical frequency. Inner emotional conflicts, stresses, and traumas create negativity in our mental-emotional bodies and these reflect in our overall vibrational state. It is felt as a hole in our emotional-spiritual bodies which causes us pain. Drugs and booze efficiently anesthetize us from this discomfort and help seal or fill the hole.

Alcohol was my drug of choice to fill the hole. Others choose pills and needles, and some even abuse food, sex, television, money, or excessive exercise. In a vibrational-sense, we are all essentially buzz-addicts in one form or another. We seek stimulation to escape the mundane and feelings of pain or discomfort. Whether we like to admit it or not, most times we get our happiness by manipulating our neurochemicals—dopamine, serotonin, adrenalin, and endorphins. Sometimes even certain acts of kindness and love are performed purely for the reward of these pleasurable brain chemicals. Can you think of anything you choose to do that *does not* involve a neurochemical or vibrational boost? True acts of spiritual love are the only exception, otherwise you are simple getting a vibrational buzz through one of the senses.

Ingesting chemicals into the body to achieve a high or vibrational boost is easy to detect and control because you are ingesting a physical substance. Pick your poison—booze, drugs, caffeine, nicotine, sugar—there's a bunch of them, and we'll find just about anything (bath salts, huffing paint fumes, etc). However, it is the non-chemical highs that are the most mischievous, elusive, and powerful. These covert stimulants boost our energy or frequencies and include such things as sex, exercise, music, thrill sports, etc.—anything that gives us a natural high, and they can be just as addictive as chemicals.

There are also the more perverse ways of hacking our brains chemicals to get a vibrational high or boost. These include gambling, stealing, having affairs, cheating, committing crimes, watching porn, starting fights, and many other taboo, illegal, immoral, or unethical things. People who partake in these activities often experience similar neurochemical pleasure as someone having sex, eating candy, or smoking crack. The magnitude of the pleasurable effect varies from person to person, but on a metaphysical vibrational level is the same as drugs or alcohol.

Most of these frequency boosters do not pose a problem if done in moderation—hence the saying "variety is the spice of life." It's when we get lop-sided and abuse a single stimulus that we get in trouble. It doesn't matter if it's whiskey, crack, porn, or gambling—once we abuse it and use it as our primary avenue for stimulation (or for numbing emotional pain), we have the chance of getting addicted. When the addiction involves ingesting chemicals such as with alcohol and drugs, we are dealt a double-whammy of both the mental obsession and physical addiction.

Once we get addicted, it's not unlike a love affair, especially when our lover is drugs or booze. Our intimate chemical friends physically please us, emotionally comfort us, and spiritually fill us in ways nothing or no one else can. They shield us from our fears and pains and provide a safe haven to hide from others. They bring out a feeling of normalcy in us, and we feel happy for once. It's hard to break up from them, especially if we built our lives around them. We will protect and hide them from anyone who threatens to take them away.

ADDICTION AND MENTAL SCIENCE

As mentioned earlier, mental science states that everything is a form of vibrational energy. Humankind exists on several energy planes including the physical, emotional, mental, and metaphysical-spiritual vibrational bodies. Any underlying emotional issues and fears we harbor will manifest internally as a vibrational discord which is felt as inner pain. If we don't mitigate these pains in a healthy rational way, they will fester and grow, and we often find booze and drugs to anesthetize the discomfort. Sometimes, the originating source of pain is often forgotten as it gets buried deep inside.

I will give an example of buried forgotten pain using an analogy of a car with alignment problems. Let's say you placed a heavy load of tool boxes in the truck of your car a few months ago. You forgot completely about these ever being there. Over time, they had shifted the far side of the trunk, which has unbalanced the rear end of your car.

This unbalanced load causes a misalignment, resulting in a bald tire, which then results in you losing control and getting in a minor wreck. You fix the car, and replace the tire. The tire goes bald again, so keep replacing the tire and correcting the alignment repeatedly over and over until one day someone points out that the cause was this unbalanced load in the trunk. The forgotten tool boxes caused the misalignment, which caused the bald tire, which caused you to wreck. If the tool box load was removed or lessened by redistributing it, this problem would never had taken place. All along you were correcting the symptoms and not the problem, the outer effect, not the inner cause.

Similarly, drugs and alcohol are the *symptoms* and not the cause of addiction. The cause is usually an underlying negative mental-spiritual state we carry *in the trunk* of our minds. To effectively cure addiction at the core, we must fix the problem in the trunk--not at the surface—we must correct the *cause* of the vibrational misalignment.

When you learn the secrets of mental science and spiritual laws, you will be able to transmute your vibrational state from negative, sick, and addicted to positive, healthy, and free. You will change from the core outwardly, and your positive radiance will materialize not only in freedom from addiction, but also in achieving your goals of health, happiness, love, and success.

This is not a load of psychobabble jargon. It is based on mental-spiritual laws, such as the Law of Attraction, that have been proven to miraculously transform people physically, emotionally and spiritually. True lasting change can only take place at the core level by applying mental science principles.

Getting "fucked up" used to be the most important thing we did every day. It was our primary preoccupation because it made us feel normal, whole, and even a little bit happy, or at least pain-free for a while. However, we not only developed a physical addiction, but more so a mental obsession for the chemical *feeling* or *effect*. With mental science, our goal is to transform this desire for craving a numb, inert, foggy mind to one of mental clarity and serenity.

To repeat, we transform from the inside out—beginning with our psychic root vibration—because, by law, every external condition (including our bodily state), always manifests from the mind-spirit. Our outward appearances mirror our inner vibrational state. Mind is always the cause, and the physical condition is always the effect.

AFTER YOU GET SOBER, THEN WHAT?

Filling the emotional-spiritual hole is only half the solution to becoming whole again. The other half is getting back on track to achieving goals of love, happiness, and success. This book will show you how to do both. As stated earlier, getting sober and clean is a milestone, not a life style.

This is why I included the words "sobriety *and success*" in the subtitle, because these mental-science principles will not only be successful in getting you clean and sober, but will also help manifest any other goals or desires you have. These unfailing mind-spirit laws and principles are universal, as they will help you achieve goals in any endeavor, whether it is sobriety, health, wealth, athletics, relationships, career, the arts, and so on.

Take note that the term "success" is not reserved solely for achieving wealth and prosperity. For me, success was firstly my sobriety and health (as it should be for everyone), and then it was followed by restoring relationships, having a successful career, and bringing back hobbies and fun in my life. From where I had come from, believe me, achieving those simple goals was momentous. So, at least in my mind, these milestones were considered a great success. But now that I've reached these, I'm on to even bigger and better goals. That's the way it works, one step or level at a time. You follow your desires as they change and grow.

To some people, success may mean artistic and athletic accomplishments, educational or career goals, new or improved relationships, buying a new house, financial freedom, and so forth. Success is defined individually by each of us. My definition of a successful life may be called mediocre to others, while to some may be a super-achievement. So long as we are growing and moving forward, success is relative to where we started and a matter of our personal desires.

For the addict, sobriety should *not* be your ultimate goal in life, but it should be your *first* goal. To be clear, getting clean should be your *first* and *primary* goal, but not the definition of your life. Your goals, desires, and wishes should be ongoing and a never-ending outgrowth of life itself, with sobriety being your natural state. Addiction is a man-made disorder that took a lot of work to acquire, and it simply needs to be undone and corrected once and for all. Remember that your addiction was purely a temporary ill condition that you will soon correct and move past.

FINDING THE "NEW THOUGHT" DOCTRINE

My thirty years of alcohol addiction finally ended after a journey that involved an extensive study on mind-spirit-consciousness. I read hundreds of books and spent countless hours listening to audiobooks, watching videos, lectures, and interviews on consciousness, spirit, and mental science It took massive research and study to finally discover the secret to filling the emotional hole inside, getting sober, and manifesting my goals. This book is the result of years of study, meditation, and a mountain of research.

The majority of the material I've presented is based on the *New Thought* doctrine, which is over a century old. New Thought is a movement based on spiritual-mental-science that took place in the late nineteenth and early twentieth centuries. Some of its best-known writers and teachers included William Atkinson, Prentice Mulford, Charles Haanel, and Thomas Troward.

Mental science is not entirely new to the world of addiction. Nell Wing, who is an archivist of Alcoholics Anonymous (AA), reported that even early AA members and founders were strongly encouraged to study the works of New Thought author Thomas Troward regarding mental science and spiritual law. Although I could not find any New Thought doctrine directly in AA's formal principles or texts, there is still a strong underlying mental science formula at work in AA's program, which I attribute to its success.

DON'T WORRY, I'M NOT PREACHING RELIGION

During my studies, I suppose you could say I had a type of spiritual awakening or an epiphany of sorts. But it did not come suddenly or easily—it took some hard convincing and developed over time. I was extraordinarily stubborn and approached these mental science subjects with great skepticism and doubt. Although I was very anxious to uncover the mental-spiritual secrets and find the underlying truths, it would take many years and huge volumes of material for it to finally reveal itself.

I mention a spiritual awakening, but I don't want the word "spirit" to alarm readers of any specific creeds or religious beliefs. In mental science studies, the term "spirit" is often interchangeable with our higher "consciousness" or "mind." The mental science philosophy that I present here, has no religious affiliations. I do, however, quote the Bible in a few places, but only in reference to mental science allegories. These same parables can be found virtually all major religious texts but Christianity just happens to be the most popular.

The deities of Jesus, Allah, Buddha, Muhammad, Messiah and others are all followed by a variety of godheads that precipitated them. These include such names as Higher Power, the All, the Universal Mind, Mother Nature, the Source Energy, the Supreme Being, Infinite Intelligence, Cosmic Consciousness, Absolute Power, God, and so on. In this book, these names are all interchangeable, but for the sake of simplicity you may see the name "God" used more frequently. Again, do not take this as associating with any specific religion or creed. As New Thought scholar Ralph Trine wrote in 1897:

"This Spirit of Infinite Life and Power that is behind all is what I call God. I care not what term you may use, be it Kindly Light, Providence, the Over Soul, Omnipotence, or whatever term may be most convenient. I care not what the term may be as long as we are agreed in regard to the great central fact itself."

Any adept student of theology will easily find that the esoteric principles and laws of mind and spirit are a commonality of major religions and are embedded in most ancient doctrines. According to the Three Initiates, the anonymous authors who wrote *The Kybalion* in 1912:

"The Hermetic Teachings are to be found in all lands, among all religions, but never identified with any particular country, nor with any particular religious sect. This because of the warning of the ancient teachers against allowing the Secret Doctrine to become crystallized into a creed."

The laws of mind-spirit belong to no one religion but are universal to all of creation. No one dogma or creed can take credit for the supreme source or infinite intelligence.

These laws and principles are far-reaching in their applications, and are used in the healing of diseases and powers of mind over matter. Remember, these are mental science and spiritual *laws*, not theories, and you will see how they are universal in healing, creation, and the achievement of goals of any kind, including curing addiction.

KNOWLEDGE IS POWER, BUT FAITH IS KEY

I cannot emphasize enough how important faith and belief in these laws and principles are. My skepticism is what kept me from successfully using the principles many years ago. I was too bullheaded and unbelieving. I demanded more evidence, more scientific proof, more validity of the claims, and more compelling supporting documentation to believe in any of these mind-science allegations. This skeptical attitude is why my research took so long and was so extensive.

It is true that knowledge is power, but you only possess power when you galvanize the knowledge with the spirit of faith. This power in faith is a spiritual law. You must search until you find your own level of truth and understanding and then you will have true faith. It is written, *"For everyone who asks receives. He who seeks finds. To him who knocks it will be opened"* (Matthew 7:8 WEB).

Speaking on faith, New Thought teacher Thomas Hudson wrote the following in 1893:

> *"This brings us to the discussion of the essential mental condition prerequisite to the success of every experiment in psycho-therapeutics, — faith. That faith is the essential prerequisite to the successful exercise of psychic power is a proposition which has received the sanction of the concurrent experience of all the ages."*

To change your body, your conditions, and your reality, you must first change your inner emotional body and metaphysical vibrational state. You do this by applying mental science and having rock-solid faith in these laws and principles. Remember faith stems from belief. In 1912, Dr. William Sadler wrote:

> *"Faith calls for a complete and unconditional surrender of one's whole body, soul, and spirit to the idea or thing which is **believed** in...Belief only requires the cooperation of intellectual powers..."*

As they say at the poker tables in Las Vegas, going "all-in" is having true faith.

A HEADS-UP ABOUT SOME FREAKY TOPICS

There are several chapters that may at first seem irrelevant (and a little weird). Their purpose is to provide a broader perspective of the mind-spirit or unseen world. You will need to learn a fundamental knowledge-base for the foundation of faith. Keep in mind that I am simply presenting the material that worked for me, and I've organized it so that you can study it in the same sequence that I did.

For example, there are chapters on atoms, the cosmos, ESP, and psychic phenomena. These subjects may have a small part to play in your ultimate mental science practice to get sober, but the underlying mental science framework and fundamentals will be important in order to develop proper faith. Keep this in mind when you are reading about protons, planets, and the paranormal—they *do* have a place in the big picture.

Knowledge of these subjects, on the fringes of mental science, are intended to expand consciousness and reinforce the existence in the nonphysical realm. The reality of the mind-spirit truths is only as real as your capacity to understand them, which is conditional on your perception and range of consciousness. By considering these peripheral subjects, you will expand your consciousness, and be open to the realities of mind powers.

For some of you, these topics may cross the border into the paranormal realm and cause skepticism. I therefore want to remind those of you familiar with a man named Jesus and his *paranormal* life. The Scriptures clearly contain many accounts of miracles, mental magic, and the presence of spiritual beings that were very commonplace in the Christ era. The instant healing of blindness and disease, walking on water, resurrections, turning water to wine, and angelic visions were all very commonplace and not considered weird or black magic to anyone then or now.

Today, however, when someone bends a spoon with mental powers, reads someone's mind with ESP, or psychically communicates with a spirit, everyone thinks he or she belongs in a freak show or circus act. We are simply displaying the modern applications of the same principles and practices that were used in ancient times.

HOW TO DIGEST THIS MATERIAL

For the aforementioned reasons, it is important to read this material experientially and empirically, and not just intellectually. Certain concepts require a base-level understanding to truly know them so you can proceed to the next higher level. To read experientially is to experience the meaning of the words and concepts in your mind and not just to read them intellectually or logically. I encourage you to stop reading, and meditate and contemplate new concepts whenever you feel the need. It is the difference between walking in someone else's shoes versus judging him or her at face value. Remember that you can only conceive and understand what you are ready to.

Another reason to digest the book carefully is that there are many concepts and terms that are probably new to you. The lingo of the mind-spirit world takes a little getting used to. But this is a *science* of the mind, not a cult or religion. We are not dealing with witchcraft, sorcery, or fairy tales—we are working with proven mental-spiritual laws that existed before the dawn of time. Again, remember that this is just a different branch of science—*nonphysical* science.

Although my study of the mind-spirit realm was extensive and took a long time, it eventually led me to the knowledge I could place all my faith in. This process was not nearly as linear and formatted as these chapters are written. I jumped around from one subject to another depending on where my spiritual query led me. You may end up doing the same thing. Or, after you read them, go back to reread and rearrange the information in your mind, or even stop and do some additional research on some of the topics.

**NOTE **If you are in an urgent rush and need to get the gist of this books, you will find the crux of the book's message is in the Chapters: "6-Vibration and Law of Attraction", and "17-Meditative Programming Technique." But please return to read the balance of the book…remember knowledge is power, and to utilize this knowledge, you must have <u>absolute faith</u>, which requires a thorough understanding of this entire doctrine of mental science.

WILL THIS BOOK BE A GAME-CHANGER OR DUST COLLECTOR?

Only you know where your head is and what you mentally are prepared to accept. Only you know your inner motivations and desires of getting sober and clean, or for achieving any goals.

Will this book become a game-changer in your life? Will it blow your mind and give you a grand illumination that will stimulate true lasting change? Or will it end up on the fireplace mantle collecting dust? Or maybe in the trash can by an empty vodka or prescription bottle?

If you gave me this book when I was a twenty years old, I would have told you to "fuck-off with this freaky mind stuff." If you showed it to me at twenty-five, I'd probably be somewhat amazed…and ten years later, I'd kiss you and thank you. Each of you will have your own level of acceptance or receptivity to this book. I'm sure an eighteen-year-old hooked on roxies has a different perspective than an eighty-year-old chronic alcoholic. Like I mentioned earlier, it took me a long roller coaster ride with many attempts to quit before this material could be received much less understood. I hope it hits home with each of you the first time.

For these reasons, I am intentionally redundant on certain concepts. So, I'm Sorry if I sound like a broken record sometimes, but I am trying to reinforce certain core principles while appealing to readers coming from varying mindsets. There are many layers of knowledge and, as you read this material, new meanings will reveal themselves as you spiritually develop and your consciousness expands. Knowingly or not, as you read, you will be absorbing the underlying truths and formatting a new paradigm that will be the springboard to your sobriety and success.

Again, if you get hung up on a topic that just makes no sense or doesn't fit in, then move on. For example, the first chapters on atoms and the cosmos contain a lot of stock knowledge and nerdy facts that may not make much sense or seem very applicable to quitting drugs or drinking. Just read on to get the gist of it, take what you want and leave what you don't. You may want to go back to that topic later when you figure out where it fits in. The underlying message of the program is intertwined throughout in many peripheral subjects, so you will find the golden thread in many different places.

THE BOTTOM LINE

This book's purpose is twofold—firstly, to fill the inner empty hole with knowledge of the truth of mind-spirit and, secondly, to learn mental science principles and how to apply them for getting sober and achieving goals.

Please keep in mind that my writings are based on my personal life experiences, my extensive study, and my success in using these laws and principles. I'm not a doctor, scientist, or engineer and I have no formal training in these fields. Mention of any research or testing results is purely my personal interpretation, as my studies included comparing vast sources of contrasting views, reports, and data. I attempted to recollect and relay the facts as accurately as possible, but by no means is the purpose of this book to make or recite any scientific or medical claims. Unless it's in quotations, it's my opinion or construal.

The absolute bottom line is that this is a book about what worked for me, and hopefully what will also work for you. Remember that when it comes to mental science, these are not opinions or theories, these are metaphysical *laws* that have been proven to work throughout history. Without your knowledge of them, these laws have already worked with exact precision to put you in the current state you are in right now, as you have created your own reality whether you like it or not.

This transformation process is not over for me, nor will it ever be. Although I have conquered my addiction to alcohol and achieved a milestone of success, I certainly have not perfected all of the philosophies and practices contained in this book, nor achieved all the goals I desire. I am the epitome of one who needs to "practice what you preach", as I continue with studying, meditating, and improving with these principles each and every day. I will use this book just like you, as a guide to achieving goals of health, sobriety, love and success.

What used to be a confusing puzzle is now an enlightening journey. My hope is that it will be exciting and illuminating for you as well. Keep an open and positive mind and enjoy!

1

My Life Part 1 The Roller Coaster

*"The father and mother give the germs of physical life and the
materials of which the physical body is composed. If these are
drink-poisoned, the child comes into the world with the drink
tendency physically implanted in the body that the parents have
given it."*

—ANNIE BESANT 1898

Okay, you're probably thinking, *"I really don't give a rat's ass about this
author's life. Just get to the part where it tells me how to quit!"*

Well, I get that, and I promise, this book will teach you things you
never read or heard about before and change your life for good. First,
though, I figured I owed a short story on my drinking addiction and the
path that lead me to discovering the mental science and spiritual laws to
cure it. I did my best to remove a lot of the personal bullcrap. So, what's left
is a brief history So here it goes.

I WAS BORN THIS WAY

For starters, I suppose I didn't quite get a fair shake at life since I was born
with two strikes against me: I was a male and a third-generation "alkie."
My dad, his dad, and my uncle were all alcoholics. So, according to medical
science, I inherited the drinking curse, too.

I was born in the early 1960s in suburban New York about an hour outside of Manhattan. I was the only boy with three sisters. We lived in a nice, middle-class community of young, working-class families with plenty of Baby Boom kids to play with. For the most part, other than my Dad's drinking, I would say that I had a pretty normal and fun childhood.

As the son of an alcoholic and otherwise great dad, it was very confusing to be both proud and embarrassed by him. On one hand, he was my hero—I idolized him as the smart, athletic, successful engineer he was. But then I'd watch as he drank himself to sleep most nights. Many nights he would preach to me about winning in sports, as his speech slowly began to slur and he'd start to repeat himself. He was a loving dad and I loved him back, which made it that much more conflicting.

When you have an alcoholic parent, the dysfunction gets ingrained at a young age and it just becomes normal for you. You get used to the fact you can't bring friends around the house because of the fear of being ashamed and embarrassed. You get used to the parental fights at midnight. You get used to conflicting feelings and the fact some things just never make sense. Children of alcoholics develop many more habits than we think or care to remember. Especially in my close father-son relationship, I'm sure I was a sponge for absorbing alcoholic habits.

Back in those days there were no outlets for this problem; you just toughed it out and played the cards you were dealt. There was no Dr. Phil or Oprah to shine a light on the subject—these were the tough old days when football players didn't complain about concussions, when fighting was the way you solved disputes in schoolyards, and when men were "real men." I suppose these were also the days when kids like me just had to learn to grow up with emotional baggage. Maybe that's why over 40 million people in the U.S. alone suffer from depression or struggle with drug and alcohol abuse and addiction.

Don't get me wrong. I was generally a happy kid and loved my dad and family—it was probably just a little more dysfunctional than I knew at the time. And who am I to complain as there are many worse traumatic situations than having an alcoholic parent. There were the kids that were beaten, bullied, physically, sexually or emotionally abused, and, of course, those born with mental or physical handicaps. So, I certainly am not *complaining*—I am simply *explaining*.

I suppose most of us have our inner demons or inner pains, it's just a matter of how or if you end up resolving them that counts. Sometimes screwed-up life-events shed right off our back, like water off a duck, and other times they bury deep within us and fester and grow into a dark hole. Who knows why some of us are more vulnerable to emotional injury than others.

As a youth, I played just about every sport, but eventually excelled in running. At eight years old, I joined a local track club and competed in AAU meets up until high school. I did very well and held several state age-group records. By my early teens, I was an accomplished middle-distance runner and was winning regional races.

My paternal granddad had also been a runner and was very excited that I also excelled at track. Back in his day, he had been his college track team's captain and school-record holder. My dad also was a college jock, so needless to say, as the only son and an athlete, I got a lot of attention from them both. You can only imagine the mental pressures I went through when my Dad would drink and get on the bandwagon about winning races, over and over.

THE ANXIETY SURPRISE

One of the first ailments I dealt with was anxiety attacks. This began when I was a young teen and it only happened at track meets. These weren't just everyday pre-race jitters either. During several races, my anxiety was so bad that during the run, I had to literally stop or slow down to catch my breath. It felt as if my lungs were being compressed and I couldn't breathe, while my heart raced and my mind fogged. I don't know if this stemmed from the mental pressure to win, or was a biological cause, but only knew it was scary.

This anxiety ended up being a long-term condition, but, fortunately, it would subside and even disappeared for periods of time. Anyone who suffers from anxiety attacks can tell you how these episodes arrive suddenly without warning, and are so traumatic that they actually instill a phobia in you. You constantly carry around a subconscious fear that the anxiety will return and strike anytime. It sounds crazy, but you soon develop an anxiety about having anxieties. In retrospect, it is now clear that I was having what is now medically termed "panic attacks." However, back in those days, no one used that term or knew much about them. So, you were diagnosed as being hyper-nervous or having heart flutters and just had to rough it out.

The anxieties did eventually subside and soon I started kicking ass in track. I was training twice a day, with morning strength training plus afternoon distance running. Now, as a young teenager, I already had set state high school records and qualified for several AAU national meets.

The reason that I even mentioned anxieties and panic attacks is they are often linked to depression, which is commonly related to alcohol abuse and addiction. It's a cause and effect condition that goes both ways. We either start drinking or taking pills as a result of excessive nervousness or anxiety/depression, or, on the other hand, we get anxiety/depression because we abuse alcohol or drugs. Booze and drugs can cause nervous system disorders that can cause panic attacks. In either case, a vicious cycle will ensue in which one will precipitate the other, which calls back to the former, and then repeats itself. Before you know it, your body builds a tolerance and you're a full-blown addict.

So, what came first, the chicken or the egg? Is it drug-induced anxiety or anxiety induced addiction? Do nervous people tend to drink? Or do people drink because they are born innately nervous? Personally, I developed anxieties before my first drink, so I can eliminate booze as the cause for my anxiety (at least at first). Was it genetic depression and anxiety that caused me to eventually find alcohol so soothing and medicinal? Or did my inherited alcoholism display itself as nervousness and depression? Who knows? Maybe my dad and granddad weren't even "alcoholics" at all, but solely suffered from anxiety and depression instead. Maybe that's why they drank in the first place—bad nerves were the cause and alcohol was only the solution to relieve it. Maybe if they had developed Xanax and Prozac fifty years earlier, no one in my family would have had drinking problems. I guess I'll never know those answers.

I had my first taste of alcohol as a fifteen-year-old and got flat-out drunk on grain alcohol shots mixed with many beers. It was at a post track-meet party at the Kansas City Nationals Track Championships. I tried to party like the college boys did, but only remember that I drank until I was drunk, and then sick. I wouldn't touch it again for many months.

For the remainder of high school, my drinking was fairly low-key. My track buddies and I would drink some on weekends, but usually only during the track off-season. I was a dedicated student-athlete at the time.

TM AND THE MAHARISHI

Other than participating in sports, one of the most important things I did in my youth was during my junior year when I took a course in Transcendental Meditation (TM). I remember my dad endorsing it because several star professional athletes were practicing TM and claimed how it made them perform better, get more focus and concentration, be more relaxed, and so on. The Beatles also made TM very popular at that time when they included TM founder Maharishi Yogi in their culture and media events. Yogi even made the cover of *Time* magazine and TM was very mainstream at the time.

The TM training course was held for four evenings over a two-week period for a group of eight of us. After several nights of education on meditation and Eastern philosophy, we were finally given our personal mantra—a unique and custom-made "sound" based on our individual personality and character. The teacher whispered my mantra to me privately, and I was told to never speak the "word" or sound out loud again. "Aum" is a familiar mantra most people have heard of, meaning "God" in Eastern yogi sects. Mine sounded like something you read on a Chinese menu.

TM is to be practiced at least once and preferably twice a day for roughly twenty minutes each session. I did it as often as my schedule allowed, sometimes daily, sometimes twice a day, and sometimes not at all. I did actually enjoy it and found it very relaxing, but it would be later in life that I learned to use it instrumentally when combined with mental science.

GOOD TIMES: COLLEGE DAZE

During my senior high school year, I was recruited and offered running scholarships by several large colleges. I decided on a large state school because of its excellent track team, but equally attractive was its party school reputation.

My prime purpose at school was running, followed in order by partying, girls, and academics. I trained very hard my first year, but my race times did not improve greatly from high school. I attributed this partly to my large frame. During the past year, I had gone through a growth spurt and had grown over an inch, plus added on almost twenty pounds. This made me a large middle-distance runner at over six feet tall and about 180 pounds. It seemed that most of the fastest guys were, on average, almost thirty pounds lighter than me, which only meant that I needed to train that much harder to be competitive.

When I wasn't running, attending classes, or doing my minimal studies, you could usually find me drinking with my friends. I had a bunch of good party buddies on the track team and we hung out like a wolf pack; we trained together and drank together. We naturally gravitated toward one another with our commonalities in athletics and partying. There were so many episodes of drunken debauchery, fights, foolish acts, and general craziness that it could fill another book. We were like the cast in the movie *Animal House*, but this one for jocks, and I was the one playing John Belushi. I was getting pretty well-established as a heavy-weight partier, a wild one.

I enjoyed drinking and learned quickly how booze was a great personality-enhancing tool. It numbed my social anxiety and gave me a warm feeling of being whole. I felt complete, funny, witty, and social. It gave me that invincibility, those whiskey muscles. Even at this early stage in drinking, it seemed that I drank differently than others. Getting a buzz was good enough for most people to feel good, relaxed, and have fun. But for me, I liked to drink until I was drunk. I was never satisfied with just a light buzz. I admit it—I liked to get fucked up.

THE ALCOHOLIC MIND DEVELOPS

When I drank, all of those little insecurities that were buried in me (intro-version, anxieties, and shyness) seemed to go away or they were at least blurred out of my awareness. I didn't know it at the time, but I already had developed a *hole* inside me, a combination of emotional flaws and irrational thinking built up from my childhood.

You don't realize that you have (flaws) this hole in you until it actually goes away and you finally feel free and normal—and what a great feeling that was. You wish you could feel this way all the time, relaxed and com-fortable in your own skin. If it wasn't for the negative side effects, I'd prefer to stay semi-drunk most of the time. It was more liberating and free.

Getting drunk a lot of your time is like taking a time-out from real life, except that the clock of life continues to tick while you're away. While the time continues to run, you stay behind in your personal inner growth. Any emotional issue you deliberately avoided with booze, not only remains unresolved, but usually gets worse. The issues and problems you protected by avoiding them, fester and grow and continue to create a bigger hole inside. If and when you ever wake up from the alcoholic fog, it can be pretty startling how big the hole really got—so startling, in fact, it usually keeps you drinking. But why would you want to dig up emotional issues and uncomfortable feelings when you can catch a buzz and feel normal and happy instead? For me, it was a no-brainer, let that damn hole inside grow…I found the secret medicine to fix it. It was called booze.

Pretty soon that emotional hole inside becomes a *black-hole* that is the catch-all for anything wrong in life. You develop a habit of burying any-thing negative there. Whether it's a bad grade in school, a traffic ticket, an embarrassing character defect, or a deep family secret—throw it into the hole and seal it closed with booze. Why feel a negative emotion? Throw it in the hole and forget it, and grab some beers to make sure you have it fully covered. This is one of the strongest binds of addiction—developing and habitually using this hole for a safe haven for anything painful or fearful. As we constantly add to the hole, we constantly must re-seal it with more alcohol or drugs. It becomes your private safe deposit box for all of your problems.

The alcoholic mind is different. For me, after getting a buzz, I'd like to mentally live out dreams, goals, and fantasies I wasn't achieving in real life—like making my dad proud of me and seeing myself on the medal podium at the Olympics one day. I didn't realize it, but I was thinking just like my dad did, dreaming big while in an alcoholic wonderland. I can recall how he would sit in his favorite chair in the den, mesmerized by the television, with a scotch in his hand, and a frown on his forehead, off in his mental dream world. You could tell he was going over problems in his head, rehashing events from the day, or maybe just fantasizing about what *could be.* The more he drank, the more he would go off into that inner thought world. I could see he was very content in that place, isolated and protected. Normal drinkers didn't drink and think like that; they didn't internalize, fantasize, and live out their dreams while high on booze. Normal drinkers socialized, had fun, relaxed.

For me these drunken fantasies made drinking even more alluring. It was such a great escape into a private world where everything was perfect and all your dreams come true. Even if it was illusory and temporary, it was worth it to feel good, to be a winner, and to play out those victories in that pleasurable, pain-free state. I could actually feel my emotions swell with excitement when I "drunk-dreamed" like this. This was the alcoholic mind that set me apart from normal drinkers. I cannot lie; *drinking and thinking* became one of my favorite things to do. You become best friends with your alter-ego, because he is the one that believes in you the most.

Maybe this is why alcoholics can tolerate isolation or even prefer to drink alone. You start out drinking like everyone else, to be social and relax. Then you realize what it does for you, how it numbs that inner pain and discomfort, and makes you feel normal and whole again. This is followed by finally feeling euphoric enough to fantasize about your dreams and goals. Then, eventually, you find you no longer need friends to drink with—you have found your best friend right there in the bottle. You never need to face sadness, loneliness, or boredom again if there was alcohol around. I wasn't quite that way in college, (quite the opposite) but I could see that was a definite path I was on. I kept alcohol "in my back pocket" for these lonesome uses later in life when I needed it for protection.

At the end of the following year in college, my running times had reached a plateau. I had only improved marginally from the previous year, whereas I should have dropped my race times much more to remain competitive. My drinking and social lifestyle certainly didn't help matters and neither did my large body frame. On top of that, I still had a mental-block about race anxiety which also held me from reaching my potential. In the back of my mind, there was always the fear that those dreaded anxieties would return, and I might have another panic attack during a race. The stress of winning would just compound the anxiety potential. So, my performance plateau was both physical and mental, and not getting faster meant not making the cut for the final championship team, which was very disappointing to both me and my dad.

MY FIRST MENTAL SCIENCE BOOK

After my mediocre track season ended, one of my coaches must have sensed this mental block I had. He recommended in the off-season that I read a book called *Psycho-Cybernetics* by Dr. Maxwell Maltz. The book is based on a self-image psychology concept. Maltz, a plastic surgeon, did a study on his patients who underwent drastic cosmetic surgery. His research found that even after a major improvement in appearance, the personalities and or performances of the majority of the patients still remained unchanged and did not improve as they should have. He determined that this was due to their fixed mental self-image. He proposed that one could not excel beyond his or her inner self-image regardless of what external physical changes took place. Exterior changes were superficial. What this meant to me was that as a runner, I probably had a self-image that I could only run a race so fast, or was too large, or that I could not beat certain other runners, and so forth. Self-limiting beliefs.

Breaking the four-minute mile barrier was a self-image restraint held by male runners for many years. At the turn of the 20th century, the world record was 4:15 and no one fathomed that breaking four minutes was humanly possible. In 1954, the record finally dropped to 3:59, and now it stands at 3:43. A thirty second improvement simply cannot be attributable to running shoe technology. This was a 99% mental, and not physical barrier.

Maltz said the self-image could be modified by using affirmations and mental visualizations. As it applied to athletes, studies found that the same muscle nerves would fire when mentally imagining an athletic event as they would during the actual race. This type of mind training—using visualizations and mental rehearsals—was gaining popularity with many Olympic athletes. Researchers claimed that visualizing an event was the same as doing it in real life—your subconscious was fooled and thus recorded it as a fact. Basically, you could develop the same muscle-memory by using your mind alone. This supposedly would work for performances other than athletics, such as with salesmen who could visualize successful pitches and deals in business, or students receiving good grades. When the end result self-image was visualized, the subconscious would find a way to make it materialize through cybernetic "hit or miss" feedback.

Receiving and reading this book was just a little too late to help my running. It seemed that time was going by too fast to make any major changes in my performance. So, the next season, I regretfully retired from the sport. The remainder of college, I would continue to run daily, but it was for my own fitness and not for competition.

For whatever reason, Psycho-Cybernetics resonated with me on a deep level. This was the first time I ever read anything about the subject of the mind. I was already taking a psychology course in college, but that was more about our social behaviors. This subject of mind was much more occult and esoteric. It was almost sexual in nature. There was something about the illusive and mysterious mind, the unseen forces, our mental powers, and the mystery of the spirit that fascinated me. It was so underground, private and secret, yet it was inside all of us, and my curiosity grew enormously.

My brain soon launched what felt like a million questions to be answered. Does the brain house the mind or the other way around? What really *was* consciousness? What made mental visualizing work—or not work? Why didn't everyone do this if it really worked? What does the mind have to do with a spirit, God, or a creator? What is imagination…. brain muscle movements or mind? Are dreams real? Are these mental powers the same forces as ESP? And on and on…I was unknowingly going down a rabbit hole that I would be digging for decades.

I suppose we all arrive at some place in our lives that we question our existence and this was my time. But my query was not about religion, a deity, or God so much as the science of mind and consciousness. To me, it seemed so blatantly obvious that mind or consciousness was the hinge pin of our existence, yet no one seemed to be making much fuss about it. Mind had nothing to do with religion, it was more primal and existential. Whether you were atheist, Buddhist, or Christian, we all still had this same "mind" or consciousness in common, so why was the topic avoided?

I continued to argue to myself, if mind controlled our behaviors, our habits, our health, our destinies, and basically our realities, why wasn't this the first thing we learned about in school? We all should have been taking mandatory "Mind 101" courses at a young age—a course about mind, the instruction manual for operating as a human being. Instead we were taught to dissect frogs and learn about cavemen, dinosaurs, and ancient history. Why wasn't this subject in every classroom and on every news stand?

I wanted answers to the questions I had but it was in the pre-Internet 1980s, so I couldn't just search Google for answers. Back then, research was laborious work and meant spending time at bookstores and libraries, and there wasn't very much free time in college for that. I did try some research in religion, psychology, and philosophy, but couldn't find what I needed. So, these looming questions went on the back burner of my mind.

One summer break, I was doing some digging for material to satisfy my search and discovered the now-famous book, *Think and Grow Rich*, by Napoleon Hill. However, instead of extinguishing the fire of my curiosity, it just added fuel to it. I managed to read a couple more mental science books during the rest of college, but was far from completing the circle of knowledge for which I was hoping to complete. It seemed that every time I found a missing link, the circle just got bigger and another gap appeared somewhere.

My inquisitiveness about this mental-spiritual question would bug me for years. Mental science became sort of a side hobby and an odd one at that. It wasn't like you could strike up a conversation with someone my age with "read any good mental science books lately?" So, needless to say, I kept it to myself.

CAREER DAYS, ANXIETIES RETURN

After graduating, I landed a good job with a large firm as a property manager handling real estate rental property. After moving around the country in a training program a few years, I ended up settling in central Florida.

My twenties were fun times. I made above-average money, drove a sporty car, dated lots of girls, drank loads, but still maintained an athletic life too. I lived the single lifestyle to the max. My daily routine consisted of working diligently at my job, running five miles after work, and then it came time for drinking and girls. I ran in races and triathlons every couple of months too. I still managed to find time to study mental science and meditate occasionally, but it was erratic and I wasn't very diligent about it. Plus, I really didn't feel I had anything to improve on in my life, all was going swimmingly in all facets.

I drank just about every day whether with friends or alone. Not much had changed from my college routine; work had just been substituted for school. It would be a rare day that I didn't drink at least a couple of beers. Once in a while, I would ask myself if I thought I drank too much, but would quickly rationalize that I deserved it—hell, I ran five miles every day and had a successful young career. Plus, I was a far cry from those homeless drunks in the alley. I had a great job, a nice car, and was healthy and fit—no way could I have a drinking problem. Plus, all the guys I knew drank a lot, too...or maybe it was that I hung out with guys that drank a lot. I didn't realize it at the time, but alcohol was slowly but surely becoming a backbone in my life.

By now I was beginning to build quite an inventory of mind-science books, but was far from having all the answers I was seeking. I still had that feeling of spiritual unrest since there were pieces missing from the mind-science puzzle. I would meditate and practice mental imaging sporadically, and read my books, hoping and waiting for it all to fall into place. I waited to be rewarded with a sudden epiphany, but it never came. For now, it was just a strange hobby that I hoped would one day uncover life's mysteries and grant me the secret to success.

I do believe however, that the meditation and readings did help me overall. I was actually doing well, advancing with my career and athletic goals. It's just that my party life kept me in check or negated any substantial progress. It was four steps forward with the mind evolution and three steps backwards from the drinking. Drinking is a chain and ball regardless how much you booze. It's just a matter of how heavy of a ball you create.

In my late twenties, anxieties crept back into my life, and I started having those dreaded panic attacks again. Again, they would strike suddenly without forewarning and would happen at the most inopportune moments, like around people at work during business meetings. They were compounded tenfold if I had a slight hangover, which was a lot of the time. Drinking the night before made anxieties worse for the next day, but drinking also made them go away afterwards (the colloquial "hair of the dog" remedy). It was a Catch-22: Drinking made them worse, but drinking made them disappear. It was a classic vicious cycle I was heading for.

These attacks were not fun at all. They made my heart race, palms sweaty, and my mind foggy and confused. It's an awkward feeling of detachment from your body as if you were losing control of your mind. The more often I had them, the more nervous I became about them, until I was in an anticipatory state of anxiety all the time. In my younger years, I used to get nervous only around running races, but now I was generally stressed and nervous around the clock. I felt trapped in many places and always needed a "Plan B" exit set up in my mind to feel safe. It takes a lot of effort and planning to deal with having these anxieties, and it wears you out physically and emotionally…especially when you use booze as your remedy.

Since drinking was so effective alleviating my nerves at night after a day of panic attacks, I figured I should try it during the day when my anxiety was at its peak. So, I started to experiment with sneaking in a few beers at lunchtime. I still didn't think I had a drinking problem—in my mind, it was simply a nerve problem that I was treating medicinally with alcohol.

Eventually I learned that what I had was a legitimate medical condition called anxiety and panic disorder. I went to a doctor and he immediately drilled me about my drinking. I knew my drinking was probably whacking out my nerves and contributing towards the problem, but the last thing I wanted to hear was that I had to quit drinking. Hell, how would I ever get a date? I totally lied to the doc so he would give me meds. He said that depression was closely linked to these anxieties, so he prescribed me an antidepressant. Things eventually did get better and the anxieties subsided once again, but my drinking remained erratic.

That period of my life was very cyclic...up and down, good and bad. I went through a couple different jobs, a few different girlfriends, and a couple different doctors and meds. The positive things in my life—exercise, meditation and mental science studies—would alternate with my drinking. It just depended on where I was on the roller coaster.

HITTING BOTTOM, QUITTING, AND SUCCEEDING...ONLY FOR A WHILE

In my early thirties, I was devastated by the news that my dad was diagnosed with cancer. We were very close and talked at least weekly. His battle would last over three years during which he went into remission for a year or so. When it finally returned for the worse, it had spread throughout his body. These would go down as my darkest drinking days to date.

I was so depressed about my dad's illness that I numbed myself with booze every day. The girl I was dating at the time didn't take long to pick up on the fact that I was pickled most of the time she saw me. She asked me to get help for my drinking and took me to see a doctor who specialized in alcoholism. He said I suffered from depression and alcoholism, and he recommended I seek treatment. No way I was ready to quit drinking—it was the only thing keeping me sane, I thought. Somehow, I appeased them both and squirmed out of any formal treatment program, agreeing to cut down on my drinking and start going to AA meetings.

This was my first exposure to AA and it wasn't too bad, at least the way I approached it. I'd drink about four or five beers on the drive to the meetings, sit in the very back, and wait out the hour meeting, bored to death. I thought how I wasn't anything like those losers, most of whom seemed to have lost everything. I'd then go home, picking up another six-pack for the drive. I did this for a few weeks, attending three or four meetings a week and then finally I just said, "Fuck it! this is a waste of my time". I never gave it a chance because deep down I wasn't ready to quit, but I wanted to at least get out of the house and pretend to show some effort.

When my dad's cancer returned from remission I was drinking around the clock for several months. Luckily, at the time, I worked at a remote office alone, with virtually no supervision, so I had plenty of autonomy and freedom. I was drinking three or four beers for breakfast, then a half-dozen miniature shot bottles during the day. I would then leave work early and drink another twelve-pack at night. I was anesthetized at all waking moments so that I wouldn't have to deal with the emotional pain of my dad. I recall how the backseat of my car was stuffed with so many empty beer cans and liquor miniatures it reeked like a barroom trash can.

My dad passed away and I went up north to the funeral and spent time with my family. When I returned back home, for some strange reason, a feeling of peace overcame me. With my dad's battle being over, my suffering seemed over, too. I suddenly felt sick of drinking, of the misery and depression it caused, and of what my life had become. I decided to honestly quit for the first time in my life. My father's death was the impetus for a psychic change in me. An overwhelming surge in my spirit empowered me with an inner strength.

Though I was not spiritually in good graces with any God, I kneeled down on my dining room carpet and prayed for a higher power or God to help me quit drinking. I then went on a three-day taper off booze so that I could stop without having a seizure. With my strong conviction, it had worked, and I would not drink again for several years. I didn't go to any treatment facility, therapists, detox units, or AA meetings. I did it cold turkey on my own. But, I didn't quit "forever" in the back of my mind.

Now sober, my life turned around completely. I achieved big success in business and became vice president with a large real estate company. I was back running five miles a day, and I was healthy as ever. I got back to reading and meditating, and I bought a house with my girlfriend.

Most of my regular friends disappeared. It's funny that when you quit booze, your drinking buddies act like you have some weird disease that they may catch, or that you "got religion" and were going to corner them to preach about their evils. I realized then that probably ninety percent of my old friends and hobbies revolved around drinking, and when you quit, you have nothing in common anymore.

I broke up with my girlfriend, and after a couple years on the dating circuit, I eventually found the girl of my dreams. We were married and had a beautiful baby boy. That little boy was, and still is, the apple of my eye. I owned my own consulting firm, we lived in a five-thousand square foot country club estate home, took Caribbean vacations every year, and I was fit and healthy. Life was good.

THE ROLLER COASTER IS BACK IN SERVICE

I slowly let drinking creep back into my life. I had gone several years without a drop, but I felt I now had control over it and could drink like a normal person, in moderation. I figured that maybe I had just needed those past sober years to reset my brain chemistry for normalcy. What was I thinking? Now that it's back to normal, I could fuck it up again?

So, I successfully drank socially for a short while, but then would have an occasional unplanned blackout night. There were times I just couldn't stop when I started, but then there were also times I could go days without a drink at all. It was very odd and cyclic. Once you have developed the alcoholic germ or allergy condition, you are on a very slippery slope when you go back drinking. You never know when you can traverse the slope successfully and normally, or when you will slip and get blackout drunk.

It wasn't long until my marriage deteriorated and my wife and I divorced. I suppose we had the typical husband-wife issues, and I'm sure my alcoholic brain didn't help matters either.

Now as a single dad, I managed fairly well over the next several years. I was still riding the booze roller coaster and binging regularly. I held good jobs, exercised regularly, and even coached my son's youth football team for about five years. I was drinking in manageable binges, but I would drink for the wrong reasons. While normal people drank for fun and relaxation, I drank just to feel normal and to numb emotions, even good ones. I drank medicinally, not socially. It wasn't good-times drinking with friends like the old days, it was alcoholic drinking—and when I drank, it wasn't to relax, it was usually to get a good buzz and preferably fucked up. I would have a three-day bender and then stay semi-sober for a few days, just nursing a few beers for maintenance. It was truly a roller coaster. I did, however, keep a promise to myself to always be sober around my son. That was very important to me. I didn't want him to have the memories that I had with my dad, so I abstained from drinking during our visits together.

To an outsider looking in, my life could be deceptively misconstrued as normal and successful—I was a business owner, was being a good dad, I exercised regularly, I was coaching youth sports, I was going on social dates, and so on. I was what they called a "functional alcoholic." It's not until you sit down, take an honest inventory of yourself, and write out a life resume, that your mishaps tell you otherwise. Looking back, it's clear my drinking career wasn't without its drama, as I didn't escape the consequences of being a classic alkie.

In my binge drinking years that had now spanned over two decades, I paid the price. The brush-ins with the law included a few DUI incidents, a couple of public intoxication citations, and several bad car wrecks that I was lucky to survive (and not kill anyone else). From these incidents, I visited jails in at least five different states, and had spent over $20,000 in fines and legal fees. Healthwise, other than a few scars from accidents and drunk bar fights, I thankfully escaped with reversible medical issues. Drinking had caused high blood pressure, depression, a bout of slight obesity, and high liver enzymes—all now back to normal. Those were just the measurable indices of drinking, the black and white issues, and luckily for me they were reversible.

The intangible (and sometimes worse) consequences of addiction are what you do to yourself, your friends, and your family. I look back and see how most of my relationships with women were definitely influenced by alcohol. Other than my ex-wife, I met most of my girlfriends while drinking or in a drinking environment—a bar or party. Partying was always a commonality and I would always prescreen my future girlfriends for that trait. If she didn't drink much, but was a pot-head or a pill-popper, that was just as good— so long as she had a vice that kept my boozing off the radar and center stage. As you could imagine, my dating criteria did not make much for solid or long-term relationships.

Of course, my social friends all shared in my taste for strong drink too. Most guys had their golfing, fishing, or hunting buddies—not me, I had drinking buds. In addition to drinking regularly at sports bars or strip clubs (with drinking as our main entertainment), we would interject alcohol at just about anything we did. We would drink while playing golf, when shopping at the mall, at movie theaters, football games, bowling alleys, music festivals, at the beach— you name it. If an establishment didn't serve alcohol, we would sneak it in. Those 7-Eleven Big Gulp cups sure could hold a lot of rum! And if you couldn't bring in a drink with you, then you just got tanked enough beforehand to coast through it buzzed. Like we used to say, if they don't serve alcohol, then "sneak it in your stomach."

ENTER "THE SECRET" MOVIE AND NEW THOUGHT MENTAL SCIENCE

Around 2006, the movie and book, *The Secret*, came out, which promoted using mental science and specifically the Law of Attraction to get rich and achieve goals. I remember at first feeling ripped-off that someone beat me to the punch and figured out the mind-science puzzle before I did. *The Secret* was a huge success and sold millions of copies. I heard how some people claimed to have made fortunes from using *The Secret*—money would come from nowhere, unexpected checks arrived in the mail, and so forth. It contended that you could get anything you desired from the universe if you asked in a proper way—like asking the classic genie in a bottle.

I anxiously read the book and watched the movie, both several times. Since I was already a self-proclaimed veteran mental science student, I definitely prejudged it and was very skeptical and jealous at the same time. After all, a woman wrote this book only after a year studying mental science, and I've been at it 20 years…what could she know that I didn't?

I think people with virgin minds in mental science would have had better luck in using the principles of *The Secret* than me. A first-time reader in mental science would have been more believing than me—my prior knowledge had caused great skepticism and attitude. For me, the material needed to be not only credulous and compelling, but advanced enough to make any impact on me. So, due to my prior studies and mounting knowledge, *The Secret* really didn't teach me anything new and was just too simplistic. I still needed to know more. What was *beyond* the secret? What was below the surface? This was just a tease and another book for my ever-increasing library.

The Secret did, however, indirectly provide me the most fantastic gift. The book sent me on the path I was seeking by introducing me to several teachers from the New Age or New Thought era of the late 1800s and early 1900s. I would soon find that *The Secret* was just the tip of the iceberg, which is what I had suspected all along. I thought that this thread to the New Thought doctrine may be the lead I was seeking.

Three of the New Thought authors mentioned were Wallace Wattles, Prentice Mulford, and Charles Haanel. After some research, I not only found the books they had personally authored, but also found huge volumes of material written on mental science and spiritual law from authors of like mind. It was as if the world had gone through a mental consciousness movement for a period of about thirty years at the turn of the nineteenth century. The subject matters varied from Law of Attraction to thought vibration; from mental healing to telepathy; from spiritual channeling to reincarnation; from autosuggestion to hypnosis; and, from metaphysics to physics. I felt like a kid in a candy store, and I started gathering everything I could get my hands on.

Over the following years, I would amass well over a hundred books relating to New Thought in just about every subject I could find. I went on a wild expedition that would take me to subjects I never expected. One day I would be reading about the Law of Attraction, which would lead me to studies on thought-vibration the next day, then off on a tangent to quantum physics, and then jumping to telekinesis, which would lead to divine hermetic principles, and then to mental healing, and on and on. There was no syllabus, format, or sequence, I just went where my curiosity took me. I was excited and finally getting some answers!

SURVIVING LIFE ON THE ROLLER COASTER

Although I had been studying these mental science and spiritual law books over the years, I don't think they were very effective since I was still in a heavy binge drinking mode. I was still riding the alcoholic roller coaster so the studies were both diluted and intermittent. Again, I counteracted any positive growth with booze.

I accepted the fact I had this drinking propensity or *allergy* in me, but that I was just going to figure out how to deal with it. I realized that success would just be a little more challenging with this handicap, but I refused to try to get rid of it. I still thought that I needed or enjoyed it somehow.

I just couldn't get off the roller coaster ride and was mentally too inert to change anything. I was always waiting for something else to change but couldn't see past the fact that it was me inside that needed to change. I blocked out booze as being any problem at all; I didn't want to get rid of my best friend alcohol since it was the only thing that made me feel normal. In my mind, the mental science hobby I had was preparing me for when I got past this drinking stage of my life—that's how I thought of it, as a stage. I thought this drinking condition, the alcoholism, was something that would just pass, like having a cold or flu, except that this bug had now lasted over two decades.

I had intermittently tried to quit drinking, several times. I read several books on alcoholism including AA's *The Big Book*. I even started going back to AA meetings, and seeing a therapist. I was never honest about my drinking to my therapist, so that was futile, and I still didn't quite feel I fit in to the AA program. So, my attempts to quit were dejecting and validated the need for booze since in my mind there was no cure for me. I subconsciously sabotaged any cure because of the lure and love of the drinking buzz.

In any case, it wasn't like I did not acknowledge I had a drinking problem; it was just that I was fighting hard to keep holding on to it, and defending it. I would rather figure out how to change everything else in life than stop drinking. I could hide from it and even escape from the addiction temporarily, but I would never divorce from it completely—the addict mind was always running in the background even during brief sober periods. In AA, they call this "stinking-drinking-thinking," when you still make stupid alcoholic decisions when you're supposedly sober. They are usually irrational, rushed, and unhealthy decisions that are often subconsciously self-sabotage to give reason to drink again.

Even during my brief sober periods, the alcoholic mindset in me would always postpone or delay decisions on things that involved any emotions until I could drink over it. I needed to hold on to that security blanket, to always have that protection or place to hide when I needed it. It was my emotional cocoon, my meeting center where I would reserve time for self-talk about anything emotional.

Football teams go into their locker rooms at halftime to regroup, strategize, set a game plan, and figure out a way to win the game. I did the same thing with the game of life, but my halftime was my drinking time. Instead of going into a locker room, I went into my "drinking room" where I would resolve all of life's issues with "Coach Alcohol". It is much easier to negotiate emotional decisions when you are completely anesthetized from pain.

Although I was still drinking in these cyclic binges, things actually went relatively well for several years with no major incidents—I kept a good job, maintained my fitness, was a good dad, and so on. When I binged, I did it professionally and would get shitfaced without anyone knowing. I learned (the hard way) to take the battery out of my phone, don't answer the door, and keep off the computer. Clean up the next morning, go to work, and hopefully with mouthwash, nobody will notice that you are still probably legally drunk. I was lucky not to have experienced any bad consequences for a while, but that would not last.

2

My Life Part 2 The Ride Finally Ends

"Just as no workman could perform a good piece of work if he were using, say a blunt chisel, a twisted screwdriver, or a hammer whose head fell off ... so cannot the real man, the inner man, the true man, do effective work on the physical plane, if the instrument whereby that work is to be performed is injured, spoilt, blunted, or stunted by any habit which injures physical life."

—ANNIE BESANT 1898

THE PERFECT STORM

After safely riding the alcoholic roller coaster for the past several years, I guess you could say I was heading for the "perfect storm" emotionally. The roller coaster wasn't slowing to a stop, it was speeding up and coming off the tracks. Suffice it to say that for some reason everything in my life was turning to shit...my job, my new long-distance girlfriend, and my family life. There's not much to look forward to when pretty much everything in life sucks 360 degrees around.

As these emotional stresses were building up, my drinking just escalated along with them. My drinking eventually climbed to a toxic level again like it had back when my dad was dying from cancer. Did an increase in drinking cause these personal failures, or vice versa? I don't really know, but I know that it made them much worse.

When these stress issues started, I visited a therapist about my anxieties and depression (lying of course about my drinking), and was prescribed another antidepressant. After a few months of ineffectiveness, I was eventually being prescribed four different medications. When you mix alcohol with these medicines, not only are any positive benefits negated, but you experience many negative side effects (hence the "don't mix with alcohol" on the label!) I was experiencing mental confusion, insomnia, sedation, memory problems, and, ironically, increased anxiety and depression—all of which made me want to drink even more. This was just another vicious cycle I found myself in.

My life had suddenly turned upside down and I went into a complete meltdown from the stress, pills, and booze. I was miserable around the clock with no light at the end of the tunnel. I worked fifty hours a week at a job I hated, I was having emotional girlfriend problems, and my family relations were strained. So, with absolutely nothing positive going on in my life, I just drank, popped my happy pills, and went through the motions of life, waiting for something to change, waiting for some magical intervention.

Once again, I dropped everything positive from my daily agenda such as exercise, reading, or meditation, and filled it with drinking. I only restrained from drinking when I saw my son for a half day a couple times a week and that was it.

MY DAILY DIET: A CASE OF BEER AND A FISTFUL OF ANTIDEPRESSANTS

At first, my drinking began as an after-work stress-relieving buzz, then progressed to getting pass-out drunk every night. Soon it crept back into having a couple beers at lunchtime to knock the edge off, and then eventually a couple more in the morning just to be calm enough to shave. Pretty quickly, I'm certain that I had an illegal blood alcohol content around the clock.

The combination of antidepressants, heavy drinking, and my jumbled stressed-out nerves began to affect me both physically and mentally.

Physically, I started gaining weight, and mentally I felt like I was having a nervous breakdown.

I thought to myself that drinking over twenty beers and taking four antidepressant pills daily was not the problem; it was the stress that I needed to get rid of. So, over the next couple of months I managed to quit my job and break up with my girlfriend.

I had a good, well-paying job that no sane, sober person would ever quit, but that was not who I was. Luckily, I had some money saved so figured I'd take some time off to get my shit together. So, that was my game plan and I abruptly resigned one morning after drinking a few beers. And breaking up with my girlfriend was no big deal either. When I last saw her, she could see that I was self-destructing, gaining weight, drinking too much, and taking too many prescription pills. She didn't have to say anything—I could see in her eyes that I was fucking up.

Quitting the job and relationship did nothing to straighten out my life and my self-destruction continued over the next few months. I was having a great pity-party being the victim of all these circumstances—the stress, the depression, the problems. It wasn't me that needed to change, it was everything else. I was waiting on something to change outside of me, waiting on someone to fix the conditions in life for me, and to get everything right again. Until this fucked-up exterior world changed, I planned on just waiting on it, and I protested it by getting drunk. I figured that I had tried in the past to do things the right way—I worked hard and all that crap— and it hadn't worked. When the exterior world was right again, I would join then back in, until that time I say "fuck it!".

You would think that since I had removed the majority of the stresses in my life, I should not have had any reason to drink anymore. But that's not how this addiction thing works. My drinking and depression continued to get worse and worse. Pretty much all my waking hours were now drinking hours and, of course, I never "went to sleep," I passed out.

My issues soon became obvious to my family, even at a long distance away from me, and at their urging I finally sought professional help.

REHAB ALLEY: MY CELL PHONE SAVES ME

Over the next eight months, I would go to four treatment places—two detox units and two eight-week residential rehab clinics. My sobriety would only last an average of a maybe two weeks after each attempt.

These places would detox me fine and I could stay sober for a week or so after being discharged, but the mental compulsion, depression, and cravings were just too much and I would cave-in. The treatment just would not stick or sink in—all the AA meetings, group sessions, detoxifications, counseling, and therapies just didn't work on me. Within a couple of weeks, I was back to my case of beer a day, pills, and couch potato lifestyle. It wouldn't be until the last treatment center that I would begin to find the cure to my addiction and at the same time solve the mental science puzzle.

The last residential rehab center was a different in that we all stayed in regular civilian apartments, not cell-like dorm rooms. We also had complete freedom to roam the small campus when not in a class or a group session, and the most amazing thing of all was that we were allowed to have our cell phones! Having my smart phone was crucial to my recovery, as you will see.

Like the other treatment centers, the days were full of classes, group therapy, individual doctor visits, recreational therapy, and many, many AA meetings. Each night we had to be in our apartments at 10:00 p.m. With no television or radio allowed, I was left with my cell phone for entertainment, which was fine with me. I usually would watch a movie on Netflix and then get to sleep around midnight.

After a few weeks of watching Netflix nightly, I had caught up with all the good movies and was surfing the Internet one night looking for something to read or watch. I came across a website that had New Thought books that you could download and read for free. This brought back memories of when I had my shit together, when I would study these books like a fiend trying to find the secret and truth to the puzzle of spiritual laws and mental science. I felt a little nostalgic and decided that I would open a few of these old books and skim over them just for the hell of it. After reading for an hour or so something kicked in psychically and spiritually—a nerve was struck and the spark came back. I felt a mental buzz. It brought me back mentally to that place I left before, where the circle of knowledge was incomplete and the puzzle unfinished. But this time my thirst for this knowledge was stronger than ever. I don't think I slept that night at all. I just read.

In an epiphany of sorts, it suddenly dawned on me that these laws and principles and the entire field of mental science was not just for getting wealthy or excelling in business or sports. They were the instructions on how we create our own reality using our mental-spiritual faculties. The laws and principles that are used by millionaires, super-achievers, mental healers, and hypnotists could also be used with addiction. These same laws and principles apply to achieving anything and overcoming any conditions. I now saw how these studies could lead me to defeat this life-long struggle with alcohol. I was renewed and excited again.

I had access to hundreds of books via the public domain libraries online, so I started to read the old ones I cherished the most. But this time, I read with more desire and vigor to finally get to the core of the truth. It was so refreshing to have this spiritual youth back in me. I was genuinely excited about life again and looked forward to lights-out every night so that I could lie in bed and have this myriad of wisdom in my hands. I digested every word, and soaked in the knowledge and wisdom like a sponge.

I soon discovered many videos, interviews, audio books, documentary movies, and YouTube clips that I never knew existed—many dealing with newer subject matter such as quantum physics, consciousness, channeled spirits, and other different mind-spirit topics. These would answer many of my queries that the New Thought doctrines had lacked.

COMBINING MEDITATION WITH MENTAL SCIENCE

I started meditating again and used TM to apply mental science to my health and sobriety goals. I started losing weight and my attitude completely changed. A month later I was discharged, but this time I went home full of life and on a mission. A new mind-spirit psychic change was in motion. I could feel this thirst for the truth inside and the big change that was taking place. Without even knowing it, I was already mentally reprogramming myself and the hole in me was being filled.

Back at home I kept on this new routine to keep sober and healthy. I decided to go back to AA meetings because I actually did enjoy the people there, plus my doctors and family insisted on it. I also went to the gym to work out daily, I started to eat a healthy diet, meditate twice a day for at least twenty minutes, and dig into the studies of the mind and spirit.

My meditations would implement the mind-science subject matter that I was studying. As I would learn new concepts in consciousness or laws of mind-spirit, I applied these in my meditations, contemplating these new ideas and beliefs or applying a new practice for programming my mind and magnetizing it toward my goals. I was getting very efficient at this new Meditative Programming Technique I had developed and it was working in transforming my life and manifesting my goals.

Most importantly I spent as much time as I could with my son. I was a grateful and proud dad, and genuinely happy to be a sober one. I also landed a great job which was to start in a couple months so I continued to study and meditate ferociously.

I stopped going to AA after a while, simply because I just didn't find it potent enough. Plus, I needed that time to dedicate to my meditations and mental science studies. I was studying this new material every waking moment. I read books in between my daily tasks, would eat my meals watching documentaries and videos, and I would even fall asleep and wake up to audio books on the subject. Even when I was driving my car or on the treadmill at the gym, I was digesting and sorting the new knowledge I learned in my mind. Meditation was becoming my new addiction, and I looked forward to it every day.

THE TRANSFORMATION WAS HAPPENING

This cramming of knowledge went on for a few months. I'm not sure when, but somewhere early on I experienced a psychic change. Along with a newfound understanding of mental science and spiritual laws, a spiritual leap and paradigm shift occurred. Somewhere in the midst of study and contemplation, I completed the circle of understanding which I had started over thirty years earlier. I found the formula and technique for making changes to my life and now understood the spirit-science of creation. Most importantly, for the first time in my life, I had developed complete faith in this new dogma which is the crucial key to making mind-spirit science work. Faith, I found, is the true key, and you can never fake it.

In meditation, I found and connected with what is called the Infinite Intelligence, Higher Power, or God, and I learned how to tap into this creative force to achieve goals. The first and foremost goal was maintaining my health and sobriety, but would soon expand to include getting a great job, a nice car, and then building great relationships again. Having a foundation of sobriety and health however was the critical part, because if you're still an addict, you can never hold on to anything else. Never forget that.

My meditations had turned into a unique mental programming period and a spiritual session in which I would create my own future, my own reality, and it worked both for sobriety and other goals.

I started this journey drinking a case of beer a day, I was depressed, 50 pounds overweight, had high blood pressure and bad liver enzymes, and was unemployed. In the short period after starting this program, I not only quit drinking (I am going on year two now), but I also lost the fifty pounds and am working out like a college age kid again. The depression has completely cleared up, I have the ultimate job, was taken off the blood pressure medication I was on for twenty years, and I'm beginning to work on meaningful relationships again. That was my personal definition of success at the time, and I achieved it All of these are direct results of the mind-spirit science I found and practiced and now want to share.

WHY NOT SHARE THIS WISDOM?

When my life turned around I wondered why others couldn't do what I did too. I saw the high relapse rate at both the rehab clinics and AA programs that I attended and figured out why they didn't work. They don't teach the universal laws of the mind-spirit that govern all creation and that dictate all physical conditions including addictions. These programs are attempting to fix the symptoms or effects, but not the cause.

In mental science, we restore our inner core vibrational state to a positive and healthy one from the sick and negative one that hosted the addict. It is fruitless to fight the outward conditions and effects if you have a poor self-image and still generate discordant inner frequencies. With mental science and spiritual laws, we fill our emotional holes that caused negative vibrations and we reprogram our mental bodies for health, sobriety, love, and success. No program I know of promotes this or can do this, and I've tried just about all of them—therapy, AA, religion, counseling, medications, cognitive training, and so forth.

When in rehab, I watched as patients got discharged only to show back up the next month. Many of those who returned had been through many other treatment programs, just like me, with no success. Realizing this mental science and spiritual law program was nowhere to be found, I decided to write this book to share in my knowledge and wisdom.

The secret of the ages of mental science and spiritual laws should be available to anyone who earnestly desires to know the truth about creation and learn the owner's manual to their mind and spirit. It can cure addiction and change your life permanently. When you learn these mental science principles, you find that your physical body and external circumstances magically remold themselves in harmony with the inner vibrations you radiate. Your body and outward conditions are simply expressions of your mind-spirit. Learn how to reprogram the inner self, and your body and external conditions will follow in like fashion. This is the Law of Manifestation.

The following chapters are a synopsis of the subject matter that I studied which led to my learning the truth about mental science and spiritual law. It took digesting huge volumes of material for me to get to this condensed state, but going through these subjects will take you down the same path I took. The subject matters vary and cover a vast array of topics. To reiterate from the introduction, some chapters may seem inapplicable, but trust me when I say that this will all come together in the end and you will start seeing the common thread that runs through all of these areas of study. It may be confusing at times, but then you will come full circle in the end and be amazed.

As written in the *Gospel of Thomas*, *"Let him who seeks cease not to seek until he finds: when he finds, he will be astonished; and when he is astonished he will wonder, and will reign over the universe!"*

Let's begin.

3

Mind in the Atom

"Science is rapidly being forced to the conclusion that in every atom there is a living principle, a vital energy; and it is this life essence, not the outward form it assumes, wherein resides the sustaining power."

—Charles B. Patterson 1904

As part of having a thorough knowledge base of mental science, you must know the origin of mind or consciousness, and this starts with studying the beginning of creation—the atomic world. When you study the light, you inadvertently are studying the dark. And when you study the physical world of matter, you are revealing the other invisible side, which as you will learn is mind.

WTF? DID YOU SAY ATOMS?

So, yes, I am going to discuss atoms in a book about curing addiction. I apologize upfront for having to drag you through some nerdy science facts, but as you will see later, having this knowledge will be a benefit. No, we're not going to learn about making THC, crack, or synthetic LSD...we're learning about the atom and its relationship to mind or consciousness.

Remember that the golden rule of mental science is possessing *faith* in the knowledge. The more thoroughly you understand the origins and core principles, the more you will believe in them, and the better they will work for you in applying mental science. The extent in which you need to know these details are all up to your own level of understanding. So, take what you need, and leave what you don't. Admittedly, these next two chapters are the most "technical" of the book, so please bear with it with an open mind.

There are two main points to studying the atomic world: First, you must understand and be able to visualize the scale of the microscopic world. Second, it is necessary to acknowledge the intelligence or consciousness that is at the core or origin of all physical matter. These two concepts will not only help in your knowledge and faith in consciousness studies, but will also provide visualization tools for meditation you will learn in a later chapter.

You may remember a little bit of chemistry from high school…about how the tiny electrons orbited around the nucleus in multiple rings in a similar fashion to the planets orbiting around the sun, with the nucleus consisting of protons and neutrons.

These protons and neutrons are made of even smaller particles called quarks, specifically, there are three quarks in each. There are many differing atomic models and theories, but the one I favor is the string theory that postulates that the quarks are composed of even tinier particles called strings. Strings are so minute that if an electron were the size of the Earth, a string would be the size of a grain of sand. There now also is the Higgs Boson particle field theory, which was discovered in 2012, that explains an even more microscopic particle than the string. This theory was mathematically defined or established to validate the existence of a field or particle that is so miniscule that it has not yet been physically discovered. It essentially is a mathematical necessity in order to explain our theories on mass and the existence of particles. Some have called this the *God particle* because it is supposedly the most fundamental substance that makes up the space between the quarks, strings, and such. In any case, we have subparticles and fields that are much smaller than the atoms' nucleus.

THE SCALE OF THE ATOMIC WORLD

The first mental science lesson is to get a visual perspective of the atom and its scale. The electrons that orbit the nucleus are two thousand times smaller than the size of the protons and neutrons comprising the nucleus. If you were to enlarge the nucleus of one of the smallest atoms (such as hydrogen) to the size of a basketball, you would fit one neutron and one proton inside of it, each of which would be about slightly smaller than a bowling ball. The three quarks inside each would be the size of tennis balls, and the strings (inside the tennis ball) would be the sizes of dust particles.

The electron orbiting this same basketball-sized nucleus would be about the size of a green pea and the scale would be a distance of *twenty miles* away in orbit! Visualize a pea that is twenty miles away from a basketball spinning at the speed of light around it. It is orbiting at 186,000 miles per second, yet somehow attractive and repulsive forces (radiating twenty miles away) keep it in precise orbit.

This huge twenty miles of open space is not apparent to us because of the density and size of the atom to mankind. To put the size in perspective, there are approximately 10 quadrillion atoms in a grain of salt, most of which is empty (the twenty mile) space. This void, ethereal space represents 99.99999 percent of the atom; thus, only 0.00001 percent contains the particles themselves, and they themselves are nothing but forms of energy.

What was in the (twenty mile) vast space between the two particles— that void between the pea and basketball? There is no air or other physical medium there, because it is atoms themselves that make up what we call "air". What is in between these particles that is allowing these forces to work? In the metaphysical world, there can be no such thing as *nothing*, there must be a substance or medium of some sort.

THE ETHER OR EMPTY SPACE

In early science years, the space or void between the particles was called "ether." The Greek philosopher Aristotle claimed that ether was the medium that also existed in outer space which explained how light could be transmitted. This term was later used to describe both the absence of a physical medium in outer space between planets and the same emptiness that occurs between subatomic particles. It is a magnetic medium that has no substance, yet somehow allows forces and electromagnetism to propagate.

As mentioned earlier, scientists today have now defined this ether as the Higgs Boson particle field. This field-particle is simply a microcosm, or finer energy form, of the same substance that is contained in strings, quarks, and electrons. It essentially is a term that was needed to explain something unexplainable. I personally prefer the term "ether" of the old days more applicable than "Higgs Boson field," as ether represents the ultimate indivisible (mind) substance that is used in New Thought texts. In 1917, New Thought pioneer Thomas Troward wrote:

"Since all physical matter is scientifically proved to consist of the universal ether in various degrees of condensation, there may be other degrees of condensation, forming other modes of matter, which are beyond the scope of physical vision and of our laboratory apparatus...it must constitute a connecting link between all modes of substance, whether visible or invisible, in all worlds, and may therefore be called the Universal Medium...."

This etheric medium is referred to by new-age metaphysicians and philosophers as the matrix, quantum soup, the universal mind, the conscious sea, or even God's mind. It is the fabric which was condensed to form what we term matter. It is the nonphysical substance where thoughts and imagination exist, and the fundamental "stuff" from which everything originates. This is worth repeating that the first particle of "matter" is simply the condensation of the ether which, in essence, is intelligent substance—there is no mass or "matter," per se.

An analogy is to think of the ethereal space field as a massive ocean that goes on for infinity—no top, no bottom, no sides, no fish or aquatic life—nothing but crystal-clear water. The first "particle" created would be likened to a swirling spherical vortex within this ocean. Visualize a powerful dense "water ball," similar to when you swirl your fist in a circular motion underwater in a swimming pool... a current-ball of compact, condensed water swirling at tremendous speed, so fast and compressed it is distinguishable as a solid object compared to the loose, light water surrounding it. It would be like the balls of water the Marvel superhero *Aquaman* throws!

But this theoretical ocean is in reality all ether, or empty intelligent substance. So, this energy vortex is purely a condensation of mind-energy. This particle, however, must contain instructions or intelligence on its creation and have consciousness to self-act. How else can an energy particle of ether, or space, form into something? Forces must follow laws, laws are organized by intelligence, and action is initiated by will or consciousness. To repeat, the root of creation is condensation of an intelligence or consciousness that manifests into any successive force, motion, or energy form. Therefore, at the essence of all matter down to the smallest particle known to mankind is an ethereal mind substance. There never was anything *physical* to begin with—just intelligence that created laws that objectified into forces.

To sum it up, creation began with mind-substance. Thus, all matter is purely mind in "solid" form—there is no true "solidity" in matter itself. It is purely the invisible cohesive forces, vibrations, and motion of the energy particles that give energy forms their physical traits.

The ethereal mind field and successive physical subparticles is analogous to a cloud of misty steam or vapor compared to its related ice particle. They both are the same substance (H_2O), but just a different density or rate of vibration, the latter form simply complying with intelligent forces or laws. Whether it is an atomic bond, chemical bond, gravitational force, or a magnetic force, they all stem from the same intelligence and result in what we call laws. The Law of Attraction is one of the most fundamental metaphysical laws we have which governs many unseen invisible forces.

The world appears to us as solid, but it reality it is simply vibrational energy. Just as on a movie screen, the actors and objects interact with each other as if they are truly "solid", so do the energy forms of matter. Your fingertip consists of cells, molecules, and atoms that are ultimately energy forms, and when you touch a rock, it is energy touching energy, not physical matter touching physical matter.

QUANTUM PHYSICS PROVES MIND EXISTS IN THE ATOM

One of the most notable experiments of quantum physics is the famous double-slit experiment. Without getting too technical, this study essentially involved sending photon waves, or light particles, through two parallel vertical slits that were cut into a protective metal sheet several yards away (like in a shooting range). The light photons passed through the slits and displayed themselves onto a backboard screen that showed the projectiles pattern. The photons normally displayed a wave pattern, just like they were a series of water waves in a pond hitting a bulkhead wall. This looked like a succession of vertical lines, characteristic of a wave—like the vertical static lines you get on an old television set when the signal goes bad.

When left unattended and unmonitored, the test displayed this expected wave pattern repeatedly. However, here's the big event that changed the scientific world: When human monitoring took place, or consciousness was present, the particles changed from a wave behavior to that of a particle. The resultant pattern was like shooting paint balls through the slits against the wall. This pattern of individual specks is called *particle motion*. This occurred during every test that was monitored. If the equipment went unmonitored, the projectile's display returned to the wave pattern.

Repeated testing was made over subsequent decades only to confirm the same results—that these particles actually did behave differently when being consciously observed by a human. The wave function collapsed into a particle behavior, only when under human observation. The actual act of observing matter had altered it, thus proving mind and subatomic particles are somehow interconnected.

What this had proved was man's consciousness somehow communicated with, and altered the outcome of the subatomic particles' behavior. This meant that the *solidity* of the "particle" does not exist until man observes, or acknowledges, it. It is a light-wave form until we conceive it, and then it becomes particular matter. In other words, the reality of solidity or matter only occurs when consciousness exists, or better yet, we create reality with consciousness.

In another dramatic test, two light particles, or photons, were placed seven miles away from a central testing source in opposite directions—thus, fourteen miles apart from each other. When one particle was stimulated with a charge to generate a response, a surprise effect occurred and the opposite particle actually responded before the test-subject particle did. The second particle would react not only instantaneously, but sometimes actually before, or in anticipation of, the stimulation.

This was reporting that communication was actually occurring faster than the speed of light between the two particles, which was theoretically impossible. These experiments proved that not only was there undetectable information being communicated between the two photons, but that it occurred faster than the speed of light, which is essentially a time warp. The "mind" or intelligence actually moved backwards in time.

Other similar tests have verified comparable results that are called "quantum entanglement." This occurs when the subatomic particles are able to appear and disappear in different places instantaneously, again, faster than the speed of light. They also would appear in the same place at the same time or coexist in multiple places simultaneously. This occurs commonly with electrons as the same electron will jump orbits and appear, disappear, and also reappear at the exact same places at precisely the same times.

All of these tests collectively support the claim that there clearly is a correlation between the behavior of subatomic particles and human consciousness. Any particle must possess an intelligence or consciousness if it can sense the intent of an experiment before it occurs. This inherent intelligent consciousness communicates with other particles as well as with human thought. As far back as 1890, Thomas Edison noticed these atomic mentality traits when he wrote, "*I do not believe that matter is inert, acted upon by an outside force. To me it seems that every atom is possessed by a certain amount of primitive intelligence.*"

If a human's thought can alter the movement of an electron or photon, this means that he or she is changing matter's vibration or behavior. When these electrons are connected with atoms and molecules in a cell, body, group, or entity of any scale, and can communicate with one another, humans can also affect the entire body or assemblage of bodies solely with conscious thought. This supports the phenomena in psychokinesis, mental healings, the placebo effect, and mind-over-matter experiences.

MIND IS IN EVERYTHING

At the origin of matter, we found the magnetic intelligent field of ether, and that the successive first particle was simply energy or condensation of this original ether-mind. Since all of these particles that make up matter (strings, quarks, electrons, and photons) all are essentially balls of energy with no mass, we could conclude that they are made of the same elementary substance, but just of opposite polarities or genders. But what makes one ball of energy different than another if they are of the same substance? It is intelligence, through law or forces, divine or otherwise that creates the duality.

New Thought teacher William Atkinson explained the attractive and repulsive forces in an atom as an act of mentality or what is termed "chemical affinity" when he wrote the following:

> *"What causes the particles to exhibit this attraction and repulsion toward each other? We have seen that the particles are attracted to, or repelled by, each other—in the matter of "likes and dislikes"; "love and hates" ... And these attractions and repulsions are held to result from "capacity to experience sensations" and the power to "respond to sensations." ...which Haeckel has compared to "desire" and "will." And if mentality is the cause of the sensations and of the response there; and the latter are the causes of the attractions and repulsions... and the latter, in turn is the cause of the vibrations; and the vibrations are the causes of the manifestations of light, heat, electricity, magnetism, and so on—then am I not justified in claiming that mind and Mind-Power are the motive-force of all physical energy?"*

Atkinson is saying that at the core or essence of matter there is a difference in personality or mentality of the smallest particles. The original particles created have no real *positive or negative* charges, only *differences in personality*. Each particle is simply at the opposite end of the same spectrum from the other: Male or female, yin or yang, thumbs up or thumbs down- call it what you like. One particle likes or dislikes the other—thus, the attraction and repulsion. Some metaphysicians say that this is the first "love" in creation, the first bond, the first positive, which therefore generated the first negative.

In other words, half the particles joined one team and half the other—shirts and skins, and this division required intelligence and consciousness. There is no change in original substance, there cannot be. The traits that the original "stuff" have are not measurable charges or quantities, but intelligent mental orientation of the energy. You could not have a negative unless you had a positive to compare it to. You cannot have light unless you know darkness.

The atom is demonstrating intelligent consciousness by being discriminative, by making choices, and by forming one gender or polarity from another. It is clearly showing a mentality if not also a personality.

It appears that substance has its own consciousness that abides by divinely created rules or laws. It simply has been designated a specific order of mentality. When you expand these personalities or mentality traits of charge, force, and vibrational rate, the result is the universe. In 1919, New Thought teacher Fenwicke Holmes wrote the following passage:

> *"Whatever is made, therefore, must be made out of Mind. Mind can act only by thinking; therefore, it is thought that takes the substance called mind and moulds it into form. God makes a world out of himself. As everything in the cosmos starts in thought and manifests in form, creation is the process by which the activity takes place. We may call it evolution or we may call it law."*

THE ATOMIC MIND SUMMARY

In summary, what I hope you take away from this chapter are the following three points: First, you should be able to visualize the scale or perspective of the atom—the basketball-sized nucleus and pea-sized electron twenty miles away. Secondly, remember the most miniscule particles are purely compacted mind substance, pure intelligent energy. The origin of what we call matter is a condensation of ether-mind substance. Finally, these particles are proven to not only have intelligence and consciousness, but also to respond to the mind of humankind—our consciousness affects the mind-substance of creation, or what we now call physical matter.

This is a core principle of mental science: All physical matter and, thus, all successive external bodies and conditions are no more than the assemblages of original mind substance in different vibratory rates. Mind, consciousness, or spirit is always the first cause and the physical world is always the resultant effect. Although everything is intelligent mind substance, only humankind has the authority, power, and volition to direct and control it.

You will soon learn how this knowledge is applied using mental science visualization techniques for changing your self-image, manifesting your goals of health and sobriety, and ultimately creating your own reality.

4

Mind in the Cosmos

"The universe is created from some power resident within. It is made out of Mind; or in other words, Spirit makes things by becoming the things which it makes. Substance, in its last analysis, is intelligence…The universe in which we live, therefore, is to be conceived of as thought and the whole existing cosmos as Mind in Action."

—FENWICKE HOLMES, 1919

Once I had studied the microscopic atomic world and its relation to consciousness, it seemed logical to move on to the opposite end of the spectrum—the macroscopic universe or outer space. This subject matter, as with the atom, is provided to expand knowledge of consciousness, mind, and creation, which plays a vital role in building faith in the mental science principles.

The cosmos or universe is simply an extension of the same laws of creation that went into the formation of the atom and original physical "matter". The creation of suns, planets, moons, and space oddities like black holes and dark energy are only different with respect to size, scale, and unique forces or laws. The origin however, remains consistent with the atom.

The same presence of mind or consciousness exists in the empty space between celestial bodies, as it did with atomic subparticles. A correlation exists between the empty space of an atom and the visible, empty portion of the universe. The "solidity," or visible part of the universe is only a minute fraction of the space—in the 0.00001 percentage range or less. And just as with the atom, these "physical" parts of the cosmos are in truth only forms of energy, just varying in scale. In 1919, New Thought practitioner Fenwicke Holmes wrote that:

> *"Metaphysics is in harmony with the postulates of science when it says energy is produced by the action of will…to will is to think, that thinking is an act of mind…That is why we can say that the universe is alive for it is made by intelligence out of itself."*

THE ETHER OR EMPTY SPACE…AGAIN

The ethereal substance of outer space is absent of any matter yet has the ability to transmit energy and intelligence just like with the ("twenty mile") void in the atom. The stars and planets, electrons and nuclei all have an intelligence that underlies the forces and motions. The empty space is not a vacuum but is a conscious sea directing the traffic of forces, intelligence, and energy. This medium also allows electromagnetic waves to propagate, which is why we can communicate with satellites and spacecraft. It is a magnetic field of mind substance.

Ancient Greeks were the first to map the cosmos and established earth, air, fire, and water as the elements composing all matter. Later, the term "ether" was introduced as the material of the stars and space. Today, scientists propose that a new type of substance exists which goes by the names of dark energy, dark matter or the plasma. All three essentially refer to the same substance and are broadly renaming what was called ether in the old days. It still remains a mystery, similar to the Higgs Boson particle field in atomic theory, except on a grander scale. Ether is the intelligent magnetic mind-field that condenses intelligent energy form into what we call matter. With celestial forces at play, this creation unfolds into the stars, planets, moons we have in the universe. The differences in the bodies are the vibrational rates.

In 1912, the Three Initiates explained how the ethereal plane is reached by exploring or dissecting matter until we find the underlying source-intelligence:

> *"When the object reaches a certain rate of vibration its molecules disintegrate, and resolve themselves into the original elements or atoms. Then the atoms, following the Principle of Vibration, are separated into the countless corpuscles of which they are composed. And finally, even the corpuscles disappear and the object may be said to be composed of The Ethereal Substance. Science does not dare to follow the illustration further, but the Hermetists teach that if the vibrations be continually increased the object would mount up the successive states of manifestation and would in turn manifest the various mental stages, and then on Spiritward, until it would finally re-enter THE ALL, which is Absolute Spirit."*

Everything in existence is part of one great vibrational continuum, with physical matter towards one end of the spectrum and the "absolute" mind or spirit at the other. Conscious intelligence pervades the entire range of the spectrum as is present in all. Mental science and spiritual law dictates that the power flows from the higher frequencies to the lower, from hot to cold, and from mind to matter. All physical conditions are simply expressions of mind-spirit—this is a fundamental spiritual law.

The Big Bang Theory says the universe is fourteen billion years old and still expanding at the speed of light from a single source. But how this single source came into being and why it was created and then exploded we do not know. The question is this: how did the original formulation or molding of the ether take place? There must have been an intelligence or power creating the original formation. One must conclude that this space or ether must have a consciousness or intelligence in order to condense itself. It must have a will or volition, a desire to self-create without any cause.

This would be analogous to a hurricane spontaneously spawning on a perfectly beautiful, sunny, calm and clear day. This simply does not happen unless there are known forces at work. There has to be causation—a wind, a storm, a pressure, thermal change, or force…a directive or an intelligence behind the resultant energy that is created seemingly from nothing. One would have to agree that there must be a deeper intelligence—a consciousness, supreme source, or divinity involved. In 1917, Thomas Troward goes on to say that:

> *"The scientific idea of the ether, as a universal medium pervading all space, and permeating all substance, will help us to see that many things which are popularly called super-natural, are to be attributed to the action of known laws…that since all physical matter is scientifically proved to consist of the universal ether in various degrees of condensation, there may be other degrees of condensation, forming other modes of matter, which are beyond the scope of physical vision and of our laboratory apparatus."*

Troward reinforces the concept that this ether or mind-substance is the nucleus of all physical matter and, therefore, is the fundamental building block of *all* creation including that beyond—the spirit world and other dimensions and densities we cannot see or measure.

You should recognize the source intelligence originating the condensation of mind-spirit into matter and also understand the forces or laws that guide them. The forces provide the laws, rules, or roadmap that manifestations will follow. These forces are no more than divinely created rules uniquely designed for each level of creation, whether it's the Law of Attraction or the Law of Gravity. All of these laws are intelligently embedded in the smallest fractal of substance and continues to the largest assemblage. In other words, every part of the ethereal field contains the intelligence of the entire universe. The foregoing statement is worth rereading.

The forces that govern "physical" science are analogous to a type of divine software which stems from a grand computer programmer or intelligent consciousness. New Thought teacher Charles Haanel wrote:

"The Universe is alive. In order to express life there must be mind— nothing can exist without mind. Everything which exists is some manifestation of this one basic substance from which and by which all things have been created and are continually being recreated. It is man's capacity to think that makes him a creator instead of a creature. All things are the result of the thought process."

We conclude that matter is created from pure intelligence and follows specific universal laws. It is in using these laws that humans can create as well. "As above, so below"—the laws mirror themselves at varying planes of existence. The particles of primary substance are the same as the particles of the cosmos. They are the spirit, or infinite consciousness, merely in a grosser, denser form. In 1910, Wallace Wattles wrote the following:

"There is a Cosmic Life which permeate, penetrates, and fills the interspaces of the universe, being in and through all things. This Life is not merely a vibration, or form of energy; it is a Living Substance. All things are made from it, it is All, and in all."

THE SCALE OF THE UNIVERSE

Moving on to the other main point in this chapter which is the scale of the universe. Just as with the atomic scale, possessing this mental visualization will provide true perspective, expand consciousness, and help with getting in the proper mind-set for meditation and mental programming.

If you were to scale the sun down to the size of a bowling ball, planet Earth would be the size of a BB pellet or a tiny bead at a distance of ninety feet away. The next time you park at a shopping center lot, count ten car-width spaces from your car and that's about ninety feet. Visualize a bowling ball (sun) at your car and you holding a small bead or BB ten spaces away. How amazing is it that Earth, as tiny as it is (the tiny bead in your hand), orbits around the sun at this distance with such exact precision?

The sun's light waves or photons travel at the speed of 186,000 miles per second. At that speed, a light particle would circle around

Earth seven times in one second. The distance from Earth to the sun is ninety-three million miles. Even traveling at this extreme velocity, it takes light over eight minutes to reach Earth. Thus, the light you see and feel is actually eight minutes old, not instantaneous as some think. When scientists see a solar flare, they are actually seeing what happened on the sun eight-minutes-ago.

Expanding the solar system further, now picture the dwarf Pluto which is one-seventh the size of Earth. It is almost four billion miles from the sun. The distance from our same bowling ball (the sun) to Pluto would measure a half-mile away, with the BB representing Earth ninety feet away, and Pluto the size of a needle head. Can you imagine that an object the size of a bowling ball can emit attractive-repulsive forces a half-mile away to keep a tiny, pinhead-size object in a precise orbit? And there is nothing in this empty space between the two less the magical ether—there is no physical medium at all.

Another interesting factoid on the scale of the universe is its enormity. Bear in mind that our sun is just one of four hundred billion stars just in our Milky Way galaxy alone—that is 1 in 400,000,000,000. The estimated number of galaxies in the universe is estimated to be up to two trillion, each containing as many stars as in our Milky Way. Scientists have speculated that there are as many stars in the universe as grains of sand on Earth.

THE BIG DIPPER DOES NOT REALLY EXIST

As stated earlier, it takes a light wave-particle eight minutes to travel the ninety-three million miles from the sun to Earth, and it takes only one second for light to travel from Earth to the moon. If you traveled at this speed of light for an entire year, you would cover 4.8 trillion miles, or what is termed a *light-year*.

The closest star to Earth besides our sun is over four light-years away, with the Big Dipper eighty light-years away. What this means is that when you look at the Big Dipper at night, you are seeing the light that was generated from these stars eighty years earlier. If one of the Big Dipper stars exploded today, we would not know about this event until eighty years from now. In other words, the big dipper may have already exploded say, fifty years ago, and we can't know this because we are still seeing the remnant "ghost" trail of light waves. So, maybe there really is no Big Dipper at all?

The distance to the farthest point across the *observable* universe is over seventy billion light-years. If you scaled the Big Dipper to be ten feet away, the farthest galaxy that mankind can see with today's equipment would be the distance literally to our moon.

If the enormity of the universe does not impress you, think about the forces required to keep it in motion, impelling perfect orbits of billions of stars and trillions of planets and moons. The precision of our orbit is so exact that we have frozen artic caps on the ends of the Earth farthest from the sun and extreme heat at the equator closest to the sun. Can you imagine what the slightest wobble or shift in orbit would do to our temperatures? A miniscule shift in Earth's orbit could result in either freezing or burning the entire planet.

Experts say that if the Big Bang and subsequent gravitational forces were 0.001 of one percent larger or smaller of an explosion or force, Earth would not exist today. There are hundreds of "engineering" parameters that had to be met in exact precision for the universe and Earth to miraculously exist today and support the life it does.

THE COSMOS SUMMARY

The key points of this chapter are twofold and similar to those with the atomic world chapter. First, you should be able to draw a deeper understanding of ether, or universal mind substance, and how it correlates with the atoms creation; that consciousness or mind is in everything including what we call space. Secondly, it's important to gain a visual perspective of both the enormity and the scale of the solar system, galaxy, and universe. Remember to merge and compare the scale of the macro universe with the scale of the micro atomic world. Keep these images engrained in your mind as you will see they provide a new perspective on the universe, which in turn expands consciousness.

The substance of physical matter, whether stars or atoms, is all the same—a condensation of ethereal intelligent mind energy. The origin of all is mind substance, spirit, or consciousness, and the physical world is simply a denser form of mind in different vibratory rates. You can say that mind and matter are the same, only different stratifications in the spectrum. The gradation goes from dense and course matter, to fine and subtler mind, to the ethereal spirit substance.

Human consciousness descended from the first cause or originating intelligence that directed these attractive forces into the first physical matter. We, as humans, have the same creative abilities in creating all physical matter—our bodies and conditions—with the same authority as did the prime intelligence. The physical world is a reflection of mind, as consciousness is the cause, and our physical conditions, the effect. *As above, so below*.

Knowledge of the origin of the supreme intelligence and how it manifested into our physical world will help cultivate faith in mental science. Soon, you will learn how to apply this faith by directing your conscious mental energy using towards achieving your goal of sobriety, health and success.

5

Earth's Mysteries

"Everybody and every living thing, including animals, trees, plants and vegetables, have some degree of mind, for everything in the universe is an impartation of the One Infinite Mind. Man, is the highest concept of the Creative Intelligence."

—WALTER MATTHEW, 1922

In the previous chapters, we learned that intelligence and consciousness exist in the creation of the atom and the cosmos, and that humankind has a power to alter and transmute these energy forms using mind. It only follows that all earthly physical forms in-between also share these attributes of mentality and intelligence.

ATOMIC MIND AMASSES INTO LIFE FORMS

The consciousness or intelligence involved in the creation of the subatomic particles and the formation of the universe also applies to manifestations of molecules, cells, bodies, and other living things. Creation therefore, is simply a series of condensations. In 1922, New Thought teacher Alice Bailey wrote:

"This fundamental faculty of intelligence characterizes all atomic matter, and also governs the building up of forms, or the aggregation of atoms. We have earlier dealt with the atom per se, but have in no way considered its

building into form, or into that totality of forms which we call a kingdom in nature...Let us now extend our idea from the individual forms that go to the constitution of any of these four kingdoms of nature, and view them as providing that still greater form which we call the kingdom itself, and thus view that kingdom as a conscious unit, forming a homogeneous whole."

The intelligence that originated in the subatomic particle builds upon itself and accumulates into larger groupings or fractals as creation unfolds to form atoms, molecules, cells, bodies, plants, and onward.

In Mother Nature's creations, there are many examples of mentality, mind, or intelligence in subjects that have no brains, thinking apparatuses, or nervous systems. This display of intelligence in inert matter further proves our point in our mind-creation dogma.

Our Earth's biosphere, where all life exists, is a thin layer about forty miles high—beginning in the depths of the ocean seven miles deep where fish life ceases to exist, rising to about thirty miles into the atmosphere where live microbes have been found. In this thin "green" layer, there are estimated to be over nine million species of land animals; three hundred thousand species of plants; twenty-eight thousand species of fish; ten thousand species of birds; three million species of insects; not to mention seven billion human residents. Thus, we have quadrillions of living species in this thin biosphere belt.

Each of these species has unique functions in the complex ecosystem of the planet that require adaptation to changes in climate, ecology, and resources. For many species, interfacing with mankind, as well as with other species, is a major concern for daily survival. This not only requires a conscious intelligence, but also the ability to communicate among their own species and with others in the community. In 1912, New Thought teacher William Atkinson said:

"Some of the lower forms of "organic" life, so-called, possess no organs, and are but masses of jelly-like matter without signs of even rudimentary organs—and yet these life-forms show evidences of desire, choice, and will. More than this,

the metals and minerals, under scientific tests, have shown "responses" that are similar to the same action in organic life—showing life and rudimentary sensation, the latter of course being a manifestation of mind."

Atkinson is asserting that mind is found not only in living organic life, but in inert metals and minerals— as was discovered with the atom in quantum physics studies. Some of you may remember the "Pet Rock" from the 1970s. This (millionaire) inventor sold millions of plain old rocks under the marketing guise as being "pets." Maybe he was not far off in his thinking that these rocks really were "alive" and had personalities after all.

Through pure biological or anatomical studies, we recognize that many living species shouldn't possess any mental capabilities whatsoever (having no brains, nervous systems, or sensory organs). However, in nature they exhibit both consciousness and intelligent communication functions. There are thousands of examples of undetected senses and invisible and unknown communications skills that both plants and animal possess. They have displayed unexplainable sensory skills to see, hear, feel, or otherwise sense in a vibrational spectrum or dimension for which humankind does not yet have measurement capabilities. The sonar of bats and dolphins, smelling capabilities of dogs, and sight talents of hawks are some well-known obvious examples of extraordinary senses. Many species have intelligence and unique capabilities that are simply not being overtly displayed—they are communicating, sensing, and thinking in ways we still have not discovered.

PLANTS CAN THINK

One of the most fundamental species is the simple plant. We all know plants grow their stems and leaves toward the sun, and their roots toward the water. They do this, somehow, without a brain or any neural activity and can somehow maneuver themselves between rocks, cracks, and crevasses. Somehow detecting what lies beyond them, they can push rocks away and creatively bend and change their shapes to get to the sun or water. Even when water and sunlight are not even remotely nearby, they will still grow in that direction, innately and mysteriously drawn to these sources. Even over vast distances, they somehow gather information without any known senses. In 1904, Erastus Hopkins wrote the following:

> *"The tiny seed of an evergreen tree which chances to fall into a crevice of a rock, ere long in the silence of its mighty spirit cleaves the rock asunder to force room for its growth, not a fibre is displaced or its bark abrazed, still its tiny rootlets a child might bend at will—such is the power of spirit."*

We have learned that plants react to a variety of electromagnetic waves, such as music, sound, lighting variations, and subtler radio and transmission waves. We now know that they also respond to the thought vibrations or consciousness of humans.

It has been proven that when people talk to plants, they grow faster and healthier than those that are ignored. Originally, it was assumed this phenomenon was a result of people breathing the needed carbon dioxide on which the plants live on. Research however, proved this CO_2 theory was insignificant, and there was something more powerful...another non-physical factor involved—mind or consciousness, and more specifically emotions.

By testing the subjects using protective shields (to prevent CO_2 transmissions), the researchers concluded the plants somehow were conscious of the positivity of the human contact. They reacted to positive vibrations resulting from human non-physical contact and communication even though they had no known senses to detect a human presence. This was proven in studies and showed how human thoughts, feelings, and moods could be communicated to the plant and positively affect its growth and thus the production of flowers, fruit, and vegetables.

THE BEETLES HAVE ARRIVED!

Besides their roots, plants also grow underground webs or strands of fine, mesh-like fibers that are a fungus root-subsystem. This net-like growth interacts with neighboring plants and trees and forms a type of communication network for the community. These root networks not only physically share valuable nutrients such as nitrogen, but also communicate and exchange information to their neighbors about a host of things. They can relay information about bad soil areas, attacks by fungi and insects, available light sources, weather conditions, and even announce new plants in the vicinity.

When certain plants get attacked—say a tomato plant by a worm, or an apple tree by a caterpillar—they broadcast their distress signals not only through the root network but also in the air. They release fragrances that warn other plants that an attack is taking place, and also to announce to insect predators that a meal is available. For the apple tree, local parasitic wasps or birds will react to the unique fragrance frequency given off which is saying that there is a caterpillar at the source and come to feed on it.

The plants and trees can tell by the specific saliva of the insect attacking them what species it is, and then determine what cocktail of fragrances to send out. This "SOS" signal-scent is not only picked up by respective predators to come get the attackers, but also to warn other plants, which can protect themselves by releasing specific toxins to deter those types of insects.

There are thousands of these fragrance cocktails or scent signatures that provide protection from attackers, as well as exchange information. This scent capability, coupled with root network communications, is the plant world's Internet. Even though they are absent of a brain or sense organs like humans, plants clearly have elaborated and specialized sensations. Without sight, sound, touch, or speech organs they still manage to see, hear, smell, and feel their environment and broadcast this data to their peers and to other species.

MIND IS IN ALL FORMS

In the molecular world of biology, similar characteristics are found with single-celled organisms, germs, and viruses. Most of us have seen videos of these organisms or looked under a microscope and witnessed how they miraculously self-perpetuate to survive. Such a simple biological entity, again lacking any brain or sense organs, can somehow communicate, eat, replicate, and make decisions.

In the Atom chapter, we found that source-energy or intelligence begins with the creation of strings, quarks, and subatomic particles. This same intelligence accumulates throughout the assemblage of atoms, molecules, cells, organs, bodies, and then groups of bodies. Life does not begin when a certain entity is created (a cell, organ, plant, or animal); it begins at the onset of the atom latent with the source energy and intelligence. In 1922, Alice Bailey wrote the following:

> *"Our body, we have been told, is made up of a multiplicity of little lives, or cells, or atoms, each having its own individual consciousness. This corresponds to its self-consciousness. The consciousness of the physical body, viewed as a whole, might, from the atom's point of view, be regarded as its group consciousness."*

A physical brain and nervous system (or even a robot or computer) can have logical intelligence; however, in order to be self-conscious and self-act, an entity must have a reflective consciousness that only living things possesses. Mankind has these attributes, and furthermore possesses the power of imagination and a higher level super consciousness which makes him superior to all other living things on Earth.

The cell of an organ in the human body has a mind or consciousness, the organ itself also has a consciousness, and the body as a whole has a greater cumulative mind. This is one of the premises of mental healings. Each entity or consciousness is part of a larger one and contains within itself smaller subcomponent entities—thus all life is one succession or assemblage of a multitude of consciousness—they are fractals. In 1892, theosophist Emma Britten wrote:

> *"We note the universality of Spirit, for though we may find it so hidden away in the mineral kingdom that we can only detect growth and decay as the result of changes in force, or the life of things-yet rocks disintegrate into vegetable forms, which again give birth to insect life, or animal forms, whilst the very lowest these, steadily march upward through various grades of expanding intelligence, without one missing link, until we arrive at the culmination of Earthly being—man."*

The aggregation of intelligence unfolds from atom, to mineral, to a living thing. Mankind however, is one step above these forms, and also possesses the creative ability to direct mind-spirit.

GROUP CONSCIOUSNESS

Individual minds can combine and thus create a new entity or group consciousness. This occurs in the human, plant, and animal worlds. The conscious subcomponent may be a cell within an organ, an organ within a body, a body among other bodies in a species, or a species among Earth's ecosystem. You can subdivide or separate mind anywhere you like, but at each level of organization there will always be a unique frequency for each assemblage of consciousness. In other words, everything has a unique mind-frequency, individually or as a group. At every subdivision, there is a distinctive frequency.

In 1912, William Atkinson stated the following:

"Psychology recognizes a mental fusion between the individual minds of units composing a community of cells, insects, higher animals and even men. The 'spirit of the hive' noted by all students of bee-life, and the community spirit in an ant-hill are instances serving to illustrate the general principle of 'the collective mind.'"

Working ants and swarming bees are examples of individual consciousness forming a larger group consciousness. The same with migrating animal herds, fish schools, or birds flying in formation. In our human society, this same principle is displayed in assemblies of people such as in church congregations, families, sports teams, corporate cultures, support groups, and so on.

The sports bookies in the Las Vegas gambling circuit are all too familiar with group consciousness. They are wise to the invisible powers that are present in a *home* game. Usually many points are given for this home-field advantage because of the intangible benefits that the crowd provides. The home team plays while immersed in a positive conscious energy field being radiated by thousands of supportive fans—clearly a definite advantage. If for some reason the energy of the stadium waivers, the loss of momentum to the team can almost be felt physically. For a football team, a couple of fumbles, interceptions, or turnovers makes the atmosphere feel as though a dark cloud came over the stadium on what was just a radiant sunny day. The metaphysical force of momentum is the group consciousness at work. As a fan, you can sense and feel this mental-momentum swing back and forth, and the players feed on it. Time-outs are often used by coaches to try to allow the psychic energy of a momentum swing to level out.

Another group consciousness example is the beautiful schools of tropical fish that move in perfect synchronicity. Thousands of fish assemble to mimic a large predator fish as they dart and move in a microsecond in exact synchronization without bumping or breaking alignment. How they communicate we don't know, and how and why they do this is only a sign of a higher intelligence or consciousness. Some say this is simple evolution, sonar, and learned survival skills, but humans still cannot replicate the precision, speed, and methods of such sophisticated intelligence-communications. Humankind may eventually replicate the robotic feedback mechanism, but the intelligence of the group and its conscious intent will never be copied. A thousand tiny minds miraculously act as one.

When you form a group or organization, you also are creating a new conscious entity. Once you assemble multiple minds into a greater one, it creates its own personality or consciousness. This again applies to groupings of minds, whether in individual humans, or in aggregations of atoms or cells. Famous New Thought teacher Charles Haanel spoke along these lines when in 1922 he wrote:

> *"As each cell has its individual consciousness, intuition, and volition, so each federated group of cells has a collective individual consciousness, intuition, and volition. Likewise, each coordinated group of federations; until the entire body has one central brain where the great co-ordination of all the 'brains' takes place."*

These so-called federations are our individual minds or conscious entities. We humans gather and form groups or entities for many different reasons, sometimes voluntarily, such as in social and sports groups, and other times by default, such as in families and by gender or race. This grouping of individuals is proven to effectively provide a psychic commune greater than the sum of its parts that cannot be brought about separately by the individuals.

This meeting of the minds is a major component in the requirements for success as outlined in the famous book *Think and Grow Rich* by Napoleon Hill. Not only do you increase the magnitude of thinking power by joining forces with another, but by combining two minds you also create a third mind in which thoughts, ideas, and inspirations come about that would not have been thought of individually. Again, the whole is greater than the sum of its parts. Discussing a problem with another individual or group will often reveal solutions that each individual would not have discovered on his or her own. This is called the *Mastermind* principle.

Group consciousness in society provides strength and support because, on a metaphysical level, we are combining and coupling positive vibrations. This positive, supportive atmosphere can be felt in church sessions when a preacher provides a passionate sermon, or at an AA meeting when a member shares his or her struggles. The group's supportive and sympathetic consciousness is being radiated and absorbed by all in its field and the cumulative effects are synergistic. One grand mind is created that is greater than the sum of the individual minds, and sympathetic minds in attendance will benefit from these like-frequencies.

There is a mental science to both family gatherings and locker room pep talks—these events are comprised of mental energies synergistically being amplified. In 1908, Prentice Mulford said:

> *"The old-fashioned revival meeting, or camp meeting, through the combined action and desire of a number of minds brought a thought current, causing for the time the ecstasy, fervour and enthusiasm which characterized those gatherings."*

I have attended hundreds of AA meetings and would hear on a regular basis how members say how they attended because he or she "needed a meeting." Or upon having a troubled day or feeling an alcoholic craving, many AA members say they "have to get to a meeting." There is more power in a group that is sympathetic to your cause, especially in cases involving mutual suffering such as tragedy, addiction, and disease. Personally, I found that the group consciousness support was the most important and effective part of the AA program. It is pure mental science at work: metaphysical group consciousness, Mental-Science 101. Go to an AA meeting and fill up your tank with psychic energy and support (and a cup of coffee) for a couple of bucks—you can't beat it.

HAVE YOU EVER HAD A "CONTACT-BUZZ"?

Getting a "contact-buzz" is the phenomenon of getting a buzz or high solely from being in the proximity of others who are high or drunk. I remember back in college when I would meet up with a group of friends that were already well underway drinking or maybe getting stoned. Being completely sober myself, by just hanging out with them for a while, and not consuming anything, I would feel goofy and high. It wasn't just me either as many others have said the same thing has happened in their experience, thus the term "contact buzz" was coined. A similar phenomenon occurs when you study at a library or office setting versus a non-studious environment, like at home. You are in tune with the vibrations of the environment and others which are conducive to learning. These are perfect examples of how our minds radiate powerful non-physical signals and combine as a group. A sympathetic mind that is attuned to any groups mental vibrations will receive these signals and harmonize with them. It works just as well in church, as in 1904 Erastus Hopkins wrote the following:

> *"The soul's vibrations are transmitted from soul to soul, as is often illustrated in a prayer meeting, when some conscientious devotee rises in fervor and power of mind and thus psychotizes by spiritual vibrations a whole congregation; and usually under such mental-spiritual vibrations it is called a glorious meeting."*

People who go to church report feeling re-energized afterward—just from bathing in the positive radiance of other worshipers.

There are many other types of groupings calling for meditations, prayers, and candlelight vigils that utilize the power of forming a group consciousness for added strength and unity. In 1901, New Thought writer Annie Besant wrote:

> *"The strong thought of a great thinker goes out into the world of thought, and is caught up by receptive and responsive minds. …The increased force that may be obtained by the union of several people to help a common object is recognized not only by occultists, but by all who know anything of the deeper science of the mind…The thought-work will be aided by the added intensity given to it by fervent prayer, another form of thought-work, fired by religious fervour."*

EARTH'S MYSTERIES SUMMARY

In summary, the main point of this chapter is to reinforce the existence of consciousness in every creation and how mind successively assembles from molecules to cells, to bodies, and to groups. This energy can be empowered by the collection of supportive or similar minds. Mind power is cumulative when there is a common goal or desire.

Although communion with your inner higher power is the ultimate source of psychic-spiritual power, association with other people with common goals can be a great vibrational boost as well. Contrarily, associating with addictive minds, or the wrong crowd, will couple the negative vibrations and pull you down equally.

Especially in your first few months of beginning your program to sobriety or goal manifestation, you should surround yourself only with positive, supportive people and conditions. The invisible vibrations of these groupings will affect your personal frequency, and thus your ability to manifest the changes you are striving towards.

Remember that mind or consciousness exists in every component of creation and is present at all levels of organizations. As a student in mental science, we use this knowledge to advance ourselves in pursuit of achieving our goals. This is done by supplementing our self-image mental energies with like sympathetic minds, and keeping contrasting negative minds afar.

6

Vibration and the Law of Attraction

"There is a force in operation which has been called 'The Law of Attraction,' by which 'like attracts like' on all planes. And on the mental plane, the 'likes' are materialized into corresponding 'likes' on the material plane. Everything that is, first existed as an idea or Mental Picture, *either in the Cosmic Brain, or in the brain of some living creature as well. There is always a mental plan behind and in every material form, shape or condition."*

—WILLIAM ATKINSON, 1909

YOU ARE CONSTANTLY "GOOGLING" YOUR REALITY

The Law of Attraction states that everything is in a vibrational state, and that like or similar frequencies will attract each other… "like attracts like." What you resonate mentally, you will draw back to yourself physically.

When you search, or "Google" a term or concept on the Internet, the results are usually returned in order of relevancy, with the strongest matches coming up first. Type in a word or concept and Google returns the websites, photos, articles, videos and so on that match, or are in harmony with, your search term. The Law of Attraction acts similarly with your predominating thought-images. The people, places, and things—or your reality—is constantly matching the thoughts you are generating. It's just as if you are constantly feeding an internal Google search engine with your thoughts, and it constantly returns the reality that resonates or is relevant to them.

When you enter emotionally painful, embarrassing, or uncomfortable thought-images into your mental-spiritual search engine, it will bring you back negative, addictive, and unhealthy results. Feed it thought-images of health and sobriety, and your world will mirror this.

ANCIENT LAW

The Law of Attraction is an old law of creation discovered by humankind centuries ago. It was an ancient hermetic secret that was brought back to light over a hundred years ago during the New Thought movement. In 1906, William Atkinson wrote the book, *Thought Vibration or The Law of Attraction in the Thought World*, which became a founding New Thought doctrine.

Most recently, the Law of Attraction was brought back to the world's attention when the book and movie *The Secret* came out in 2006. As I mentioned earlier in the book, tens of millions around the world watched and read it. While a great number professed their attainment of wealth and success as a result of it, there also were those (including myself) who unfortunately did not find any success. Why is this, if it is a *Law* of Attraction? Why did it work for some and not others?

The Law of Attraction is a simple concept, but the mental science principles behind it needed to apply it can get very complicated. We can't just ask the universe for a million dollars and expect checks to arrive in the mail. Nor can we merely think ourselves sober or thin by making a mental picture of it and then transform into that image. The Law of Attraction is simply a branch of the mental science tree, just like optometry is a branch of medical science.

The study of mental science principles and spiritual laws must be comprehensive and thorough so that a solid foundation of faith is developed. As you will learn, a surefire program for change first requires knowledge, then faith in this knowledge, then application of the knowledge.

EVERYTHING VIBRATES, INCLUDING YOUR THOUGHTS

Everything is energy, and the difference in its physical manifestation is purely a matter of its unique vibrational frequency or signature. In 1912, The Three Initiates wrote the book *The Kybalion* which stated:

"Nothing rests; everything moves; everything vibrates…the differences between different manifestations of Matter, Energy, Mind, and even Spirit, result largely from varying rates of Vibration."

H_2O is the same in many forms, and the difference between ice, water, snow, and steam is all in the rate of vibration. The same goes for what differentiates the colors of yellow, blue, and red. Atoms and molecules, cells and organs, plants and animals, bodies and buildings, and even thoughts and emotions, all vibrate. Each radiates on a dimension or plane with a specific power and frequency.

Most of us are familiar (from high school science) with the spectrum chart that shows us the frequencies for visible light, x-rays, sound waves, and radio waves. What this chart does not show, however, is the frequencies of mind-spirit which is in a dimension and density of its own. In other words, it's *off the charts* of measurable frequencies. If the entire electromagnetic spectrum was stretched to 2,500 miles long, just about coast-to-coast, that the visible portion would only be two inches long! Just think about the enormity of frequencies that we don't know about.

The non-physical world however, is powerful in that it controls the denser cruder physical world. For example, with solar energy, a (physical) photoelectric silicon cell converts (nonphysical) sunrays or photons into actual electricity. This electricity can then move a four-thousand-pound bulldozer, which then can take down a mountain of dirt. So, you can say for a fact that from ninety-three million miles away, a form of non-physical energy, the sunlight, can move a mountain. It's all in the transmutation of the initial mind-energy into material or physical expression.

Likewise, with the mind, we have the ability to change or create matter or physical conditions by powerfully directing our invisible, nonphysical thoughts. In 1911, William Atkinson wrote:

"Everything in the material world is in vibration—ever manifesting a high degree of motion. Without vibration, there would be no such thing as a material universe. From the electronic-corpuscles which science teaches compose the atom; up through the atom and molecule, until the most complex forms of matter are manifested, there is the ever-present Vibration."

Vibrational frequencies have specific characteristics. Low frequency vibrations are darker, colder, and slower. These correspond to radio and sound waves on the electromagnetic chart, and represent fear or depression on a metaphysical emotional chart. On the opposite end, high frequencies are hot in temperature. These correspond to light or gamma waves in the electromagnetic field, and represent love and enthusiasm in the emotional field. The flow of energy is usually always from the higher frequency to the lower, from hot to cold, from light to dark, positive to negative. You cannot add darkness to a lighted room, but you can add light to darkness. Just as hot air will always move in to neutralize colder air, faster moving frequencies and particles overcome and invade the slower ones. Happy positive thoughts are much more powerful than negative sad ones—its metaphysics.

The mental science vibrations we are dealing with are the nonphysical—thoughts and consciousness. These cannot be seen or measured. Scientists can measure a person's *thinking activity* by electrical and magnetic detection of neurotransmitters, but this is physical and not metaphysical. Our brain waves differ completely from our esoteric mind-thoughts; the latter holds our consciousness, imagination, and intelligence. Science has yet to find a method of detecting mind or thought.

This entire spectrum of the nonphysical, or metaphysical, exists in tandem with the physical world. Our mental-spiritual bodies simply exist in a dimensional plane or density that is much subtler and finer than its denser course physical counterparts. Each physical component has a corresponding archetypical form, just in a different dimension or density—a type of astral ghost or shadow. For every "physical" form, there is an unseen metaphysical form which precedes it as the ethereal skeleton behind its existence.

Thoughts are real vibratory things and not just idealistic fantasies, dreams, or lofty images. Mental currents are as real as radio waves, sun waves, and X-rays; they are just more subtle and undetectable. Metaphysical and spiritual in nature, they are finer than anything we know in the physical world, yet the most powerful.

The Law of Attraction states that when thoughts are mixed with emotions, they generate powerful vibrations that attract those people, things, and circumstances that are in harmony with the frequency that is being radiated. This vibrational state not only affects conditions external to ourselves, but also works internally to affect our brains and bodies, as proven in mental healing and placebo effect studies. In 1904, Erastus Hopkins wrote:

"TO THINK IS TO PRODUCE VIBRATIONS...by its agency the Visible Universe is built up or can be destroyed. The so-called physical body of man is no exception to the Law of Vibration. We cannot think without producing a vibration of some kind, which is at once recorded in the brain and transmitted throughout the whole nerve system of the body. We are mind; mind and soul are one and the same. Mind thinks thoughts, and in doing so produces vibrations which radiate and reproduce themselves indefinitely."

YOUR SIGNATURE SELF-IMAGE FREQUENCY

Your cumulative thoughts and emotions at any given moment are represented by a specific frequency. This is your identity or signature self-image frequency. You feel it as your mood, level of enthusiasm, and general feeling of well-being. It is reflected in people's auras. It is the harmonic tone or *song* your mind-spirit is singing. It brings you good luck or misfortune, success or failure, and health or sickness.

This emotional-body has all the attributes of your self-image. It is not a single frequency, just like a fire is not a single flame. You are constantly radiating frequencies on hundreds of your personal desires, ranging from health to wealth, from love to material possessions. Your individual thought-images amass to create a holographic self-image, and it is this resultant self-image that radiates outwardly to create the world you live in. When it is a harmonious frequency we are happy and healthy. When it is discordant or misaligned, we suffer sickness and misfortune, and this is when addiction come into play.

You may have thoughts and feelings about specific things throughout the day, but unless they are believed to be true, and absorbed into your belief system, they are no more than inert thoughts. We only act upon thoughts we accept as truths. They have no vibratory power without belief.

If you keep repeating a lie to yourself long enough, you may begin to believe in it, and that lie will become a reality. Constantly tell yourself that you are powerless over alcohol, and your reality will soon reflect this negative thought. Your body will remain weak to it, you will have cravings for it, and the people, places, and things in your world will harmonize with this belief. You will be attracted to others who also are weak or powerless. Concentrate and believe you are beyond the condition of addiction, and you will live in that reality, and attract healthy and positive people and conditions, and your body will be strong and resistant.

HOW THE LAW OF ATTRACTION WORKS

The Law of Attraction proves that like frequencies tend to group together or harmonize. Like attracts like, and vibrations of the same sort will gather together or be attracted together. The physical world is simply an expression of mind. Physical reality is the mirror of the thought frequencies that desired it into existence.

The vibrations set up by the mind will transmute into their physical counterparts. Thoughts of health and sober living will not only attract healthy conditions to you, but your body will also react positively biochemically. Cells, organs, and the body as a whole will mirror the frequency that the mind projects. When you apply the Law of Attraction to your self-image, it is extremely powerful in transforming both your body and your life's conditions. In 1897, Ralph Trine declared:

"There is in connection with the thought forces what we may term the drawing power of mind, and the great law operating here is one with the great law of the universe, that like attracts like. We are continually attracting to us, from both the seen and the unseen side of life, forces and conditions most akin to those of our own thoughts. This law is continually operating whether we are conscious of it or not."

Keep in mind that as you think, you evoke images. As you imagine, feelings are created. And as you feel you vibrate, and as you vibrate, you attract and manifest that which you desire. If your dominating thoughts are negative, they generate dissonant vibrations and return more negative conditions. These eventually manifest in outward conditions—both bodily illness and unfavorable circumstances. *As above, so below.* The outer world is always reflecting the inner. When this happens, a change to right thinking is needed—a reversal or refreshing of the mind and knowledge of mind-spirit laws. You will bring in the light to the darkness, with thoughts of the truth. A simple change of mind will stop this cause-and-effect chain from ever starting to unfold.

Your vibrational state is a nonphysical emanation. Think of it as your metaphysical song, but with a cosmic resonance. If you could describe your inner being as a type of music, would it be a smooth melodic rhythm, a fun rock beat, a heavy-metal riff, or a disharmonic jumble of noise? What "song" represents your inner frequency? Beethoven, Led-Zeppelin, Garth Brooks, Bruno Mars, a bird singing, or the sound of a busy intersection? This inner vibrational state has a sound, color, melody, and feel, but on an astral, nonphysical level—a plane with different dimensions than the physical realm.

Back in 1899, New Thought teacher, Ralph Trine, reinforced the Law of Attraction when he wrote:

"The type of thought we entertain both creates and draws conditions that crystallize about it, conditions exactly the same in nature as is the thought that gives them form. Thoughts are forces, and each creates of its kind,

whether we realize it or not. The great law of the drawing power of the mind, which says that like creates like, and that like attracts like, is continually working in every human life, for it is one of the great immutable laws of the universe."

Very simplified, the formula of the law looks like this: thought-images plus emotions equals vibration, which attracts.

When you set goals, you are setting up thought-images which have a vibrational frequency. When you think, feel, and act in vibrational alignment with them, you change your inner being and thus manifest your desires.

This is the basis of the Law of Attraction. If you want to see how your thoughts and frequency has been directed in the past, then simply look around your conditions right now. Stop reading for a moment and take a quick inventory of your life; this is a mirror of your past thinking and vibrational state. Whether you are healthy or an addict, wealthy or broke, gainfully employed or jobless, living in luxury or on the street, in loving relationships or alone—all result from past thinking, your past frequency. You received exactly what you were radiating.

Remember that the Law of Attraction works off the feelings you vibrate, not the inert thoughts or images. Faith and enthusiasm in the goal as being already fulfilled is the most powerful state to manifestation. When you achieve an inner vibrational state of a sober, healthy, and happy person, you will become so—it is law. But there is no fooling the inner self if there is any doubt. It must be believed as a fact. Mental science says you can change any vibrational state by believing in it with unwavering faith.

THE LAW IS BOTH THE CAUSE AND THE CURE OF ADDICTION

Whether you realize it or not, you have developed a certain addict's lifestyle. You may have been covert and sneaky about it, or maybe blatantly obvious. The people, places, and things you've associated with, all have your addict's touch to them. Worse yet, your personality, habits, and physical body also reflect this lifestyle. The way you dress, the way you look, your moods, and the health of your body. Some people see right through the mask you put on and can see the trouble behind it, yet you may completely fool others. Everything in your world harmonizes with your mental preoccupation with your addiction. This is because it is a vibrational frequency you resonate from a core level. Deep down, the addict *loves* his or her drug to the point that they are using the Law of Attraction to draw it to them.

You are now learning how to reprogram old thinking habits and positively charge your vibrational state. When your mind is magnetized with a new goal self-image of being clean, sober, healthy and happy, your vibrational being will change and your external circumstances will mirror this. You must believe in the law. It cannot be done with half-assed belief.

One way or another, your addiction, depression, and bad circumstances are a result of your past thinking and vibrational state. Granted, many of us have suffered from trauma and emotional damage in our youths that were not our fault and unavoidable, but your internal state that governed your outward conditions was in your control. That, however, is all in the past, and what is critical is the now and the future. Your future depends on how you change your vibrational frequencies, which is the result of today's thoughts, images, and feelings.

Your negative thoughts and images manifest in you like a virus does in your computer. You don't want a slow, corrupt, and faulty computer nor do you want a depressed, sick, and addicted brain and body. A computer virus is only a pain in the ass, whereas the negative thoughts and beliefs are a pain in the heart. You must clean out the viruses of your mind and reprogram yourself with a positive goal self-image vibrational state.

Negative thoughts will attract like thoughts and, if pursued, will manifest into discordant vibrational states. In worldly conditions, this negative state will display itself as bad luck, failures, missed opportunities, accidents, conflicts, and so forth. Your negative frequency also directly affects your physical body and will produce depression, sickness, and disease. These same inharmonious vibrations that cause this vibrational discord or pain are triggers for addictions. A simple small problems can snowball into a discordant emotional body. You will learn that right thinking, goal self-imaging, and maintaining a positive vibrational state will prevent this from ever occurring.

LAW OF ATTRACTION SUMMARY

The Law of Attraction stipulates that at all times you are attracting to yourself whatever your focus, attention, or intention is. At every moment, you are thinking and feeling and creating your future. You cannot escape this law. Open your mind and become aware of what is in your core frequency, and with mental science practices you will learn to replace and reprogram these with positivity, health, and sobriety.

Bear in mind that the state of your body, your present situation, and your present conditions, were all your choices, whether they were consciously selected or not. Mankind always has the ability to choose his thoughts. In 1921, Fenwicke Holmes wrote:

"He has no devil to blame. There is no luck good or bad; there are no mistakes except his own; and the inharmony he feels is the inharmony he makes. We are living in a universe of pure intelligence, infinite in power, continuously creative, and impersonally manifesting in poverty or wealth, sickness or health, according to the dictates of our own selections. We set the mould into which Spirit shall pour Itself out into form for us. If we are rich, it is by no chance. Either consciously or unconsciously, we have kept the law; we have sowed faith in supply."

The Law is always at work whether you choose to control it or not. If we don't actively control our vibrational state with positive programming, we are like a ship without a sail, drifting and vulnerable to outside forces. If you don't first see it, plan it, and believe it in your mind, then you will simply follow the course set by others and external conditions. Master the laws of mental science and you will master your physical body and conditions, and control your destiny.

With the principles, you learn and apply here, you will change your vibrational state to that of a healthy, sober, loving, and successful person.

The Law of Attraction will return to you the reality that reflects your inner state. Use this law and always be aware that it is working at all times. Remember, thoughts and beliefs are your choice—no one can put them in your head except yourself.

> *"When your understanding grasps the power to visualize your heart's desire and hold it with your will, it attracts to you all things requisite to the fulfillment of that picture by the harmonious vibrations of the law of attraction."* --Genevieve Behrend, 1921

7

Maya, Our Dual World

"Everything flows, out and in; everything has its tides; all things rise and fall; the pendulum-swing manifests in everything; the measure of the swing to the right is the measure of the swing to the left; rhythm compensates."

—THE KYBALION, 1912

Through mental science and spiritual law practices, we will learn to control our destiny, and achieve our goals of health, sobriety, love, and success. In doing so, we use mind and thought, which function in the invisible world of unseen energies. We have already learned about the powers of group consciousness and the effects of others minds on ourselves, but there are also more esoteric forces at work. In this metaphysical world, there are other energies around us that are constantly balancing and harmonizing the world. We must recognize, heed, respect, and adapt to these energies in order to maintain our positive vibrational state.

Maya is a term used in some yogi and Sanskrit sects meaning the illusory nature of the universe. It is the contrast we experience—the duality in nature. It is the yin and yang, ebb and flow, light and dark, hot and cold, male and female, and the positive and negative. Without maya there would be no light and shadow, nor sound and silence... it is real, yet it is simply vibrational energy that follows laws. Newton's Law of Motion, which states that "for every action there is an equal and opposite reaction," is a law of maya in which it follows that "what goes up, must come down". Maya is the contrast required to have extremes, and without it there would be no variation, no motion, no life—nor would there be any desires.

THE DUALITY IN NATURE

The true ancient masters and wise yogis were those who could see past the mayic nature of the world and perceive the underlying truth. They lived a life of harmony and balance and did not ride the exhausting and sometimes extreme waves of maya. Maya was the illusion that kept humankind from wisdom and to overcome it was to achieve wisdom and defeat ignorance. One way the magical yogi masters proved their supremacy over maya was by performing feats such as levitating their bodies in defiance of gravity. There were even great masters known to walk on water, and the ultimate mayic miracle, resurrect themselves from death. They used both the negative and positive forces of maya to create what they desired.

You may be wondering what this subject has to do with curing addiction and achieving our goals. The answer is that in using the mental science principles, we must be cognizant of the forces of nature that may influence or affect our energy and moods, and thus our vibrational states and goal achievement efforts. There are powerful energy currents that should be recognized and heeded, and we should understand these forces as well as acknowledge the contrast in the creation of all things. Maya not only identifies the dual nature in life that gives root to our desires, but also to the rhythmic action that nature is constantly undergoing. In 1912, The Three Initiates also wrote:

> "*Everything is Dual; everything has poles; everything has its pair of opposites; like and unlike are the same; opposites are identical in nature, but different in degree; extremes meet; all truths are but half-truths; all paradoxes may be reconciled.*"

In my use of the word, the Law of Maya is a broad term and includes several other related doctrines. These include the Law of Rhythm, the Law of Gender, the Law of Polarity, the Law of Duality, and the Law of Cause and Effect.

Gaia, Mother Nature or planet Earth has many contrasting entities and forces at play—the sun and moon, the high and low tides, light and dark, the weather cycles, and so forth. There are invisible life currents that circulate around us at all times that contrast in polarity or duality and are constantly changing. These all can affect how we feel mentally, physically, and emotionally.

TAKE HEED OF THE EMOTIONAL PENDULUM

The physical body has its cycles and rhythms, too. We experience pain and pleasure, joy and sadness, energy and lethargy. We work in the daytime and sleep at night. Like a pendulum, we work hard (swing up), then rest (swing down).

Highs are sometimes balanced out by lows, but this is not a bad thing—it's just a balancing act of nature. After getting a natural high from jogging five miles, having sex, or eating a chocolate sundae, you must let the ensuing "down" pass. We don't attach to it, fight it, or take it personally, it's just the dual mechanics of the universe. This is why meditation after a physical workout is more effective. After exercise, you are naturally going into a physical recovery-mode, so you just "ride this wave" down to catapult yourself into deeper level of consciousness.

There is also dualism and rhythm in the emotional or mental world. Sometimes we find that periods of elation and happiness may be followed later by depression or sadness. This is very pronounced at celebrations, birthdays, and so on when we go from one end of the emotional spectrum to the other without really knowing why. This is no more than the momentum of the emotional pendulum swinging back on you. The extreme opposite is often experienced when we hit one extreme emotional state. As William Atkinson wrote in 1919:

"Persons who dwell principally on the plane of the emotions live in a state of alternate heaven and hell. Now enjoying to the fullest the upward swing, they revel in the ecstasies of emotional feeling until they feel as

if they were indeed gods. Then comes the backward swing which plunges them into the hell of depression, melancholy, remorse, regret or feeling of impotence and uselessness. The more emotional the person, the higher and lower in the scale of feeling does he travel."

This is not saying that it is wrong to experience strong emotions, but only to be prepared for the backlash that may occur. You will be more careful in managing your emotions once you experience and understand these rhythms. "There's no such thing as a free lunch" …you pay for getting high (even a natural high), it just depends on if you learn to ride the resulting wave or fight it.

When we realize that we are attracted to one part of a spectrum, we should be careful about the opposite end coming into play. To go to extremes in exercise will result in fatigue, just as periods of rage often end in that same person expressing opposite feelings of friendship or even love. A lovers' quarrel is a perfect example of going from one extreme emotion to its opposite. You also may know people who are referred to as "drama queens." They are usually very exhausting to be around because of their extreme emotional reactions, and they are always finding themselves in cyclic good luck-bad luck situations. They love to ride the cyclic emotional waves.

The peak emotional highs and the ensuing bottom-out crashes are the critical ones we need to heed. Using drugs or alcohol can send dopamine levels off the charts. They say that crack can boost dopamine levels over ten times the normal level. The crash that follows is usually just as extreme, usually becoming an impetus to get more drugs or booze into the system to level off the freefall before the crash. These cycles of ultra-high to severe depression does wicked things to your nervous system and brains chemistry, not to mention your metaphysical state. It not only takes time and meditation to heal the damage, but we also need to correct the loss of sensitivity of our senses and awareness. We need to restore and reestablish our mental focus and sharpness, and consciously seek out the subtler energies present in everyday things.

Once you understand the mayic world you will actually find more variety in life. Drugs and alcohol numbed this experience in the past and raised thresholds of perception. We now need to jump the psychic railroad tracks and find other highs to replace the old, artificial ones. We need to explore new avenues for highs once we heal and restore our normal pleasure thresholds. As you heal, your threshold for pleasure will return to its natural level and you will soon find that simple contrasts in life are once again stimulating. Rock star Alice Cooper swears that the game of golf saved his life by keeping him sober. He found a natural high in the sport, the landscape, and the serenity of the game. Just remember to keep the balance and harmony—as ex-addicts, we tend to take everything to extremes. When you do find a natural passion or high, always be prepared for the pendulum to swing back, knowing it's a natural phenomenon.

These same laws of rhythm apply in the metaphysical realm of vibration and goal manifestation. You may find yourself progressing forward toward your goals and then one day feel that you are idle or even going backward. This is just the rhythmic cycle in the metaphysical world balancing out the ups and downs, pluses and minuses. This may put you in a crappy mood out of the blue for no reason. Don't take it as a personal issue, there is probably an unknown force of maya at work, so you just need to relax and let that stage and mood pass by. It's like the athlete who lifts weights to gain strength. In order to gain muscle mass, he or she must tear the muscle tissues so they grow back stronger and larger. The athlete does not get depressed after a workout when his or her muscles are sore and torn down. He or she knows they will soon rebuild stronger than ever. The downward cycle is heeded and accepted because of knowledge.

It is difficult to constantly maintain a high frequency rate without a period of rest, and you cannot be positive and upbeat all of the time. Just as a dieter should spoil themselves with an occasional sweet, you can let yourself slide and get away with some slack times as well, as long as it doesn't involve drinking or drugging.

BIORHYTHMS AND ASTROLOGY PROVE OUR CYCLES

These human emotions and cycles of moods and performance have been scientifically studied. Biorhythms is a study based on the premise that every human body has three cycles—one each for emotional, intellectual, and physical—which are twenty-eight, thirty-three, and twenty-three days long respectively. When plotted on a X-Y graph, these functions display as three intertwining sine waves on the chart. The cycle starts the day you were born. So, a simple calculation could tell you exactly where you were today in each of these three categories—at the peak, the bottom, or somewhere in between. All three waves will align every couple of years and you will experience what is called a triple high or triple low, depending if they align on top or bottom of the chart. Otherwise they are a mix of the three. For example, one day you could be physically a level nine, emotionally a level two, and intellectually a five, and then every couple of years you will hit that peak 10-10-10, or 0-0-0. If you follow biorhythms, I'd stay home on the triple-0 days, and play lotto on the triple-10's.!

Astrology is similar to biorhythms in that it bases personal predictions on the period you were born and the cycles that follow. These, however, are based on celestial positions of the sun, moon, and planets in the zodiac. Although I don't follow either biorhythms or astrology, I still try to be sensitive to the fact that sometimes there are outside forces nudging at us or pushing us certain directions. I firmly believe, that we create our own reality with our thoughts and beliefs. If you believe and have faith in biorhythm predictions or a horoscope, you are engaging the Law of Attraction in making them become self-fulfilling prophecies. Humankind has mental-spiritual capacities to surpass the common forces of maya, so you do not need to be wary that you are doomed by these astrological or biorhythmic cycles. They are simply unseen tendencies which mental science practices can overrule. If you do not practice mental science, and instead just flow with life, then you are vulnerable to all mayic conditions including astrological and biorhythmic.

MAYA SUMMARY

Keep in mind not to take the downward swings personally and let them upset your momentum or motivation. Many times, we misinterpret bad moods or feelings of inertia for something negative, when in fact it is solely coming from the rhythms of maya. The cause can be from any of the different planes at work—earth, body, mental, or metaphysical, psychic. You need to learn when it's time to rest and just to acknowledge these swings in the pendulum. Do not fight it. Step to the side and let the pendulum swing past you and not drag you back with it.

To succumb to the downward swing of maya is analogous to going out in the ocean for a swim. When a breaking-wave approaches, it is much easier and more efficient to simply duck or dive under it effortlessly. If you try to swim through it and fight it, the wave not only sets you back several steps, but also wears you down. The master surfer learns not only to avoid the wave, but to go forward in spite of it.

Keep in mind that your emotions and moods reflect your inner vibrational frequencies and are our compass for telling us if we are on course or not in achieving our goals. You must consider the facts of maya when you get in a bad mood for no reason, or you suffer a slight setback in achieving your goals…it is not always your fault. It may not be you at all, but just the natural swing in universal rhythms. Learn to differentiate an attitude or mood you can control versus just a natural passing feeling. Recognize them, flow with them, and keep focused on your goals. The mayic cycle will pass.

There are always two sides to maya. It's up to you to decide on how you will experience it. A partly cloudy day is still partly sunny, and a half-empty glass of water is still half-full. Just remember that knowledge, right thinking, and wisdom cures the riddle of maya.

8

Spirit Messages

"The word supernormal simply means that which is above the normal and not that which is unknowable. The word occult includes many very illusive phenomena—phenomena which though recognized by scientists as facts, yet seem to baffle all explanation. Certain metaphysical phenomena called psychical, with which Spiritualism deals, will someday cease to be mysteries because other human powers or sources of knowledge not now recognized by modern psychology will become operative..."

— J. C. F. GRUMBINE, 1910

WHY I BELIEVE

I still vividly remember a strange experience I had as a youth. As I mentioned in my life story, I was a competitive runner growing up, and my grandfather had also been a runner himself. To reiterate, he was both his college school record holder and team captain.

When I was ten years old, my grandfather passed away and his wife died shortly thereafter. He had just begun to see my early running achievements when he died, and I know he would have loved to see me follow in his footsteps and become a champion runner like he was.

A couple of years later at age twelve, I had already accumulated over a dozen trophies for various sports and probably another fifty or so running medals. On the walls of my bedroom, my dad built bookshelves for my trophies and rows of wood molding that held my medals. The medals were mostly in plastic cases that sat on the wood ledge leaning against the wall and were secured with double-faced tape. On the back of each medal case, I wrote the race results: the event, my time, and what I placed. Not many kids had a room like mine, and I was proud to show it off to my friends after school.

One evening in the middle of the night, I was awakened by a sharp crackling noise. I recognized this noise as my running medals because of the plastic-metal rattling sound that it made, along with the direction from which the sound came. I was startled and scared. My bedroom was in a remote part of the house away from the others, and I knew no one else would have heard it.

I was lying on my side and slowly squinted open my sleepy eyes wondering what it was. There in front of me, about five feet away, were two glowing white ghostly figures. They were silhouettes, but I clearly recognized them as my grandfather and grandmother. I closed my eyes in fright, and then a few minutes later, looked again, squinting ever so slightly, so I would not be noticed to be awake. My heart began to beat faster as they stood there staring at me. I froze in fear, as my heart continued to pound. I started sweating, but I lay still, pretending to be asleep. I was wide awake inside and terrified. I would look again a couple more times, with the smallest unnoticeable squinting of my eyes, and I could still see them. They stood there holding hands in a white astral glow, staring at me. After about twenty minutes, which felt like hours, I looked again and they were gone.

Like a baby, I yelled out loud for my mom and asked her for some water. She came and turned on the light and saw me sweating, so she asked if I felt sick. I said that I had just had a bad dream. I did not want to sound crazy to her by telling her what had happened, plus I was pretty confused by it all.

After she left, I turned the light back on and walked over to my medal display. Two medals were lying on the sofa below the shelves. I saw that they were very secure in the way they had been mounted, and it took some effort to make them dislodge from the adhesive. I thought again about the vision I had and my young mind simply did not comprehend it. Was my granddad looking at my medals that night and checking on me?

Thinking this dream or vision was just too strange, I never mentioned it to anyone. But subconsciously it did instill a belief in me of spirits and the after-world that molded the views I have today on life and death. I *do* believe that I saw my grandparents that night, and therefore have a belief in an afterlife.

So, this next area of study was a natural attraction to me, not only because of this experience I had as a youth but also because there still were missing pieces of the puzzle revolving around the concept of consciousness and spirit. I already learned about the source of intelligence, the atom, the cosmos, and mind, but I was curious about the conscious entity or spirit behind it all. Mental science was the practical use of the mind-spirit, but what else was hidden behind that?

I wanted to verify if the concepts on mind, consciousness, and mental science resonated in the spiritual world. Since mind and consciousness were of a nonphysical source, then people with knowledge of the afterlife should be able to confirm or verify the reality of its existence.

I had read of these strange cases of people that reported firsthand knowledge of the spirit world and wanted to investigate it further. There were several groups of these people which included psychics, channels, and near-death experience (NDE) patients.

I AGREE, THIS IS WEIRD STUFF

This chapter may make you feel like you're entering another weird zone. But as I mentioned before, people get uncomfortable when dealing with the occult, or things our five senses don't perceive. I suggest you read it and believe what you will…just keep an open mind. At worst, it will provide amusement, but hopefully will also provide enlightenment. In 1910, J.C.F. Grumbine explained this unwillingness to accept these paranormal things like this:

"Any function, faculty, sense or power of the soul which is not known to science may be termed occult. This does not imply that it is unknowable or that it

is unthinkable, but that it is at present, so far as science or experimental knowledge is concerned, outside of the field of hypothetical or known causality."

Keep in mind that this book is a study course in mental science. So, we are exploring all of the facets this subject matter offers, including some topics on the outskirts or fringes. By introducing these extracurricular subjects, I'm trying to reinforce the fact that we live in both physical and nonphysical realms, and I'm trying to present the extension beyond the mind or consciousness that we call the spirit.

It almost seems like cheating to get secrets about the afterlife. If there were legitimate cases of people who had information on our existence from the *other side*, then I definitely wanted to know about it. It would be like getting your opposing team's playbook before a football game. Why struggle and try to figure out the game of life the hard way when someone has already been to the source and brought the rule book back with them? Why not get all the secret plays, passwords, and shortcuts from an experienced veteran who has already played the game? They would know all the answers about life after death, our destinies, and about our mental-spiritual abilities.

I've always suspected life after death, I suppose because of my grandparents. There is also a scientific basis stating that energy or forces can be neither created nor destroyed, they only can change form. I believe this is a universal law and that it applies to the mind-spirit world also. Instead of physical forces and energy being conserved and converted, we are dealing with its counterpart of consciousness and spirit. Consciousness or spirit only changes in densities, planes, or dimensions and never ceases to exist. In 1919, Swami Vishita wrote about how these fine subtle spirit vibrations are perceived by mankind:

"All our sensations are due to the impact upon our sense-organs of vibrations in some form…Some vibrations are too rapid and some too slow to affect our senses, and therefore we have called to our aid various mechanical contrivances which enable us to recognize existences which would otherwise remain unknown. But it is still conceivable that there

may be, and doubtless are, conditions of vibratory energy that escape us, and which, if we could develop finer senses, would yield wonderful results and extensions of our power and knowledge. Today, indeed, we are coming into contact with forces, possibilities, and personalities which amount to a revelation of a new universe of things."

Please take note of the last sentence: *"Today, indeed, we are coming into contact with forces...and personalities."* Having extrasensory capabilities not only allows for one to sense the fine mental vibrations of others, such as with ESP, but also sense finer frequencies or densities, such as spirits or "personalities."

So, I proceeded to investigated three different types of afterlife groups. These were: Spirit entities channeled by mediums; medical cases of near-death experience (NDE); and, stories of Eastern yogi recitals on reincarnated or resurrected spirits.

At first, I was very skeptical of all of these stories and claims. I put them in the same category as circus fortune-tellers, crop circles, or Egyptian pyramid conspiracies. But I suppose these subjects couldn't be too far-fetched, because there are currently several television shows about psychics and mediums, with one series going on its eighth season. So, there is evidence that much of mainstream America is beginning to believe in this.

It took hundreds of hours of study and research with an open mind for me to come to the conclusion that many of these stories and cases are legitimate. After thoroughly investigating many subjects, I found a golden thread that ran through all of the material—what they all said completely concurred with the mental science principles and spiritual laws that I had already been studying. This was one of the main purposes of my inquiry, to see if this spirit world collaborated with the mental sciences I learned in books. And it certainly did, which just reinforced my faith that much more in the dogma I was building.

All of these spirit-sources had experiences confirming that once the physical body is shed, there is only a consciousness, spirit, soul, or higher being remaining. Death of the body is seen as the birth of the spirit, or as a change in the texture of the body from atoms and molecules to a subtle astral light on a different dimensional plane. The soul or consciousness remains, but just in another nonphysical bodily form, as in accordance with the law of energy conservation.

ABRAHAM, BASHAR, AND SETH

The first three of the subjects that I studied were mediums—people who "channel" or connect with nonphysical entities or spirits of those who had passed on. A medium usually enters a trancelike, meditative state, and the spirit entity connects with the medium. They then communicate with a third party who typically asks the questions. Apparently, when the spirit communicates to the medium, it is not in any particular language, but is described as "information blocks" consisting of images, feelings, and messages. Some of these may take the medium a few seconds to translate and some that may take hours. It all depends on the complexity of the subject matter. I guess it would be like you or me briefly looking at a painting or post-card and then trying to describe it to someone.

I watched hundreds of channeling videos and many are truly entertaining. These entities or spirits could conduct a normal conversation with someone on the outside world while connected to the medium's body. They could have interviews and question-and-answer sessions, just like having a normal conversation (maybe with just the slightest delay in response time). Their ability to have live conversations was one of the factors that made me a believer in these select mediums. Their impromptu answers, quick wit, and the information they would share spontaneously without any delay told me that it was coming from a direct source, and wasn't fabricated by the medium. The subject matter and manner in which it was delivered was a direct contrast to the actual personality, knowledge base, and intellect of the medium's true self. After studying and observing hundreds of cases, I was convinced beyond a shadow of a doubt that these mediums were not faking it—there was no way they could have this knowledge and answer these questions in a split second unless they truly were the source of the information.

Seth was the first spirit I studied. Seth is a (passed-on human life) spirit who used Mrs. Jane Roberts as a medium back in the 1970s and 1980s.

I've perused many of the books about Seth written by Jane Roberts, and also watched and listened to numerous video and audio clips of the actual channeling of Seth.

Seth was spiritually deep, metaphysical, and philosophical, but also conveyed very practical mental science lessons that resonated with New Thought doctrines.

His most famous and eternal quote was this: *"You create your own reality…your beliefs form reality."* This was recorded during a live session and can be accessed on the Internet today. Jane followed this statement by expounding upon details and knowledge of the science of the spirit.

Seth, through Jane Roberts, wrote over two dozen books that included topics including mental science, mind and consciousness, the afterlife and spirit world, reincarnation, the soul and psyche, and the subject of reality. Some think that Seth's material is too extreme, occult or metaphysical. As with any subject matter, you should disregard or discard what doesn't fit your beliefs, and take what does. For me, I was interested in the mental science portion and in how to advance or evolve as a human being—how to use mind powers properly—and Seth's material provided a great deal of this information on this.

What I found most interesting was Seth's knowledge and insight into human metaphysical life and how humankind creates his or her own reality using thoughts, emotions, and desires. Seth said that humans can change the outcome of their lives when they change their thinking, beliefs, and intentions or expectations. The subconscious mind will accept and act upon human thought images, imagination, and perceptions, and thoughts and beliefs are the only creating forces in one's reality. Seth affirmed that the events of today are materializations of past thoughts and beliefs, and that your expectations dictate your future. These teachings were spot-on with the mind-science teachings I was already learning in New Thought.

The next channeled spirit I studied is named Abraham, who is still active today. Abraham actually is not an individual, but a group of non-physical entities or a collection of consciousness. Their teachings and messages are interpreted by channel Mrs. Esther Hicks.

Esther Hicks is very popular and has published many books and videos. One of their bestsellers is entitled *The Law of Attraction*, which was called "the secret of *The Secret*" by Oprah Winfrey. I guess channeling can't be too weird if Oprah follows it, right?

Abraham is very popular on YouTube, in radio interviews, and live in lectures and workshops around the world. During these workshops, Mrs. Hicks goes into her trance and Abraham surfaces and teaches lessons on their co-creation philosophy and answers questions from the audience. The lectures and Q & A sessions cover many current event issues and practical social and psychological topics from a metaphysical standpoint. I consider her to be the "Dr. Phil" of the mediumship-spirit world. She is very personable and offers great practical advice from a very wise source.

Abraham's teachings also validated the mental science dogma I was building. They agree that within the philosophy of the Law of Attraction, everything exists in a vibrational state. We are all vibrational beings and should strive to be in alignment with our source energy, or our natural higher self. Your source energy is your core frequency and the essence of your purpose and the creator's design—it is the highest form of vibration. With respect to desires and goals, to flow with your natural being or source energy is akin to being alone on a small boat with a paddle—you can allow yourself to flow naturally and coast downstream, or you can go against your source energy and paddle upstream against the natural flow.

The natural flow of things is harmonious with love, health, and happiness. This translates into being sober, healthy, fit, clean, and having abundance and joy as our natural vibrational state. Addiction to drugs or alcohol is paddling upstream in the metaphysical sense. When our thoughts, emotions, and visualizations go astray with wrongful deeds or desires, we lose our vibrational alignment. I've seen how this happens when people think egotistically, materialistically, or fearfully and those negative frequencies engage the Law of Attraction to return similar or matching conditions.

I learned that we are an eternal consciousness in temporary physical bodies seeking connection with our source energy, or our creator. We are brought here on Earth in this physical form to create, and we do this by using our thoughts and emotions vibrationally. When the goal you set is formulated, it should feel good to be in true alignment with your source energy if it is to be manifested into physical form. You should feel a natural state of excitement if you truly are aligned with your source energy. Abraham concurs that *"You create your own reality,"* which was the foundation of Seth's mental science premise.

I think Abraham's teachings are also spot-on when you relate them to addiction. When we are not in vibrational alignment due to an underlying pain or fear, we find remedies by numbing ourselves with drugs or alcohol. This negative disharmony also could manifest in misuse or abuse of food, money, sex, or other ego driven diversions. Anything to avoid dealing with the underlying pain or fear.

What we resonate is what we attract. If we are vibrating a negative frequency, it is dark and low and then we attract those people, places, and things that correspond—the boozers, bars, drug dealers, and bad crowds. When we radiate positive frequencies, these negative people and conditions will simply not fit into our vibrational alignment; they just don't match-up. We will reject them and attract healthy, positive people, places, and things in harmony with our vibrational states. The respective frequencies directly affect our physical and mental health similarly.

The third channeling subject I studied was a nonphysical entity named Bashar, who was channeled by Mr. Darryl Anka. However, in lieu of being a passed human spirit, Bashar claims to be a nonphysical intelligence from another dimension. Bashar was brought here to teach humankind mental-spiritual advancements and explain how we operate in the mind-spirit world with regard to changing, growing, manifesting, and evolving consciousness.

It is truly entertaining to watch Bashar perform when he takes over the body of Mr. Anka. He is very intellectual and insightful and can be very animated, funny, and witty. You can see this for yourself via his website archives and on many YouTube video clips. Like Abraham, Bashar is also active today and does many live interviews, seminars, and lectures that you can attend, and he also distributes his readings and videos online.

Bashar shares many similar teachings as Seth and Abraham, but I feel that he is the most scientific of the three. He also states that we are transitional beings that are creators of our own realities. Bashar says that we are also vibrational beings and create our realities by changing our current vibrational frequencies to match the frequencies of the desired end result. We are shifting realities all the time, and our states of being or existence are matters of changing frequencies using feelings and thoughts.

The condition of our physical world is simply the outer ring of our inner vibration. It is analogous to a stone thrown in a calm pond. The center splash impact is our consciousness, and the outer rings are the manifested reality created in the physical world. One must first change the inside, inner vibrational frequency, and then the outside changes. It's not the other way around; that would be the old-school way of causing change and involves hard work. Rather, we create our reality from the inside out.

All realities exist right now, and it's just a matter of tuning into the desired frequency that we wish to live in. There is a world that exists with you as a sick, depressed addict and another one of you as a healthy, happy, sober person. The frequency that you radiate from within will determine the world you live in. There are an infinite number of these parallel worlds, each matching a frequency of the reality you are projecting.

Your present life, health, and external conditions are a result of your vibrational state. Just as we can tune a radio to different stations, one can change their inner frequency using the power of thought-images and feelings, to a different world. This means that when you create a new vibrational self from the inside, you literally cause a change in the outside reality. In some New Age groups, this is termed *reality shifting*—when we change our frequency to align with the frequencies of the new realities desired. We change within, and awaken to a changed world without.

This is not some hokey-pokey paranormal jargon—your perception and belief in the frequency you interpret will determine how your world will be interpreted. In the physical world, we can perceive many different visual frequencies depending on the "glasses" of perception we wear. Have you ever seen an x-ray, thermal imaging picture, or night vision scene? With normal vision, you do not see these frequencies; you must change your reception so that it resonates with that you wish to see. Likewise, this equally applies to non-physical frequencies. These frequencies already exist, you just need to tune into the ones you prefer to perceive.

Another concept shared by Bashar with the others is the idea that what excites you is your true cause or path of your core self. When you feel true inner excitement, you are demonstrating the vibrational harmony with your true core self. This excitement is a naturally high frequency. When your intentions and thoughts are focused on these excited desires, they materialize very quickly. This is because you have found the path of least resistance in the manifestation process. This will also expose your natural talents and be your most joyful path.

You may find your natural excitement in music, art, poetry, parenting, coaching, athletics, or otherwise. Whatever it is, you will find that this is what you excel at and find easiest to achieve success in. Health and sobriety belong to all of us naturally; we were born with an innate desire for this condition. Addicts have somehow *unlearned* natural health in order to become sick or addicted. Addiction is a man-made unnatural calling which goes against the grain of life. Follow your inner excitement of health and sobriety effortlessly, or go against nature with drugs and alcohol. Like Abraham says, you can flow downstream naturally or paddle upstream unnaturally, it's your choice. Drugs and booze take effort and work because it's an upstream unnatural path.

Your ideal core being is your full potential realized. Most people do not strive to achieve this state because the desire to do so presents a lot of stress and we don't have faith in accomplishing these goals. We therefore lessen our desires for perfection so that the stress is reduced. What most don't know is that to live in accordance with our core being is our natural effortless way. It's just a matter of finding our path, talents, and purpose. Once you learn mental science principles, you will gain the faith to achieve these desires.

EVEN OPRAH BELIEVES

One interesting fact is that Abraham/Ester Hicks has actually been interviewed by both Oprah Winfrey and also by the late, great self-help guru, Dr. Wayne Dyer, author of *Your Erroneous Zones*. Dr. Dyer, whose books have been read by tens of millions, had interviewed Abraham a couple of years prior to his death in 2015. In the interview, Dyer states that Abraham's teachings are the *"wisest and most profound on the planet today."* How much more credibility could you ask for than to be endorsed by a huge self-help celebrity known to tens of millions?

I found it very coincidental and uncanny that all three of these medium entities from the nonphysical world spoke of almost the identical conclusions about human metaphysical world from three entirely different times and perspectives. All three concur with the Law of Attraction and the concept that vibrations and frequencies of thought-emotions create our realities.

I highly recommend that you expand your mind and further study these sources. You will see that these mediums are credibly translating valuable information from sources not available to you and me. The website information for these three can be found in the appendix of this book.

In 1909, New Thought teacher Janet Young explained perhaps how we can get these receptions from spirits when she wrote the following:

"The subjective mind is the spiritual estate of mankind. In this vibratory domain, the electrical spirit transmits and receives messages. The mind is interpenetrated by impressions from the higher planes of intelligence and existences of helpers to which the thought is directed by fixity of purpose.... Divine Orders of Beings exist who overwatch, guide and guard mankind—respond to entreaty and trust—reveal the hidden mysteries ... Concentrated thought attracts the assistance of these spiritual helpers and forces through the energy of mental action..."

Over a hundred years ago, Janet Young knew that spiritual knowledge and "hidden mysteries of God" were available to all of us on a deep, subconscious level and that through concentration, we "seekers of higher wisdom" could access this knowledge and wisdom. We can do this ourselves, like the Buddha or yogis, through meditation and thought control, or we can trust others who have learned this art of communication, such as with Bashar, Seth, and Abraham.

After studying these mediums, I continued seeking other sources of spiritual knowledge of spirits from the afterlife. I next was drawn by those who temporarily left their bodies in near-death experiences and returned to describe the other side.

DEAD MAN TALKING

Supplemented by the advent of cardiac resuscitation equipment, there have been millions of reported cases of near-death experiences (NDE). These are usually either medical surgery patients or victims of accidents who have been clinically determined to be dead with brain or heart functions ceasing anywhere from a few seconds up to several minutes. Then there are those who slipped into comas for minutes or hours, and some that stayed comatose for days and years. Although these latter cases are not true "NDE" cases, their conditions and stories are very similar, so I viewed them in the same vein.

I found that the most common trait of an NDE journey was the ascension of your "being" through a white tunnel, entering an angelic realm, a world of beauty, and having feelings of warmth and unconditional love. Nearly all of the NDEs I studied had made a similar claim. The presence of a greater power, a white energy, and loving warmth leaves the majority of these NDE travelers never fearing death again and usually having a total change in their core beliefs and values when they return. Sometimes, the mood, expectations, or emotional state of the patient beforehand determined how the journey goes. In other words, your inner belief system may influence the path you take.

On the Internet, you can watch and listen to hundreds of these NDE stories and hear testimonies about how this other world exists and how small or insignificant our Earthly life seems. Although I did not hear many stories of mental-science wisdom or knowledge being transferred during these experiences, I did gain knowledge that reinforces the fact that not only does a higher intelligence exist, but also that our souls or spirits are eternal. This stay on Earth is but a step in the great staircase of our ultimate existence, and our spirits are eternal; they exist before and after our physical earthly life.

One of the best documented cases proving consciousness exists without the physical brain is that of Dr. Eben Alexander. Alexander is a

Harvard-trained neurosurgeon, with over twenty-five years of experience in practice and teaching. In 2008, he went into a seven-day coma due to an acute bacterial meningitis infection of the brain that should have killed him. The infection completely shut down his brain and body, and he rapidly slipped into a coma. It was a bizarre incident, as the odds of spontaneously acquiring this infection as an adult was roughly ten million to one.

He later wrote two best-selling books, *Proof of Heaven* and *The Map of Heaven*, which are documentations of his afterlife experience, and how science and religion are merging to prove that this spirit world of consciousness exists.

Having heard many of his interviews and lecture videos, I found his story not only very credible and fascinating, but also in complete resonance with the metaphysical philosophy behind mental science. His philosophical interpretation of his spiritual journey echoes both the worlds of quantum science and spiritual philosophy that I had already encountered.

Alexander's meningitis infection was so deadly that it incapacitated the neocortex thinking area of his brain. On a clinical and medical basis, he was brain-dead—with absolutely no ability to use his brain for thinking. The attending doctors gave him a two percent chance of surviving at all, and then if he did, he'd be in a vegetative state on a life-support machine. They said he would never recover from this dead brain state.

When he awoke from the coma, he had lost all memory of who he was, of his past twenty-five years as a neurosurgeon, of his spoken English language, and of his family and friends. It would take months to regain both his memories and physical skills, but the memory of his spiritual journey was clear as day.

Alexander would later tell how, during the coma, he left his body and went to a beautiful world with stunning features of colorful rainbows, flowers, waterfalls, butterflies, and landscapes. There was transcendental music everywhere that helped guide him. He was blanketed with a warm feeling of unconditional love and everything was communicated by vibrational feelings.

A bright, white, sparkling orb appeared, which Alexander sensed to be the prime source. He felt unconditional love from this powerful intelligence. This would attract him with musical tones and melodies and would ascend him to a gateway realm at the source and to different levels and planes of existence.

He learned that our existence or consciousness is not dependent on the physical brain. He was literally brain-dead, but he somehow successfully thought, conceived, felt, rationalized, and remembered the experience clearly and vividly. All communication was nonverbal, yet the information was transferred perfectly and with all detail. He states that before the coma, he had a strong scientific conviction from his medical education and career that consciousness was an outsource of the brain's physical functions. This has now changed 180 degrees. He knows now that consciousness exists without the physical brain.

Other important lessons he learned were that consciousness is universal and interconnected not only among humans, but also between all living things; that the source or creator loves us unconditionally; and that unconditional love of all things should be our goal as well. Lastly, that our material world is the real dream state, the illusion—the spirit world is the only true reality and is much more real. This last part reminded me of a passage in *The Kybalion*, written by The Three Initiates in 1912 which read:

> *"And Death is not real, even in the Relative sense—it is but Birth to a new life—and You shall go on, and on, and on, to higher and still higher planes of life, for aeons upon aeons of time... You are dwelling in the Infinite Mind of THE ALL, and your possibilities and opportunities are infinite, both in time and space."*

Dr. Alexander's story is a fascinating and uplifting one, and I recommend his books or lectures to anyone interested in hearing more details of his spiritual journey.

YOGI SPIRITS

My final spirit study was that of Paramahansa Yogananda, an Indian yogi that lived from 1893 to 1952 who was responsible for introducing many

Westerners to the yogi way of life. He promoted the unity of science and religion, and the practice of mind over body. He taught that correct, truthful thinking and meditation would bring freedom from physical and mental disharmonies (maya), and that people should strive to evolve through meditation and mental practices into God consciousness. He believed that spiritual ignorance was gravely wrong, likened to a sin.

Yogananda is most famous for writing his life story *Autobiography of a Yogi* in 1946. It's a fantastic book that I've read several times and still often refer to it. Even the late, famous Apple Computer founder, Steve Jobs, was a big fan of this book. Jobs not only read it religiously each and every year, but he incorporated many of its Eastern philosophies into his Apple corporate culture. The book was known to be so important to him that five hundred copies of it were given out to the attendees at his memorial.

Yogananda lived a life full of magical and spiritual events. He witnessed and participated in many miraculous performances with his yogi peers including physical transformations, mental healings, mind-over-matter feats, and spiritual reincarnations.

One of my favorite chapters was *"The Resurrection of Sri Yukteswar"* in which Yogananda's yogi master, who had just recently died, reappears to him as an astral being. Sri Yukteswar, in this astral-ghostly form, explained that he now lived in an astral world in which everything consisted of "light" forms like a dream state. Beautiful fountains, waterfalls, rivers, flowers, fruits, and landscapes are made, not of matter, but of beautiful, clean, cosmic light. His soul had moved on simply to another astral form.

This encounter of Yogananda's reminded me of my similar experience as a youth, lying in bed and squinting to see my grandparents standing there in front of me in this same astral form. Both of these visions also strongly resembled the experience of Dr. Alexander. Yogananda again, confirmed the existence of the non-physical self which survives the body, and also how our spirit-consciousness directs and forms our physical reality.

SPIRIT MESSAGES SUMMARY

Both metaphysicians and modern-day mentalists teach that both our spiritual bodies and thoughts are vibrations that radiate in eternity and never die or fade. Furthermore, these vibrations are such that they do not obey the rules of time.

It is believed by many that time is an illusion and that the past, present, and future all exist right now—everything coexists in a collective consciousness or universal mind matrix. In an 1887 lecture, Hiram Butler spoke about man's expanded mind and relation to space-time saying:

> *"The consciousness of being spirit is equal to the consciousness of being God, and such a consciousness is infinite in its nature. It is what I might term an all-consciousness. It pervades all things, cognizes all things, and is everywhere. It annihilates space, destroys time, and causes the past and the future to become merely one eternal now."*

Psychics, great inventors, and artists simply tap into or get into alignment with these frequencies that already exist. They are not creating so much as they are discovering what is already there. Some mediums and channels are merely picking up on spiritual frequencies or thought vibrations that match with which they are resonating. It is just like tuning in a radio station on a receiver; if you're a country fan, you'll find the country station, and if you're a sports fan, you'll find the ESPN show, and so on. These mentalists are simply tuning in to subtler frequencies we are not accustomed to. In the universal mind matrix, there is a frequency for every-*thing*, and every-*one*.

The great metaphysical philosophers all agree that we are not physical beings that have a spiritual part, but are spiritual beings that have physical part. Mental science studies in quantum physics, the cosmos, and the spiritual realm prove that human consciousness is eternal and exists without the brain or body. To realize that we are eternal is to realize the power of mind and consciousness.

Mind-spirit is always the cause, and the physical world, always the effect. Your body and external conditions in life are simply the physical expressions of mind-spirit. Using mental science, you will learn to direct these mind-spirit energies toward the attainment of the goals of health, sobriety, love, and success.

9

Mind Talents

"There are such things as etheric vibrations proceeding from human personality...in fact that we possess an additional range of faculties far exceeding those which we ordinarily exercise through the physical body, and which must therefore be included in our conception of ourselves".

—THOMAS TROWARD, 1919

IF IT'S ON THE TELEVISION, IT MUST BE TRUE

Well, if you thought I was done writing about weird stuff, you were wrong. It would be remiss not to include the subject of paranormal psychic phenomenon (PSI) in a book related to mental science, right? So, here comes another freaky subject chapter.

PSI studies include subjects such as ESP, psychokinesis, and clairvoyance. This is another one of those *fringe topics* that is not the "meat and potatoes" of mental science, but is still important to have knowledge of. The essence of mind or consciousness is still at work in PSI, but is just displayed in a different, more obscure nature. J. C. F. Grumbine explains why we call this stuff *weird* when, in 1910, he wrote:

"A thing is said to be normal or natural because it is object of or subject to the law of a material cause and effect as comprehended by our five physical

senses. A thing is supernormal or supernatural because it is object of or subject to the law of spiritual cause and effect as comprehended by the intuition or conscience, or any power above the sphere of the five physical senses."

Just as psychic mediums are being shown on popular television shows, so are PSI mind talents. Just recently, I watched the trendy television show *America's Got Talent* and saw a couple calling themselves, "The Clairvoyants." Over the past eight weeks they performed unbelievable feats of mind-reading that simply could not be attributable to magic or trickery. Millions of viewers probably will go away scratching their heads, dismissing it as weird, unexplainable, or just well-performed magic. Unfortunately, in order for many people to believe in a new phenomenon, it usually requires that the evidence is presented by a scientist or doctor in a white government uniform. It's unfortunate that the psychic displays shown on television are presented as entertainment and magic, and not for the true scientific phenomena they truly are.

The public had the same fake-illusionist opinion of famous Uri Geller who fascinated audiences back in the 1970s with his ability to bend spoons and stop watches with his mind power. Although he performed these feats hundreds of times in every imaginable blind test condition, there still were mainly skeptics and doubters. Sometime the finite mind of mankind cannot comprehend the infinite realm of the true reality.

We have all come to believe in the existence of unseen radio waves and x-rays but there is only a small percentage of us who believe in the finer and subtler vibrations of mind transmissions of thought. The person who exhibits PSI mind powers merely is in tune with ultrafine frequencies to which most of us are not mentally adapted. They are simply more sensitive in this *sixth sense*, or should I say less ignorant of it.

Just as a dog has specialized hearing and smelling, great artists and musicians also are able to perceive special visual and audible harmonies because their minds are aligned to these highly-refined melodic frequencies. The psychic, or person with ESP skills, has similar talents in sensing or directing subtle energies. Great musicians, artists, and psychics are all tuning in to special frequencies with extraordinary reception.

EXTRASENSORY PERCEPTION (ESP)

I think everyone has experienced some type of ESP at one time or another. I recall back in college when backgammon was a popular game, I would play it daily with my college buddies after classes. I remember several occasions when I could uncannily predict the roll of the die not just once or twice, but several times in a row. I did this deliberately; it was like a game within the game. I had to be in a particular mental zone for it to work, concentrating in a special way. I would call the numbers out loud as I released the dice onto the table and they would be right on target. The odds of doing that five or six times in a row must have been a million to one. But I don't know if I was predicting the outcome or causing it—ESP or psychokinesis. In any case, it was a little spooky. My friends could also do this on occasion, too. It was kind of like a little psychic ESP game we had going on. We all have these capabilities…they are sometimes just displayed when unexpected.

The people who get in these mental zones at will are often called psychics, seers, paranormal, or sometimes just weirdos. In any case, we are again dealing with people who can sense or direct nonphysical, unseen energy, or the supernormal.

In the 1930s, scientist and doctor, J. B. Rhine, performed a psychokinesis study with rolling die using a mechanical tumbler with a psychic dictating the outcome. After over 650,000 die rolls, the outcome favored the psychokinetic subject's outcome with odds of ten thousand to one. These studies were replicated more recently using modern random number generators and results also favored the fact that human conscious intention proved to alter the outcome. This may remind you of the quantum studies in the chapter on the atom in which we discovered that human consciousness affected the behavior of subatomic particles simply by observing them.

In the 1970s during the Cold War, both the United States and Russia spent millions on the research and implementation of PSI programs. They trained *"ESP-ionage"* agents called *"PSI-Spies"* who had proven psychic talents that would perform psychic surveillance and headhunting on enemy spies and assailants. They also could perform remote viewing—mentally seeing locations of the enemy's hidden military installations from remote places. The government is still suspected of covertly employing persons with psychic abilities for ESP-ionage today. It is also becoming very commonplace for law enforcement to hire psychics in criminal investigations and missing persons' cases.

Even though the subject matter of PSI is on the fringes of the science of psychology, a huge amount of research has been performed. One very credible source where you can find thousands of these positive paranormal test results is at the website *www.noetic.org*. This is a site and organization dedicated to the study of mind and consciousness. Their labs have researched subjects including ESP, mental healing, energy fields, conscious intention, distant healing, and prayer. They are a great resource of information in this field with reports verifying factual claims of the existence of paranormal talents. Let the facts speak for themselves and you will feel the same as me in that PSI is truly a legitimate science—it's just that we are at the infancy of understanding how it works.

The person with a psychic mind somehow has developed or restored mental faculties that can sense these subtle vibrations. These talents are not reserved for a select few either. Many say that everyone has these psychic abilities and that we simply have forgotten how to use them over generations. Past generations have deliberately shunned or ignored our abilities because they were treated as taboo, witchcraft, or evil. Like other traits and habits, our ignorance has layered over successive generations, and we have buried these natural psychic abilities.

These intrinsic powers are still in all of us. We all still have this innate ability to sense and control these esoteric thought vibrations—it is all a matter of *unlearning* certain beliefs about the brain and mind by using mental science, meditation, and by applying special knowledge. We have been trained so well to trust only our five senses and the external, objective world that we have lost our sensitivity to the subtler mind-spirit-thought frequencies. Great artists, musicians, poets, inventors, and those exhibiting PSI mind powers, are the minority who have tapped into this thought world of sensing at a higher, subtler vibrational plane. Getting more attuned to psychic waves is not necessary for mental science applications, but could be helpful to being more receptive to beneficial hunches and intuitions.

PSI SUMMARY

PSI research and performances reaffirms the existence of the nonphysical mind world in support of our mental science dogma. It is in this same invisible realm that we will use our mental science applications to cure our addiction, and achieve our goals. When we use thought-images in mental science, we are using them for creative purposes—to obtain wishes and desires. When we mix emotional frequencies with them and think *from* the image and not *of* the image, it creates new programming and changes our future realities.

The knowledge of these mind talents is not to learn ESP, but to reinforce our knowledge and belief in the unseen world of mental science and powers of mind. These same invisible thought frequencies are combined with desire and faith to wield powerful forces that positively charge our vibrational states for goal manifestation.

The fact that thought frequencies can be sensed and directed by people with specially developed faculties should come as no surprise to one who knows the truth about consciousness, creation, and mental science. Our aim is to use these powers in a creative manner, to achieve our goals of health, sobriety, love, and success.

10

Healing Science

"History informs us that in all the ages man has recognized the existence of an intelligent power capable of creating diseases in the human body, and of healing them independently of material remedies or appliances. This Power, being invisible and intangible, was very naturally referred to mental or spiritual agencies, good or bad, beneficent or malevolent, as the symptoms in each particular case seemed to indicate."

—Thomas Hudson, 1903

PSYCHOSOMATIC SICKNESS: MIND OVER BODY

Medical doctors are finally realizing that the mind of humankind is the chief creator of all sickness and disease. The term "psychosomatic illness" refers to sickness with no medical basis that is created by the mind. Most of us correlate psychosomatic sickness with common minor ailments like colds, headaches, and backaches. However, doctors and scientists are proving now that more serious illnesses such as heart disease, addiction, and cancer also stem from the same mental and emotional issues, or psychosomatic cause.

Recall that, on a metaphysical level, we are still dealing with the fact that all matter including the human body, is basically composed of the courser spectrum of mind substance. In 1921, Fenwicke Holmes wrote that:

"The body is but a manifestation of spirit; **matter is but spirit at its lowest level.** *Therefore, when you have a case of supposed difficulty, you must get into a heightened consciousness of spirit. The greatest healer is simply the one who can most completely become conscious of spirit, who can know that all is mind."*

The mind and emotions are particularly instrumental in regulating the immune system which, in turn, is responsible for combating sickness and disease. Studies have proven that as much as ninety percent of all illnesses are psychosomatic or created by the mind. If wrongful thinking and negative emotions can cause illness and disease, then it stands to reason that the process can be reversed using the same methods. Addiction is nothing more than a manifested ill-condition that can be treated by correcting the underlying metaphysical discord. Mind and body are cause and effect—the nature of our thoughts is the *cause* that produces the bodily *effect*. In 1922, New Thought teacher W. John Murray wrote:

"The physical sciences all assure us that the starting point of everything in the world is the invisible nucleus which gathers around it by the Law of Attraction whatever is necessary to its complete manifestation in form. If our thought nucleus is one of fear, it will at once attract unto itself the same quality of thought...If our thought nucleus is one of sickness or poverty, it will coalesce with other thoughts of sickness and poverty until it registers in us as the finished product in bodily discomfort."

As Murray says, the end result of a negative thoughts will be illness. Before we ever get too sick, however, we usually try to combat the pain and discomfort with avoidance and medication, and for the addictively inclined, this means booze and pills.

Our negative thoughts are to our bodies and physical conditions like a virus is to a computer. If your PC gets infected, it runs slow, gets corrupted files, loses data, functions irregularly, and may even damage the hard drive. We must purge the system of the negative program, replace it with the correct software, and install an anti-virus program. Likewise, with the body, negative thoughts left unattended will manifest as pain, illness, and disease. In mental science, we remove these originating negative thoughts and beliefs with correct thinking, we reprogram the mind with positive goal self-images, and we recharge our vibrational states with high frequencies of desire and faith

Mental science related programs and alternative treatment centers are now beginning to crop up for treating disease and illness. Some of the new-age treatment centers realize the power of the mind and emotions play a huge role in treating and curing cancer, and thus have implemented nontraditional programs. These newer clinics feature holistic mind-body programs including meditation, acupuncture, relaxation techniques, guided imagery, visualization, hypnosis, and yoga. The big hospitals, rehab centers, and pharmaceutical companies don't like this. They will do, and say, whatever it takes to keep their beds full, so be wary of their motives of discrediting these alternatives. Unfortunately, they still have all the money, so will keep bombarding us with advertising to reinforce that we need them, the external source, in order to heal. In mental science, we realize that all healing comes from within.

I've learned of many terminal cancer conditions which have been reversed with mental science techniques. The tumors disappeared, and cancers went into spontaneous remission. Studies have shown that by improving the mental-emotional state and using visualization techniques, stress is reduced, the immune system is strengthened, and the illness is removed.

In 1922, New Thought writer Walter Matthew wrote about the mind-body connection:

"The conscious mind can and should be ruler and governor of the subconscious, but, if through ignorance or carelessness, it permits cinema pictures of sickness, disease, poverty, fear, hate, revenge, unhappiness, etc., to be impressed upon it, the subconscious will go to work to actualize these pictures in or on our body, circumstances and environment. The

subconscious mind accepts every premise as the truth, so, if the premise be false, it will act on it just the same as if it were true, and the result may be far different from what we wish to come into our experience."

What Matthew is saying is exactly what the hypnotist knows and uses for his rules of engagement. Once the conscious mind is silenced, the subconscious will act on the information fed to it as reality. It does not argue, weigh, or measure the conditions of the information or instructions presented; it just acts on them as if they were true facts. You will learn how to apply these principles in a similar fashion, using a powerful self-programming exercise called "Transcendental Meditative Technique."

THE PLACEBO EFFECT

One of the most important outcrops of the mind-body connection is the placebo effect. Placebos are inert, fake drugs (sometimes called sugar or bread pills), where a patient believes he or she is taking a real pharmaceutical drug. The placebos come in any form that the real drug does—pills, creams, liquids, injections, and so forth.

There are even *placebo surgery* procedures, in which patients are taken into a fake surgery setting. During the pretend surgery, the areas being operated are covered in a tent fashion (for lower body surgery), and the semiconscious patients watch videos of prerecorded successful surgeries on a video monitor above, thinking that the videos are of their own bodies being operated on. Superficial incisions are even made to make the surgery appear real. The results were positive, in both placebo drug applications and surgery procedures, proving that mind and belief were the factors in healing and not the medical procedure or medications.

I learned of a recent study made to determine whether placebos were effective in the treatment of depression compared with real antidepressants medicines. The testing clinically proved that the placebo patients not only felt relieved of their depression, but that actual biochemical changes took place in their brains, even more so than those taking the real medicine. This double-blind study used sensitive brain imaging equipment to study the patients' brain functions before, during, and after the testing. The placebo patients actually showed more neurochemical activity resulting from the placebo than did the patients taking the real antidepressant medicine. Apparently chemical reactions required to balance specific levels of serotonin, endorphins, and dopamine were occurring by the power of the mind alone, with no pharmaceutical aid whatsoever. People literally were thinking chemical changes into their brains. In other words, placebos made actual measurable physiological chemical changes in the body... the patient did not just imagine him or herself cured.

This same type of placebo study was performed on pain patients. In these studies, the placebos not only helped free the patients of any *sensation* or *feelings* of pain, but again caused actual physiological and chemical changes to occur in the patients' brain. In this case, it was the brains natural opiate levels. The fake pills actually caused the brain to produce pain-fighting opiates just like, and sometimes more than, the real medications produced with the other patients. The pain relief was not just in the patients' imagination—their brains actually produced anti-pain opiates by thinking the pills were real. As William Atkinson said in 1912:

> *"It will be seen that just as is health the result of the normal functioning of the Subconscious Mind, so is disease the result of its abnormal functioning. And it may also be seen that the true healing power must come alone from and through the Subconscious Mind itself...."*

Remember that in order for a thought to graduate from the conscious mind to the subconscious, it must first be believed. If you believe you are vulnerable to drugs or alcohol and they have power over you, then your brain-body will reflect this reality you created by weakening your willpower and increasing your subconscious desires, urges, physical cravings, and chances of relapse. When you learn mental science, you know you have full control over the addiction. It's your pure choice and will to allow drugs or alcohol in your body and to deflect these cravings and urges.

Sometimes the law works in reverse and the body affects the mind which then alters the inner vibrational state which starts an addictive cycle. In this case, it's body-over-mind, instead of mind-over-body. This happens when we get injured, infected, or, of course, when we pollute and sicken our bodies with drugs and alcohol abuse. Our physical body has its metaphysical energy centers which get weakened and misaligned when these negative physical events occur. There are techniques that correct the body's energy such as acupuncture and reiki healing. Reiki healing is concerned with correcting or balancing the body's energy nodes or chakras. Acupuncture utilizes a similar map of energy centers within the body and opens blockages and corrects energy flow. The masters proficient in meditation and mind control can often perform these energy corrections with pure mentality. Most people have a hard time separating their bodies from their minds, so when they are sick, hungover, feel overweight, or are injured, it reflects in their moods, emotional body, and frequency they vibrate. This is why keeping the body healthy and energized is important, so that any physical negativity does not seep into the mental-emotional body and begin a cause and effect cycle.

Placebo studies clearly show that the mental state of expectancy and faith go into producing the amazing positive effects proving mind-over-body. According to New Thought author Orison Marden, this same mental attitude of belief is also required for traditional medicine to be effective. In 1910, he wrote:

> "It is expectancy, implicit faith, complete change of attitude, that heals disease, changes habit and character. Expectancy of relief and unquestioned faith in the remedy or the physician are much more healing potencies than either the remedy or the physician. Faith in the physician, in the reputation of the remedy, faith in the change of climate, play a tremendous part in the healing, restorative processes. Faith has ever been the great miracle worker of the ages. It has endowed a spoonful of water, a bread pill, a black ring, a horse-chestnut carried in the pocket, with marvelous healing powers."

He asserts that the 'marvelous healing powers of a bread pill' and even a legitimate medical physician are both contingent on the patient's mental attitude of belief to be effective. Since we have placed so much faith in doctors and medicine over the past generations, we seem to be born and raised with an innate belief that they are the only ones who can cure us, and unconsciously this may be true because of these ingrained beliefs. This deep-seated subconscious belief that only doctors and medicine will cure us is strengthened and reinforced throughout our childhood development and solidifies in our belief systems. This is why many people with colds and flus go to the doctor's office, and after receiving nothing more than a short consultation, immediately start feeling better afterwards. It's sort of like your mother's chicken soup…if you are raised to believe it will alleviate your cold or flu, then it will. Sorry mom, but it's just the science of mind over body, and not your boiled chicken that worked.

Unless you have become a true master in mental science like the ancient yogi, I strongly recommend that traditional medicine is not forsaken. Especially in the cases of any severe physical or mental injury or illness. Personally, if medical cures are available for an ailment, I still use them, but they are always supplemented with mental science practices. Mental and physical sciences are both realities with their own laws, and it is purely a matter of knowledge and inner faith as to which will actually work.

JONESING FOR A FIX IS CURED JUST BY ANTICIPATION

A study proved how an addict's mind actually produces the pleasurable effects of drugs or alcohol before they even ingest them. The brain starts working purely by the anticipation of using. The study showed that an addict's dopamine level rises solely with the thought that he or she is getting hooked-up with drugs or booze soon.

When addicts know that they have a drug or drink coming into their bodies imminently, withdrawal symptoms are reduced, depression lightens, and their moods get better. A slight euphoric feeling of pleasures will actually start kicking in before any chemical is even ingested. You may recall this happening to you, when the inner discomfort and pain starts to go away on the drive to your dealer's house or to the liquor store. It's like drug foreplay, and very much a mind over matter placebo effect.

I remember in my heavy drinking days, I was so miserable in the afternoons while imprisoned at work. The three beers I chugged down at lunchtime had already worn off and I was irritable, depressed, and anxious. I'd kill to have a miniature of liquor hidden somewhere. I would look at the clock every fifteen minutes, wishing it was five o'clock so I could get to the gas station down the street, buy a six-pack, and taste that cold beer flowing down my throat and performing its miracle on my mind. When it got to about 4:40 the discomfort would magically dissipate and I'd get in a great mood and a have burst of energy to finish the day. It was mind-over-body, my mind already preparing chemically for the alcohol. I would suddenly get calm, relaxed, and happy. This is just more proof of the mind's ability to make chemical changes in the brain by thoughts alone.

PLAYING MENTAL PAC-MAN CURED HER CANCER

There are many different mental techniques to correct physical sickness and disease using the mind. One success story I heard was of a young woman with a cancerous tumor who was attempting to use visualizations to heal herself. She decided to visualize her body in a video-game manner to the theme of PAC-MAN. Several times a day she would meditate on the image of the tumor being eaten away by a *health* cell that resembled a PAC-MAN. The PAC-MAN would eat away at this imagined dark cloud area where her tumor was located at each visualization session. After several weeks, she was at the point in the game where the PAC-MAN cells had nothing left to eat...there was no dark spot left in her mind. She was later scanned and, to everyone's amazement, her tumor had completely disappeared.

Another story that is well-circulated is that of a woman who cured terminal cancer by merely changing her routine to watch the funniest movies she could find, day in and day out. She filled her every waking hour watching comedies and refused to pay any attention to her cancer, nor did she allow any negative feelings about it in her mind. Soon her cancer went into complete remission. Metaphysically, she simply changed her frequency from a negative, dark state, which was a host of sickness and disease, to a positive, bright one, which did not allow for illness to survive—they were vibrationally in conflict. Per the Law of Attraction, sickness does not resonate with a positive mental-emotional frequency and therefore is rejected. In 1922, Eugene Del Mar wrote:

> *"Disease being a product of thought, the human form being the physical composite of many thought pictures, and disease those characteristics of it that are in correspondence with ignorant beliefs and erroneous opinions; it results that the fundamental disease is mental. If an opinion is the cause, the result may be altered by a change in opinion. If the original opinion was the cause of destructive conditions, then when that opinion ceases, it will no longer produce any results"*

Remember that if you believe that you are an addict, it will manifest as your reality. What you believe—your opinion of the truth, is what governs your physical conditions, and your world.

NEGATIVE VIBRATIONS MANIFEST AS DISEASE AND ADDICTION

Fearful, negative thoughts are major causes of disease or illness, and mental science laws prove that by reversing the thoughts and emotions, you can preclude or reverse these effects. If a past trauma or emotional pain is causing a negative mental-emotional state, then we must correct it by removing or at least diffusing the problem and replacing it with positive energy. The mental focus on this pain generates an undermining and discordant vibrational state that can be corrected by right thinking and proper mental science techniques.

Negative emotions have many subcategories, but fear is at the top of the pyramid, as it is the mother of them all. Fear of sickness, failure, embarrassment, and loneliness are the most powerful damaging negative emotions that we entertain as addicts. In 1911, New Thought practitioner Leander Whipple wrote:

> *"FEAR, when active within the mind, is a devitalizing influence, that destroys the equilibrium of action and generates a negative condition of*

unrest, because of the mental doubt; a veritable state of unease or dis-ease. —Fear in the mind results in sickness which may culminate in disease, either mental or physical."

The negative seedlings that are buried deep inside are the ones that grow and manifest as your illness. These fearful falsehoods and negative beliefs result in a disharmonic vibrational state that cause our immune systems to falter and open the door to sickness and disease. Del Mar added that *"Truth thoughts are allied to health and false thoughts generate disease."* If you believe. with feeling and conviction, you are powerless over your addiction, then you are commanding this reality to manifest, it will come true. You set up a negative frequency and attract the conditions to make this belief materialize—ranging from causing cellular changes in your brain and body to attracting negative destructive people and circumstances into your life.

When we are pulsating a discordant frequency, we feel emotional, physical, and sometimes spiritual pain and then reach out for drugs and alcohol to anesthetize us. Unfortunately, the drugs and booze only mask, conceal, and exacerbate the underlying condition and delay their needed healing. The drugs and alcohol create a vicious addictive cycle where the depressing, negative state self-perpetuates and recycles itself, getting larger and larger. Remember your vibrational state stems from your thought-images that are mixed with feelings and are believed to be true. This belief may be subconsciously ingrained which is where mental science will come to your aid in reprogramming false thinking.

As New Thought writer William Towne put it in 1910, *"Hate, fear, and evil are but mortal, erroneous conceptions of the All Good. To entertain fear and hate obscures the Truth and keeps us in bondage to disease. Love wipes out the error and restores harmony."*

In other words, Towne is saying that the vibrational frequencies of disease and sickness are the result of believing in untruths or wrongful thoughts based on fear and hate. These can be remedied when the patient realizes this truth, releases the resistance, and realigns himself or herself with the natural flow. Towne further wrote, *"If you have realized unity, faith, and love in your consciousness, harmony should be the result...harmony is the manifestation of Divine Mind or Truth."*

Discord, disease, or sickness therefore is a human-made creation that is induced by living in a falsehood of thinking based on fear or one of its sibling emotions. This is unnatural and disharmonious. Fear disguises itself frequently as competition, ego, pride, and materialism. The reason that you drink or drug can probably be traced to one of these core fears— and remember that self-pity, guilt, and resentments are also tied into this same family of negative emotions.

The mind-over-matter phenomena was also written about by Canadian New Thought leader Charles Brodie Patterson who, in 1901, stated:

"At times, our minds become anxious and even fearful; perhaps we allow anger, or malice, or jealousy to find lodgment therein. This wrong way of thinking and feeling makes the mind discordant and unrestful, expelling all real happiness and mental peace. Moreover, mental discord and unrest are manifested in physical sickness and disease, because our bodies and souls are more dependent for health and strength on mental harmony and brightness than on either food or drink."

WATCH OUT FOR "HEALTH WARNING" TV COMMERCIALS

False subconscious beliefs can be accepted as truths inadvertently and even subliminally. When a man with a heavy drinking problem is told by a television commercial his drinking is causing liver disease, this message often exacerbates the physical damage when he continues to drink. If he consciously or subconsciously perceives this as a truth and allows this claim to exist in his reality, it will psychosomatically cause liver damage. Each future drink is that much more injurious since now he visualizes the cells being destroyed by the alcohol chemicals. The smoker who watches television commercials showing images of black lung x-rays does the same each time he takes a drag or a cigarette. With every puff, he or she subconsciously flashes that black lung picture in their subconscious which directs the body to take action and follow this belief. And people who had a bad bout with drugs or alcohol who are told that they are doomed by a genetic disease of addiction will adopt that mentality as their reality and the truth—they will play the victim role and blame their weakness on their DNA. To fear something and believe in it is to inversely pray for it—you still engage the Law of Attraction. In 1912, Dr. William Sadler wrote:

"Those who fear disease most are likely to catch it. Those who fear it least are less likely to contract it…. The fear of disease is often so intense and acute as really to cause one to fall a victim…"

Television commercials, advertising, and literature intended to help can actually hurt by providing graphic details of the sickness and disease on which the person is trying not to focus on. Instead, people use these pictures and information to psychosomatically cause more damage. They may do this subconsciously, but all the same it is there causing not only more damage, but also more guilt. Doctors, hospitals, pharmacy companies, and rehab clinics spend billions of dollars trying to convince you that you have an illness, disease, or condition that will get worse or kill you until you buy their product or service.

Where your attention goes, energy goes—what you focus on, you become. If you are constantly told that you will become sick and die, you become sick and die. If you're told that you are powerless and have an incurable disease, you will live that way and have to fight the battle the rest of your life. When you have learned that mind is the cause of all physical manifestation, you will be the master of your life, and control your health and sobriety. In 1910, Wallace Wattles wrote:

"Use your will-power to withhold your attention from every appearance of disease in yourself and others; do not study disease, think about it, nor speak of it. At all times, when the thought of disease is thrust upon you, move forward into the mental position of prayerful gratitude for your perfect health."

Reinforce the fact that addiction is a temporary condition of the past that you went through. There is no need to study this disease or dwell on it any longer. It is the past, you've learned your lesson, and now you've moved on.

It's better to show a focus on the goal of health, not the threat of disease. This means living in hope, and not in fear. You want to have a positive vibrational state reflecting the goal-image of a sober, healthy, and happy person enjoying life, not one that is fearing addiction, disease, and death. It is better to hope than to worry, but it is even better to believe than to fear. Know the facts of the negative consequences, but tuck them away in a mental filing cabinet and focus on who you want to be, not who you used to be.

HYPNOSIS: MORE PROOF OF MIND-OVER-BODY

Hypnotism is another powerful mind-body treatment that is effective in healings. As most of us know, this is the process of placing a person in a trancelike, nonconscious state, such that his or her subconscious mind is susceptible and receptive to suggestion.

There are two operations of mind: conscious and subconscious. The thinking, conscious mind deals with the five senses and outside stimuli. It filters, organizes, rationalizes, argues with, and objectifies data before passing it on to the subconscious. The subconscious mind takes the information passed on to it as a true fact and acts on it.

Charles Haanel states that the subconscious does exactly what it is told as this is always perceived as a truth. In 1922, he wrote:

"Receiving any suggestions as true, the subconscious mind at once proceeds to act thereon in the whole domain of its tremendous field of work. The conscious mind can suggest either truth or error…The subconscious mind cannot argue; it only acts. It accepts the conclusions of the objective mind as final."

The hypnotist silences the body and conscious mind, and then has direct access to the subconscious mind which is the seat of all behavioral habits. When the conscious mind is removed, the person will do exactly what the hypnotist suggests, as the conscious mind is bypassed.

Hypnosis, similar to other healings, works to detach the physical body and conscious-thinking brain and work directly with the person's subconscious. To cure sickness and disease, the healer-hypnotist would need to change a person's negative, diseased mental-emotional body to a positive one, making the healthy positive tone the strongest and most dominating.

Just as proven with placebo effect studies, hypnotism has proved that chemicals can be produced in the brain by mind power alone. As far back as 1893, Thomas Hudson knew this when he wrote:

"It is well known, and no one at all acquainted with hypnotic phenomena now disputes the fact, that perfect anesthesia can be produced at the will of the operator simply by suggestion. Hundreds of cases are recorded where the most severe surgical operations have been performed without pain upon patients in the hypnotic condition."

We already learned in placebo effect studies that mind can cause the brain to produce opiates, dopamine, serotonin, and several other chemicals by the power of thought alone. When a person believes that he or she is taking a pain pill, his or her brain actually produces opiates; when a sugar pill is said to be a tranquilizer, the person's brain produces serotonin, and so on.

One study showed that when subjects under hypnosis were told they were being touched by a burning iron rod they actually produced blistering skin, redness, and swelling. In actuality, the rod was only a room temperature pointer, yet the body still produced the same effects as if it were scorching hot.

Hypnotherapy is now used by clinics for treatment of both drug and alcohol withdrawals, cravings, and overall addiction therapy. The efficacy of the treatment is conditional on both the condition, beliefs, and receptivity of the patient, as well as the integrity of the hypnotherapist. There is no reason that properly applied self-hypnosis would not be just as effective, so long as a person has proper faith in it. The Meditative Programming Technique you will soon learn is a mental science program incorporating self-hypnosis fundamentals.

DEEP HYPNOSIS DISCOVERY

A fascinating story is that of Mrs. Delores Cannon who spent almost fifty years as a hypnotherapist before passing away in 2014. She was dedicated to studying mind-spirit sciences and authored over seventeen books while lecturing to thousands on these subjects. Cannon began her career as a traditional hypnotist, and then she moved on to specialize in regressive hypnotherapy, which explores a person's deep psyche, getting to the historical roots and origins of current ill-conditions and issues.

In her later years, Cannon discovered a phenomenon that was an outcrop of her extensive years of deep hypnotherapy practice. She found that when putting patients under a deep meditative-hypnotic state, they not only benefitted from the regressive hypnosis therapy, but entered a state where they were capable of receiving miraculous healings and accessing sacred universal knowledge.

She found that people in a somnambulistic subconscious state reached a new level of consciousness or what she called "oversoul." It was at this deep level that her subjects accessed an intelligent source and received deep spiritual knowledge. This was a common occurrence throughout thousands of subjects; the people would change but the source's message remained universal and constant. She states that this source intelligence or supreme consciousness appeared to be a type of collective soul that was universally available to all of these subjects. This was the ultimate source, not only of knowledge and wisdom, but also of miraculous healing powers.

It appears that this oversoul, or universal intelligence, is the same source as the cosmic consciousness found by meditators, or the God within by many spiritualists. As word got out about accessing this source energy, thousands of people around the world with serious illnesses flocked to see Mrs. Cannon for her services and were miraculously cured. She started a program dedicated to helping others called the "Quantum Healing Hypnosis Technique," which is still available today. What she had discovered was a spiritual dimension or plane that is inherent within all of us. While on this deep spiritual plane, not only did these subjects reveal great mind-spirit wisdom, but also received miraculous and powerful healing energy. This spiritual plane reminded me of the place that the channeled spirit Seth had communicated from, as it is the same collective consciousness available to persons of any time period.

EPIGENETICS: MIND OVER DNA

New findings have been made in genetic science called "epigenetics." This science proclaims that we are capable of altering our genetic code or DNA structure, thus rendering us capable of escaping the inevitable outcome of inherited traits and diseases.

I learned of a recent study, where two identical simple cells were encased in separate petri dish cases and placed in two notably different external environments. Instead of growing identically, which was expected, the cells actually mutated in accordance with the external conditions they were surrounded by. Furthermore, they caused actual DNA changes required to adapt to these conditions. What this suggested was that somehow these cells were *conscious* of their surroundings and adapted accordingly, thus modifying their genetic code. It was concluded that in order to do this, the cells must possess some type of intelligence or consciousness to see, feel, and sense the environment outside their encasement. This may remind you of the studies on the plants and their intelligent root network, or of the atomic subparticles response to consciousness in quantum physics experiments.

Epigenetic scientists have postulated that DNA acts as both a transmitter and receiver of photons, energy, and intelligence. It sends and receives intelligence, thinks about it, and alters its behavior, cellular makeup, and genetic code accordingly. Using electromagnetic vibrations was one of the effective methods of transmuting these genetic codes. Since we know that both mind and heart are powerful electromagnetic generators, it was only logical that mentality or thought also would be effective transmuting DNA. If mind or thought can alter electrons in quantum studies, and send thought vibrations across the planet in remote healings and ESP, it can also change the composition of yet another molecular structure, namely DNA.

These epigenetic studies have changed the way many in the medical society now perceive the *permanence* of inherited traits and diseases. If mind or mentality can alter the innate behavior of cells and molecules, then it can also alter their outputs of traits and bodily conditions including disease. These so-called inherited problems are not as irreversible and permanent as thought in the past, and now appear to be subject to change by mind and consciousness. In 1922, Eugene Del Mar wrote:

"No one consciously desires mental inharmony or physical disease; but often, perhaps even as a matter of habit, he thinks the thoughts that cannot result otherwise. When his thoughts are of falsity, mere beliefs or opinions founded on physical sensation and hence interpreted wrongly, he really desires, invites or looks for disease; and looking he finds, asking he receives."

HEALING SCIENCE SUMMARY

Modern science is proving what ancient mental healers, alchemists, and metaphysicians already knew—that the mind-force not only can alter atoms and molecules, but also cells and organs, and therefore ailments and disease. Drug and alcohol addictions are simple physical manifestations, albeit disorders, that fall under the direct control of the mind. Addictions are mere expressions of a misaligned inner core which can be corrected with mental science.

Using mind powers to cure physical and mental conditions has proven effective in a variety of operations: direct and remote mental-healings, self-applied visualizations; placebo effects; and, hypnosis. Which of these applications will work for a particular patient is determined by his or her faith and belief in the method or process. In 1902, New Thought writer Stanton Davis wrote:

"If faith is operative in reacting upon drugs, upon inanimate objects of veneration, upon traditional concepts...What if we placed our faith in Thought, which is itself an active agent, a spiritual force—creative,

constructive, potent? In fact, faith itself is but a mental attitude of confidence and expectancy, and is thus in itself witness to the efficacy of thought directed to certain ends…We must learn to place our faith in the Unseen rather than in the phenomenal, in the Substance rather than the shadow, for that alone fails not."

Our expectancy, faith and belief, which are deeply rooted in the subconscious mind, are what our bodies ultimately act upon—not upon the physical molecules of the medicine. Somewhere along the way in evolution we developed an inborn subconscious trust in doctors and medicine, and lost our belief in the mind and spirit. Once we realize this, we can restore these capabilities, take back control, and transform ill-conditions back to health.

Mental science dictates that when you apply desire and faith to your visualizations, and see the end result as a true existing fact in your mind, it will become a reality. This applies to both positive and negative thoughts and beliefs—whatever seed you plant in your mind will sprout into a reality. Your addiction is simply the outgrowth of a bad seed that you've allowed to grow.

If the powerful mind can stop pain, heal cancerous tumors, produce biochemical changes, and even transmute our own genetic code, it can succeed in curing the conditions of alcoholism or addiction. By using this knowledge and applying mental science techniques, we have the ability to not only to prevent addiction, but to reverse and cure it.

11

Emotions and the Heart

"Keep your heart with all diligence, for out of it is the wellspring of life."

—Proverbs 4:23 (WEB)

Thoughts and images are inert, flat, and two dimensional without the added element of emotions. As the saying goes, *"sticks and stones can break my bones...but words will never hurt me."*. The sticks and stones are no more than thought-images injected with emotional power and put into action. It is the emotions that add power, energy, and action to our thoughts and images, and it is the heart which is the main broadcasting and receiving mechanism.

We do not create our inner vibrational frequency using plain thoughts, images, or words. Our emotional and mental bodies are established with thought-images mixed with feelings. The resultant frequency or vibrational state then engages the Law of Attraction to create our physical body, conditions, and world.

THE HEART: MUCH MORE THAN A BLOOD PUMP

The heart is the source of our metaphysical vital force. It manifests in our emotional body as a spiritual warmth when positive energies are flowing, and as a burning pit in the gut when negative energies are generated. Emotions are no more than vibrational frequencies. When placed on a metaphysical scale, love and fear are at opposite ends of this frequency spectrum.

The magnitude or strength of any emotion is determined on your belief and faith in the thoughts you are associating with it—what you believe to be true, your perception of the current reality. Remember that if your perception is distorted with drugs or booze, your body, and worldly conditions will mirror this in like manner—a twisted confused mind will reflect in a sick body and dysfunctional life.

The overall self-image frequency that you maintain about yourself on a constant basis throughout the day and night is what establishes your overall vibrational state. This is the metaphysical "song" that you sing, the aura you radiate, and persona you give off. It is this inner melody that engages the Law of Attraction to create your reality and manifest your health.

When mixed with the correct emotions such as faith and love, thought-images transmute into powerful vibrations that materialize your thoughts to achieve your goal desires. Thought-images magnetized with emotions will radiate outwardly and affect everything from mental and bodily functions to changes in external conditions and circumstances.

When concentrated toward the goal of sobriety, emotionalized thought-images will help heal our failing organs, relieve our cravings and depression, and lead us toward healthy and happy living. They will attract people and circumstances that align with our vibrational state. If you think and feel negatively, you will get depressed, have bad luck, and attract the wrong crowd. When you think and feel positively, project a healthy, sober self-image—good people, places, and things will magnetically gather around you.

Most of us have experienced the fright of witnessing a pet or child run out in traffic and felt the jolt of fear go through our hearts with a speeding car approaching. Or how about having that warm feeling in your heart when you see a cute baby smile and laugh, or a puppy playing? These both are examples of good and bad, loving and fearful heart vibrations. These feelings are felt in the heart itself, as well as in the bundle of nerves in the upper stomach or solar plexus—the pit in your stomach.

EMOTIONS AND THE LAW OF ATTRACTION

When we use the Law of Attraction to achieve goals, it is our vibrational state or emotional bodies that are doing the attracting, not the simple pictures and words. Successful millionaires that use the law do so consciously or subconsciously, and generate feelings of wealth from the heart within. They develop the *feeling* of having universal abundance in their vibrational state, and then they attract wealth automatically. These millionaires feel wealth in every endeavor from their heart, whether it regards experiencing fine dining, living in luxury, wearing expensive fashions, driving a Porsche, paying all of the bills, or buying whatever they desire. They feel rich and wealthy from the inside-out, down to the core. It shows in the way they act, walk, and talk even before they ever make any money.

It is important to distinguish mere mentalizations from heartfelt feelings. When we use mental science, we feel from the heart, visualizing our goal already taking place as if it were already a fact. We see, feel, and believe ourselves doing these happy, healthy and sober things, and being disgusted by drugs and alcohol in a subjective manner. We strive to change our inner core vibrational frequency to this goal image. This is much different than just thinking or picturing an event.

Idle thoughts and feelings do very little to us. For example, when we watch a horror film, or have a bad dream, we stir up fearful negative emotions. But movies and dreams don't turn us into addicts, failures, or attract bad things into our lives. In order for visualizations and thought-images to impact our emotional body, we must internalize them, place faith in them, and believe they are a true reality. We must see, feel, and believe ourselves in a certain manner, not just have fanciful thoughts about it.

The goal of weight loss is a good mental science example. The successful dieter who goes from 180 to 140 pounds in a couple of months does not do so by posting the ideal weight of 140 on the wall and constantly picturing those numbers. This person does not repeat self-affirmations that he or she will lose forty pounds in sixty days over and over, and keep checking the scale every day to see if the numbers match yet. This would never work.

Dieters are successful when they change their vibrational frequency to that of a healthy lean person. The inner self-image must be heartfelt or emotionalized, making the dieter already feel great about this new thin self. He or she already must think and act like a thinner person, visualizing with great feeling what he or she would do when in possession of this goal. This dieter visualizes doing the "thin-things" they desire— running, exercising, playing with the kids, looking sexy, dressing sharp. When absorbed in this new self-image, the dieter will subconsciously begin to exercise more, eat healthier…his or her metabolism will actually increase, and the weight is lost almost miraculously. The body will be magnetized with this new goal image and, without conscious effort, will change its appetite for specific food types to the caloric, fat, and carbohydrate contents that match the goal image attainment. Change the inside and the outside will mirror it. When the end result is mentally magnetized with faith in its attainment, the means to getting there is sometimes unplanned.

"I WON'T DRINK TODAY…"

Alcoholics won't quit their addictions by repeating, "I won't drink today" over and over. They won't do it by going cold turkey one night and taking sleeping pills to get past the cravings. They won't do it with idle prayers, or going to meetings and listening to other alkies. These are superficial attempts to cure an inner vibrational discord using the brain and will power. The truth is that only heartfelt mind-spirit practices will work. The thought-images must be truly believed and come from the heart. A genuine love for the new sober self-image must be felt deep down.

The successful mental science cure to addiction deals with removing the compulsion of that *feeling* or *effect* of getting high or drunk. When we try quitting, we don't miss the smoke in our lungs, the powder in our noses, or the burning alcohol going down our throats—we miss getting fucked up! We miss that buzz, that blissful feeling, that numbness, that euphoria, and that need for escape.

We can overcome the physical addiction relatively easy with a safe detox program, but the remaining part, the mental obsession with the "buzz," is not quite as simple. We must find a true inner desire for this natural serene sober mental state, the peaceful clarity of mind. When this mental state is your heartfelt desire, your vibrational frequency reflects this, and the chaotic frequencies of drugs and booze simply do not resonate or harmonize with this new paradigm.

In other words, when you truly desire, love, and appreciate the state of mind of peace and mental clarity, the thought of drugs and booze will no longer be appealing, and eventually will disgust you. They will be vibrationally incompatible and not harmonize with your new vibrational state. On a metaphysical level, you are no longer compatible with drugs or booze.

THE HEART'S SECRET BRAIN AND EMANATIONS

An organization named *Heartmath* has provided a great deal of this information on the heart, emotions, and consciousness. The group, found at www.heartmath.org, performs fascinating research for the global benefit of humankind, and I recommend you check them out.

Studies found the heart as the largest generator of electromagnetic waves in the body, even more so than the brain. This research has shown that the heart generates electrical and magnetic fields that are detectable with EMF medical devices up to several yards from the body... They also have metaphysical characteristics like thought vibrations; which are unseen and subtle yet powerful and intelligent. They say that dogs and bears can detect fear and other emotions in humans. This is simply the heart radiating fearful vibrations which the animal has extraordinary reception for. Some psychics can also see these invisible emanations as colorful auras around people. The different colors represent different vibrational frequencies, corresponding to moods and personalities.

Have you ever been in a checkout line at a store and someone is standing behind you too close, violating your personal space? You don't see them but can feel them. Or how you know when someone is staring at the back of your head from across the room? What you sense are these unseen vibrations and waves that are being emitted and received just like a radio broadcast tower radiates sound frequencies and a receiver picks up the signals. They come from both the heart and the mind, intelligence with emotional power

These energy fields are intelligent in nature and result from emotions generated between the heart and the brain. In Eastern sects, this corresponds to the second and third chakras of the energy chart, which is the middle eye and the heart. The heart emanations consist of fine, ethereal feeling-images and when combined with the intelligence of thought results in a powerful force. In the practice of mental science, we use this powerful mixture to manifest goals and transmute our realities.

The heart not only generates these vibrational frequencies, but is also a keen receiver of them. These thought-heart signals that radiate through space often bypass the objective conscious brain, and thus are not rationalized, so the feelings come to the heart as unfiltered and pure. When this happens, we receive gut feelings or hunches, because they have not been processed and rationalized by the brain. These are felt in the lower heart and upper stomach called the solar plexus region. This is also known as the yellow energy chakra. These intelligent receptions are often felt and intellectualized before the brain has time to process what is actually happening in the external world.

In addition to being a powerful broadcasting and receiving mechanism, the human heart is also a thinking source. Scientists have found the heart literally has cellular brain matter in its tissues and retains memories of our identities and traits similar to the cerebral cortex of our brain. This explains why recipients of a heart transplant often report strange incidents of having new personality characteristics of the donors. Countless heart-transplant recipients have reported that after their surgeries, they suddenly began experiencing new skills, and have new talents or tastes. After the surgery, they suddenly possessed new personality traits or talents. Some would start drawing or painting, or playing tennis, eating spicy food, wanting to speak a foreign language, were suddenly great at math, turned ambidextrous, and a host of other new personal characteristics. They would later discover that these talents and traits were the same as those the heart donor had possessed. How could an organ share this information unless it had some form of memory and thus intelligence, or mind?

I read of a story of a female heart donor who was sadly killed during a brutal rape and murder. A male was the recipient of her heart transplant, and had no knowledge of the donor or the cause of death. Soon after the transplant, he was haunted by detailed visions of her rape and murder. He relived the entire incident during several horrific daydreams. He was so traumatized that he reported it to his doctor. His doctor, who knew of the female donor's history, made the connection, and told the patient the story. It was as if a movie was stored in the heart's tissues somewhere.

When the heart is in its natural positive state, it resonates this to the entire body. Scientists learned when heart rhythms of test subjects were measured, joyful emotions were displayed as smooth, regular, uniform, flowing waves, whereas fear and anger were exhibited by jagged and irregular waves. Knowing that every emotion generates a like response by the brain and nervous system, it can be seen how the heart's feelings affect our overall well-being and vibrational state. Remember, it is the heart generating our feelings, not the brain. Thoughts, images, and words are simply the tools that ignite the emotions from the heart.

METALLICA VERSUS MOZART

One of the most notable experiments showing the effects of heartfelt thoughts and feelings on physical matter was done by Dr. Masaru Emoto in the mid-1990s. He placed several containers of water on separate tables in a public setting. Each bottle had a different positive or negative theme to it represented by pictures, music, and/or text. Some bottles represented love and peace and others had connotations of hate and anger; some had pleasant, serene themes, others negative and hateful.

Imagine for example, if you had one bottle of water with a picture of a cute baby playing with a puppy on the label along with Mozart melodies playing in the background. Then picture a second bottle stained in blood, with a picture of Adolf Hitler on it, and death-metal music blaring loudly in the background. Visiting viewers observed these samples while contemplating their unique themes. Days later, the water samples were taken away, frozen, and put under a microscope to analyze the crystalline structures.

The "love-water" displayed beautiful snowflake crystals with geometric symmetry, whereas the "hate-water" featured jagged, chaotic, and incongruent crystalline patterns. This test has been repeated by many other groups with different variables, but the results remained the same. They all proved that human feelings and consciousness effected the molecular composition of water.

If both the human body and planet Earth contain 60 to 70 percent water, then what does this say about how our thoughts and feelings affect both our body's health, as well as the planet's ecology? This test should remind you of the effect of human consciousness on the health of a plant, or the movement of the subatomic particle in the quantum double-slit test, or even in the placebo effect studies. All of these efforts prove the existence of mind over matter, and superiority of consciousness over the physical world. It is this mind power that we harness when we use mental science.

The strongest emanations by the heart are the positive ones generated by the emotions of love, faith, and desire. This is our natural, intended state of being, and creates positive heart rhythms. Contrarily, stress and feelings of fear, hate, and anger constitute an emotional and vibrational misalignment. Recall the woman who cured her cancer by constantly watching comedies and refusing to allow negative thoughts to enter her mind.

When the Law of Attraction is engaged, the thought-images and subsequent feelings can become a vicious cycle. A negative thought generates a bad emotion on which you then focus your attention. This causes you to breed additional similar thoughts, and these provoke even stronger emotions which become depressing and emotionally painful. This eventually results in breaking down the immune system and causing pain, sickness, and disease. The pain precipitates the need to find an anesthesia and thus we reach for, and abuse, drugs and booze. This will continue to spiral out of control unless correct thinking and mental reprogramming is brought in to correct it. Remember however, that this same cycle can occur with positive thoughts and emotions too.

CRAVINGS AND URGES

Usually when an alcoholic or addict has strong cravings or urges, it stems from either a physical withdrawal, or the need to numb a form of inner pain or conflict. The pain is usually a result of ill-thinking which originated from a negative thought such as a fear, resentment, anger, or just a past negative memory. Remember, the conscious brain would first have to accept this thought signal as a truth or reality in order to act on it. The thought then must be given focus, attention, and strength with emotional energy. The heart then gives the conscious thought the power to turn into a physical craving or an urge. A thought is simply a thought, but a thought believed to be true, mixed with heart emotion, causes action. An alcoholic won't have a craving looking at a picture of an ice-cold beer unless his subconscious mind projects him into action, drinking it, and feeling the effects in his imagination—and all that can happen in a split second.

Sometimes cravings or urges (and relapses) seem to come from nowhere. This happens when information bypasses the conscious brain and goes straight to the heart and you have a gut reflex. All of the sudden, you don't know why, but you just need a drink, pill, or your drug really, really badly. An impulsive, overwhelming feeling of fear and gloom overcomes you for no apparent reason. You get emotionally knocked down, so you reach for an artificial lift to get back on your feet and feel normal again. It's like out of nowhere someone just put a spell on you that instantly put you in a physically nauseating and mentally depressed state. This is no more than negative information (or one of your emotional triggers) being perceived by your subconscious and heart without having the chance to be rationalized, filtered, or argued with by the conscious brain first. It is the heart using its powerful intelligence and receiving functions, and lacking the brain to filter, rationalize, and protect you.

When your core vibrational state is negative, it's hard to deal with pain and fear. Cravings and urges will be powerful, since the immunity of your emotional body is weak and vulnerable. One of our prime goals in mental science practice is to positively charge our core vibrational state which provides a psychic shield from triggers and negative thoughts. When you are spiritually and emotionally grounded, and have positively magnetized your mind, it will deflect these signals instantly and thus you will avoid the adverse feelings that generate cravings or urges. You will have created a mental barrier or emotional fortress that won't allow negative thoughts to penetrate. Since they are not in harmony with your new vibrational state, they are rejected on a metaphysical level before they can act on the physical plane. These old triggers are rejected in accordance with the Law of Attraction; they no longer are attracted since they do not resonate with your new self-image frequency. You are now tuned into the frequency of sobriety, health, love, and success and can only receive and perceive signals that resonate with it. You change your inner core vibrational frequency such that your emotional body radiates positively. You have created a new reality and will only receive and perceive vibrations that are in harmony with it.

When addicts are convinced they are genetically doomed with an incurable disease, they will always feel weak, and remain susceptible to emotional triggers. Once you realize and believe that addiction is only a condition of mind that can be healed, reversed, and cured with mental science, you will subconsciously ignore and deflect these negative signals, and remain immersed in your healthy, sober self-image.

Mental science is built on the foundation that desire, love, and faith are the strongest positive emotions when mixed with thought-images and they will change one's frequency to manifest any wish imaginable. Just remember that the emotions of fear and hate are equally as strong and will objectify into form just as efficiently. It's your choice of thought.

PRAYER IS MENTAL SCIENCE; WORRY IS INVERTED FAITH

To fear something and put focus and attention on it is dangerous because it may lead to its creation. Remember the saying "be careful what you pray for because you might get it"? Any emotion combined with thought will cause it to perpetuate and grow by the Law of Attraction. Fearing or concentrating on a relapse, police arrest, embarrassment, past failures, or disappointments will all have the same results. On a metaphysical level, this is the definition of worrying—it is inverted prayer.

The effectiveness of prayer or worrying is directly proportional to your faith or belief. To make the desire (or worry) realistic, it must become a fact in the imagination—it must feel already in existence. In 1921, Genevieve Behrend wrote about the science of prayer, stating:

> "*The fundamental necessity for the answer to prayer is the understanding of the scientific statement: 'Ask, BELIEVING YOU HAVE ALREADY RECEIVED and you shall receive' ...once you realize that everything has its origin in the mind, and that which you seek outwardly, you already possess. No one can think a thought in the future. Your thought of a thing constitutes its origin. THEREFORE—The Thought Form of the Thing is already Yours as soon as you think it. Your steady recognition of this Thought Possession causes the thought to concentrate, to condense, to project itself and to assume physical form.*"

The act of visualizing your sober, healthy self-image goal as already accomplished is a powerful metaphysical technique of reprogramming the mind. Contrarily, when you see yourself *possibly* failing, relapsing, or using again, you are setting up the visualization of the act already being done. In 1887, *Esoteric* magazine explained how prayer can be used accidentally with negative thinking or worrying about fearful things. An unknown source contributed the following:

"Prayer may be unconsciously offered for evil to self as well as for good or supposed good. Prayer, desire, demand, is the working of a great law or force in Nature, and this force may be used with evil result as well as good."

Worrying is inverted faith, or prayer in reverse. When you worry, you are imagining end results while attaching strong, fearful feelings to them, thus causing the Law of Attraction to create these bad conditions to materialize. If you worry that you might slip up and have a drink at a party tonight and visualize it long enough with added fearful feelings, then you are just creating your future reality. Instead, you should be picturing yourself enjoying a coke or a bottle of water and having fun while relaxed and at peace. Successfully visualize overcoming the trigger event in your mind, otherwise you might set up failure by fearing the worst. When you have faith in mental science, you will have faith in yourself, and your ability to control your destiny.

An interesting observation the *Esoteric* author made regarding prayer was the fact that when we wish or desire for a goal achievement, we not only attract the physical manifestation, but also the mental attributes that go along with it. The author wrote:

"The asking process will draw qualities of mind and character as well as material things. If you feel lacking in courage, confidence, patience, cheerfulness, decision, in ability to control temper or appetite, you may also draw to you more and more addition of these and other qualities by the same law of persistent demand."

When we place sobriety and health as the objects of our desire, we will not only manifest the physical conditions, but also attract the mental qualities of strength, willpower, and confidence.

Do not rehearse and relive the negative events of the past. Don't try to go back and fix them in your mind and mentalize "what-if" scenarios. Learn a lesson from them, forgive yourself, and know that by using these new mind powers, you will overcome any minor setback. Concentrate instead on your positive, healthy self-image. Never forget the past lesson you learned, but do not keep reliving the mistake and giving emotional energy to it or it will fester and return. We don't concentrate on our drinking and drugging days, we focus on the sober healthy future. That's the difference between a sober mental science student and a "recovering addict". One is past tense, while the other is still fighting.

Keep attuned to your heart and gut like they were your wise mentors. The heart and solar plexus region are receiving bodies for hunches, feelings, and intuition. They are our indicators or feedback telling us where we stand emotionally, and thus what frequency we are generating. By using feelings as feedback, you can tell if you are emotionally on the right vibrational path aligning with your inner self and goals. Feelings are your guidance system or internal GPS telling you where you are now and where you're going.

When you have good, joyful feelings, then you're most likely on the right route; bad guilty feelings mean something is wrong or off course. The heart will alert you when you are around good and bad people, places, and things, and it will tell what decisions or choices should be made. Again, you should trust in your gut feelings or hunches more often, as they originate from the truthful source.

EMOTIONS CAN BE DANGEROUS WEAPONS

Since emotions are the biggest culprits for causing cravings and relapses, they should be treated with respect and be somewhat guarded, like having a gun in your house. Although the thoughts and beliefs that create the emotions are the ultimate underlying problem, sometimes our feelings manifest and take over our bodies so quickly that we don't have time to analyze their origin. We just suddenly *feel* like getting fucked up without knowing why. Again, this is the heart receiving and processing intelligence before the brain does.

To addicts and alcoholics, emotions are like sharp daggers that stab our hearts and guts and cause pain that we need to quickly numb with booze and drugs. Addicts usually have a very high sensitivity to both good and bad emotions because we are so used to anesthetizing them. We've gotten used to cutting off the highs and lows of the feeling-spectrum. We are comfortable right in the middle: inert, unemotional, and numb. The slightest bad problem or even a good reason to celebrate can be a total emotional nightmare to an addict. Slight emotional ups and downs that are insignificant to a normal person, can be a huge problem to an addict. Mood swings were negated with booze or drugs, and we eventually learned to not to deal with emotions at all—we hibernated in isolation while depressed, dormant, and inert—where it was safe.

The heart-mind emotions are obviously evoked when something happens in real life, but are also induced purely by the mind or imagination—this is the same basis of hypnosis. The same emotions are produced when an event is visualized vividly and believed, and when you act and believe as if the imagined event was already a true fact.

THE HEART SUMMARY

It is the heart that adds power to, reinforces, and carries the thought-images created by the mind. Good and bad thoughts will generate respectively loving or fearful feelings. The heart has neither judgement nor ego, as does the objective mind. When the mind and heart (thought and emotion) are blended in unison and meditated on for a desired end result, it constitutes a powerful spiritual force that literally creates a new reality. The heart will provide the strength and action to your intentions.

Remember that the heart is both a powerful broadcasting and receiving unit that not only receives and perceives intelligence, but sends it out powerfully greater than thoughts can alone. Trust in hunches and gut feelings, and let the heart be your guide telling you if you are following your desired path or not.

Know that by using these infallible mental science laws and principles you are becoming that new sober healthy person right now. By adding love and faith to your thoughts and images you are creating powerful vibrations that will, in turn, not only heal your mind and body, but also protect you from negativity and create your future reality. When you positively radiate your new self-image with your heart, it is spiritual law that you will rendezvous with the likeness or product of the original heartfelt image.

12

Start with Desire

"In order to attain a thing, it is necessary that the mind should fall in love with it, and be conscious of its existence, almost to the exclusion of everything else. You must get in love with the thing you wish to attain..."

—WILLIAM ATKINSON, 1906

If you didn't desire to get sober and clean, then you wouldn't be reading this book. The question is how authentic and heartfelt is your desire? Do you have true passion to get clean and sober? Do you *love* that sober and healthy image? Is that new self-image always in your mind's eye?

One of the most important principles in the Law of Attraction and mind-spirit laws is that of desire. It is a fundamental requirement of mental science needed to ignite the fuse of emotions required to achieve goals. The strength of our desire, our intent, and our focus determine the attracting force the law will provide. We must have a love of that which we wish to manifest.

We create a burning desire for what we want, and do not give any attention to that we do not want. To cure our addiction, we should not fight against the drugs or alcohol, but instead should intently desire sobriety, health, joy, and serenity. To change a room from dark to light, you do not try to fight and vacate the darkness, you simply bring in the light. In 1909, Edward Walker wrote the following:

"Thoughts are mental Things, and tend to become material Things. The Ideal becomes Real. Our dreams come true. Our desires are seed-thoughts that have a tendency to sprout, and grow, and blossom, and bear fruit— and the blossom and the fruit are of the same nature as the seed-thought. We are sowing these seeds every day."

DESIRE AND LOVE ARE ONLY FREQUENCIES

Desire, like faith, consists of a special creative frequency that gives our vibratory structure direction on where to proceed. Once desire is nourished with thoughts and emotions, it grows into conditions and experiences. When you truly desire sobriety, health, and happiness, the ideal path is paved for your physical experiences to follow.

Desire is found in the attractive forces of subatomic particles, in the cosmos, and in all the laws that rule creation or manifestation. In 1905, Elizabeth Towne wrote:

"The Law is inherent in each atom of the universe, and in each organization of atoms. The Law manifest is the simple sensation we call Desire. Desire is the voice of God. Desire is the Law of Attraction recognized. Desire is the unreasoning and unerring cry of the ego—every ego, from the original atom to the Christ man—for that which is related to itself; for that which is a necessity in the process of unfoldment."

You may think it is silly to say that desire exists in an atom, but it is an attractive force created by the source intelligence or supreme consciousness, so it very much exists. We call this some special atomic bonding coefficient, but the attractive force is of desire, which is likened to the frequency of love. So, yes, love exists in atomic structures, too.

I'm one of those old-school people that thought love was reserved for the "lovey-dovey" affectionate people, over-the-heels love-struck couples, sappy songs, and poems. I never understood what love meant in all those great Beatles songs, and I thought the "peace and love" hippy movement was a bullshit reason just to get stoned. It took learning about mental science for me to understand that love exists not merely as one of our human emotions, but as a metaphysical frequency in mental science.

Love is a vibrational frequency on the unseen metaphysical spectrum, situated on the pole alongside faith and desire, and opposite the pole of hate and fear. Love and fear, and any emotional frequencies in between, are available for us to use—it's simply a matter of choice. It's purely a decision of using correct thinking, and of developing proper mental thought control. You simply change the dial to the frequency you wish. It may take some relearning of bad thought habits, but it is truly a choice.

In Napoleon Hill's famous book, *Think and Grow Rich*, a burning desire was paramount to achieving any success—this was the starting block to any achievement. Whether we are seeking money or sobriety, we must first have an obsession for its attainment, and then develop faith that we can and will have it. Desire is the beginning of any change or creation.

Philosophers and metaphysicians have written that if you have the ability to desire something, then it is law that it must be a potential reality. According to ancient metaphysical law, it is impossible to truly desire anything that is not an actual possibility or within the realm of you actualizing it into reality. And one thing is very certain: You will never experience a reality unless it is desired and imagined first. Whether you realize it or not, your path in life thus far was already played out in your mind first—although for most of us was most likely subconscious. If you can simply *imagine* a sober, healthy, happy lifestyle, then it is your spiritual right to own that existence and be that person. You must forge the mental pathway first in your imagination.

WHY DO YOU REALLY WANT TO GET SOBER?

Keep in mind that with the Law of Attraction, it is much more powerful to attract the thing you love and desire versus one for which you have little or no feeling. When the heart is drawn to something, it is a powerful force and the heart's emotional participation is critical in manifesting it into reality. There must be strong intention or desire that stems from the heart.

This law applies to achieving goals of any sort, whether it's for sobriety, financial gain, weight loss, athletic achievement, and so on. Materialistic or ego-driven goals and desires are much weaker in frequency, and thus more shallow and temporary than those stronger desires attaching heartfelt feelings. You must dig deep inside and find the right reason for sobriety. To want health and happiness, you must feel you deserve it. You may need to forgive and forget a lot of guilt, resentment, and regret, but somehow you must be emotionally clear enough inside to allow this loving feeling of desire for your health and sobriety.

You must want sobriety from within and must know, feel, and imagine how the benefits of getting clean will transform your life down to the smallest details. You must get genuinely excited and emotionally charged when you envision your new life as a sober and healthy person. You must imagine the rewards and already see yourself with improved relationships, health, and finances. Just imagine the freedom alone!

Visualize yourself free from addiction and genuinely happy. From deep in your heart you must desire and get excited about living with a clear mind and not one fogged, confused, and depressed. Desire must be emotional and not inert as in wishing. In 1909, Edward Walker wrote the following:

> "It may be urged, all ideals do not become real, all hopes are not realized, all aspirations are not possible of expression and attainment—why? The answer lies in the fact that the majority of people do not know how to desire—do not know what they want. So far as desire is concerned, they content themselves with mere 'wishing,' or 'wanting' or fretting because they haven't the thing—real, active, burning, creative desire is foreign to their natures."

So, how sincere and strong is your desire for sobriety? If you are getting clean just to please another person or situation, it's not a true burning desire. That's not a true, heartfelt desire from within. It's not true desire if you're getting sober because you just got a D.U.I. and it freaked you out, and you have to show the judge you went to AA for ninety days. It's not true desire, if you're quitting only because your spouse threatened to divorce you and you can't afford the financial consequences. It's not true desire, if you're getting clean only because your boss or parents gave you an ultimatum that you'd get fired or booted out of the house if you didn't quit. In these situations, you only have a *need* to get sober and not a desire. Desire is internal, personal, and heartfelt. In order to manifest your goals using mind-spirit sciences, it is important to enlist all of the emotions in support of your new vibration and mental image and desire is critical. You cannot fake this.

One of the biggest obstacles with desire and goal achievement is the fear of failure or disappointment. This results in weakened faith, which equals weak results. It is understandable that, if in the past, you failed at staying sober, or in achieving any other goal, your confidence may be low. To try again and put your heart one hundred percent into another attempt is taking a big emotional risk. You may think to yourself that if you fail again, you know the fall is going to hurt, and even more. So, what do most of us do? We play it safe, we "hedge our bets," and simply don't get our hopes up—we wish and desire with half-ass effort. We say to ourselves that if we fail, it's no big deal because we'll only have a short fall—we are prepared for it. So, you only climb up half the ladder of desire, not to the top. This won't work.

You must forget about all past failures at getting sober or achieving any other goal and know that this time it is different. Dream big again—you are starting fresh with a huge, powerful arsenal of knowledge of mental science laws you never had before.

Be mindful that once you learn the powerful laws of mind-science and realize these are fail-proof principles, you can put all your eggs in one basket and trust one hundred percent that the outcome will be as you wish. You must have complete faith and abandon any crutches, excuses, or "parachutes" you have for possible failure. Your belief in these laws and principles are critical to your success.

To generate the proper vibrational frequency for goal manifestation, you must fall in love with your new desired self or the end result you wish. You must have such a burning desire for your new self that you feel actual love for this image. You should literally feel your heart warm and flutter in your chest when you ponder the possibility of this new self-image becoming a reality.

To add fuel to your burning desire, think of all the circumstances, events, and experiences you will gain by having this new life. Visualize in detail how the staff at work would think if you showed up for work looking fit, twenty pounds lighter, sober, and sharp. Or if you surprised your young child by being his or her new soccer coach. Imagine the happiness on your family's faces to see you go for a run after work instead of drinking a six-pack. Or the joy in your parents' or spouse's hearts to see you celebrate six months, and then a year, clean. Think of the feeling of not having depression anymore, the freedom to have that monkey off your back, and to have a clear, serene, and positive mind.

Mentally live out all of these ideals in your mind that sobriety will bring you: Finding happiness, fixing finances, mending relationships, feeling and looking healthy, and being truly free. See and feel how great that would be. As you assume the feeling of being healthy and sober, you will change your vibrational state and mold your world to resonate in harmony with it.

You must take the emotional risk of feeling these things as accomplished in mind already, not as an idle wish. Reinforce to yourself that this time it is different because you now possess the secret powers of the mind required to achieve anything you desire. You can heal yourself and change your entire life with these new mental powers. Foster this desire so strong until it becomes an obsession. In 1906, William Atkinson wrote this about desire:

> "Desire is a manifestation of this Universal Life Love. So, I am not using a mere figure of speech when I tell you that you must love the thing you wish to attain. Nothing but that love will enable you to bear the burdens of the task. The more Desire you have for a thing, the more you Love it; and the more you Love it, the greater will be the attractive force exerted toward its attainment..."

EMOTIONAL CROSS-TRAINING

When you truly desire you generate the feeling of love and excitement from your heart. A "trick" method for applying true desire to your goal can be accomplished with the following technique. Begin by focusing on a memory of anything that currently generates love or excitement. This may be a spouse, pet, child, girlfriend/boyfriend, favorite vacation, chocolate, music, an idol, or whatever. It may be a memory, or just a fantasy, but it must genuinely excite you. Feel how your heart pulses and warms and generates gentle reverberations, how your metabolism increases, how you get authentically excited.

While radiating these positive vibrations in your mind and body, simply transfer this feeling over to the thoughts of your desire for health and sobriety. Let those good vibrations bleed over to your self-image goal. Develop the habit of thinking of your goal-image whenever these emotions of love and enthusiasm are warming your heart and getting you excited. It's just like a type of "emotional cross-training" trick—get warmed up with your natural excitement, then play the game of living out your desires in your mind while in this state. It impresses upon your subconscious in powerful ways.

Successful athletes do this all the time. They get fired-up for games by raising their excitement level listening to their favorite motivating music, while visualizing their successful performances. While in this excited vibratory state, their goal visualizations are given strength and permanence with these added emotions. They are creating neural pathways of successful achievements, and also positively charging their inner vibrational state. You can do the same whenever your vibrations are high from another source, and simply mix those energies with your new goals. Whatever gets you excited, do it while visualizing yourself in possession of your sober, healthy, successful goal.

The goal of sobriety and health is a natural normal desire. It's not like you are asking to be a millionaire, a rock star, or to be quarterback in the Super Bowl (not yet at least). Sobriety and health is our God-given natural state we are simply trying to restore.

New Thought author, Orison Marden, wrote about having faith in your desires, and not to giving up on them. In 1910, he wrote the following:

"Many people allow their desires and longings to fade out. They do not realize that the very intensity and persistency of desire increases the power to realize their dreams... It does not matter how improbable or how far away this realization may seem, or how dark the prospects may be, if we visualize them as best we can, as vividly as possible, hold tenaciously to them and vigorously struggle to attain them, they will gradually become actualized, realized in the life."

Your sober self-image and happy, healthy lifestyle should be your first desire in life and held in the forefront of your mind at all times. Remember that you are not focusing on the act of quitting drugs or drinking, you are concentrating on the self-image of health and sobriety. Everything else will manifest from this healthy and positive core vibrational state. Keep this image fresh and alive in your mind's eye, and never let the desire go away or fade. It is law that it materializes into reality. Marden continues with:

"What we yearn for, earnestly desire and strive to bring about, tends to become a reality When we begin to desire a thing, to yearn for it with all our hearts, we begin to establish relationship with it in proportion to the strength and persistency of our longing and intelligent effort to realize it. The trouble with us is that we live too much in the material side of life, and not enough in the ideal. We should learn to live mentally in the ideal which, we wish to make real."

Marden is saying that you must live more in the inner thought-world or ideal world of your goal-image and not base your feelings and actions on what the outer world is saying. This is not living in fantasy; it is living in the world that you are creating. Don't forget that the outer physical world is simply a mirror of your inner world. When you desire and imagine your goal self-image with faith in its actualization, you build a powerful inner vibrational state, and your reality will soon reflect this.

We all have unique personal desires that will vary as to how we want to live our sober lives. Each of us define health, happiness, and success in our own personal ways. What is luxurious to one person is mediocrity to another. What is healthy and fit to somebody may be slovenly or handicapped to another. What is a great career to you may be insulting to another. Some of us live contently renting an economy apartment, while others are not satisfied until they become a millionaire or superstar living in a mansion. Some people even get comfortable living with physical ailments—bad backs, high blood pressure, obesity, and so forth. They are content this way, and don't care about getting well, even if a remedy or cure is available. Mental science does not tell you how to live your life, what is a good or bad life...only how to achieve that which you desire. So long as sobriety is your prime desire, what you do with the rest of your life is purely subjective, and your choice. Just remember that with mental science practices, anything you desire will manifest in miraculous fashion.

Our desires for these ideal worlds and realities are individually personal and unique for each of us. The one commonality is that addiction is unnatural, dysfunctional, and disgraceful regardless of any socioeconomic level. It is looked down upon in all sectors of society around the world.

DESIRE SUMMARY

Ultimately, our goal is to change our self-image vibrational state to that of a clean, healthy, serene, happy, and successful person. To do so, you must have a clear self-image of this, a strong desire for its obtainment, and faith in mental science that it is already becoming a reality. It is the frequency you resonate that attracts you to your goal attainment, and desire is what kick-starts the vibrational sequence. Desire and faith are the emotional fertilizers that empower our mental images to grow from thought-seeds into physical realities.

Once you understand these mind-science principles, you will realize that you are one hundred percent in charge of your life's conditions. There is no one else, and nothing else, that can get in the way of changing your inner being—only you control what goes in your mind. You must trust mental science with complete abandonment and have faith in these mind-spirit laws, and you'll realize the power and control you possess over all conditions in your life.

Desire is the beginning to making permanent change using mental science. You must have a heartfelt desire to be the new clean and sober person and have a true love for this new self-image. See all the benefits this new life will bring you and know that with these mental science laws they are already becoming true.

I hate to be the one to tell you this, but if you remain addicted after reading this book, it simply means that somewhere deep down you have a desire to be that way. You've decided that you prefer to hold on to negative thoughts, punish yourself, and never change. You have become who you are today because of your inner desire and choice of thoughts, images, and feelings. You will become who you want to be tomorrow, by starting with a heartfelt desire for a new sober self.

13

Meditation-The Gateway

"The subjective mind takes cognizance of its environment by means independent of the physical senses. It perceives by intuition. It is the seat of the emotions, and the storehouse of memory. It performs its highest functions when the objective senses are in abeyance."

—THOMAS HUDSON, 1893

THE DOOR TO THE SUBCONSCIOUS

Meditation is a gateway to the subconscious and a powerful tool for applying goal-achievement techniques in mental science. It is a means of removing the outer world and directly accessing the inner-core mind. You will soon make it part of your daily routine for reprogramming your subconscious, restructuring and charging your spiritual vibration. Meditation, combined with self-directed mental science, is the most effective tool for change.

Anyone can meditate, it simply involves getting relaxed and passively concentrating on rhythmic mantras, your breathing, heartbeat, or music. The goal is to get your brain into the alpha-theta brain wave state of deep mental relaxation and receptiveness. You go into a state of being that is void of the five senses, disconnecting mind from body and allowing your inner consciousness to surface as your objective self is quieted

Meditation by itself is a great aid for relaxation, stress reduction, and expanding consciousness. There are entire books and online videos on meditation in which you can find meditation music, listings of mantras, relaxation techniques, and instructions. I am going to explain some basic fundamentals of what is necessary in order to get to the receptive state. This will be needed to apply mental science visualizations and programming which you will learn in an upcoming chapter titled, "Meditative Programming Technique."

I was taught Transcendental Meditation (TM) as a teenager, which has been a blessing. Little did I know how important a role it would play later in my life. TM is just one of many meditation techniques. You can use just about any meditative relaxation method you like. If you decide to use a recorded music mantra, just don't use the guided meditation ones that contain voice commands as this will interfere with the programming you will soon be doing.

The silence you find in meditation is a learning experience where you become aware of the nonphysical world. You will find that when you go into this silence or deep meditation, your creative mind is awakened and many answers to problems will surface. Usually if you go into meditation with a question or problem, you come out with an answer or solution, as all of the knots in your mental network seem to loosen and get untangled.

HOW IT'S DONE

To perform meditation, you should first find a quiet place. You can even use headphones and sunglasses if you're in a busy environment. Physically you should be comfortable to sit upright, in a chair or on the floor; lotus position is fine, but certainly not required. I myself sit in a regular office desk chair. Your back should be upright and straight, with your legs limp in front of you on the floor. Your hands should be in your lap gently clasped, and your head should be vertical, not resting on a headrest, and tilted back slightly so your forehead (third eye) views above the horizon beyond. Your shoulders should be relaxed and limp. Remember to relax all your facial muscles, too. Your spine should be vertical and erect with your shoulders slightly back but without strain.

You can meditate to relaxing yoga meditation music, use a mantra, concentrate on your heartbeat or breathing, or any combination of these. I actually mix several together. The purpose is to busy your conscious mind with simple rhythms to achieve this non-sensory state of mind. I play Zen music at low volume, repeat a mantra, and monitor my breathing. My attention will shift from one rhythm to the other while I let thoughts float by. I find that the more I have to focus on, the quicker I can forget the external world, and the faster I go into the meditative state. In other words, the more I distract my conscious brain, the quicker it gets preoccupied. In a way, you are busying and confusing your brain to the point it simply shuts-off.

The use of sound is fundamental to meditation. Sound, which uses harmonics, is a natural healer, whether this is listening to your breathing or heartbeat, a mantra, or Zen music. The sound waves permeate your entire body from the atoms, molecules, and cells to organs, muscles, nervous system, and bones. It also levels the frequency of your brain's neurobiological activity and aligns your thought vibrations, thus settling stress and emotions. There are many YouTube videos, audio clips, and CDs in which you can find meditation music and mantras. Music with headphones is especially beneficial if you have distracting outside noises.

First start by getting physically comfortable, and then you begin your mantra-music and concentrate on the sounds, your breathing, and how relaxed your body feels. As you listen, thoughts will come and go and you should allow them to float by; just let them flow freely without attaching to them. Acknowledge your thoughts, and what they represent, and let them go in the thought stream again. Think of these thoughts as birds flying by overhead in the wispy clouds; just acknowledge what kind of bird it is, the colors, and its behavior, and let it just keep flying by. Don't give it any special attention that would draw the bird to you, and let it go into the distance out of sight. You will find that your mind will settle, like the snow in a Christmas snow globe. Just let the snowflakes settle at the bottom; do not stir them up with thought waves.

Passively concentrate on your breathing, your heartbeat, your mantra, or the music. By keeping your attention on more than one thing at a time it will quiet the mind faster. Again, let your thoughts drift by and just listen to the inner rhythms of the sounds.

Once you've relaxed, it's time to expand your consciousness. In the chapters on the atom and the cosmos you were given graphic examples of the scale of each using bowling balls, basketballs, BB pellets, and peas. Use these visions in meditation to expand your awareness, and gain a space-time perspective. Keep in mind that you are not your body, you are a consciousness-spirit that has a body, so treat it as a separate entity in meditation so you can direct it to relax more effectively.

As you relax, visualize the scale of the atom and the universe—remember the analogies of the bowling ball and pea, sun and Earth, then the atom and electron, and then the expanded giant universe. Playfully zoom in and zoom out from one to the other. You'll find that you get objective about your body, feeling more detached, tiny, and insignificant, whereas your consciousness gets larger.

Go to that place in your mind where all creation seems to be pure consciousness or divine intelligence. Sink deep to the core where all creation started—the origin of consciousness, the condensation of ethereal mind substance. In your mind ponder and meditate on the concepts of the beginning of all—how this concentrated mind stuff in the ether began the act of creation.

Confusing concepts and questions about creation and the higher power may arise in your mind that you do not have answers to right now. You do not want to start an investigation or internal debate. Those queries can be reserved for another separate special meditation period, but for now we want to meditate in order to perform mental science programming. Acknowledge challenging thoughts and then let them float by. Just go to that inner calm place, the beginning of the beginning, the warm, deep, blue spot, for the feeling of abyss in the presence of the eternal consciousness. Expand your mind from the scale of the atom to the limits of the galaxy and then back to your body. Recall the scale of the solar system and galaxy with respect to the atom and drift back and forth. See how the mind and consciousness are present in everything. The act of expanding your mind with these visions will put your consciousness and body in perspective and promote a feeling of serenity and peace.

Passive concentration on your selected sounds will put you in a deeper, trancelike state. Practice this exercise and soon your mind-body will automatically relax when it hears the mantra or music.

PAVLOV'S DOG

A best-selling book called *The Relaxation Response* was written in 1975 about a mind-body phenomenon. They found in studies that when we associate a certain word, phrase, or mantra with a deep relaxation state, we can elicit these same mental and physiological effects in times of stress just by recalling these sounds or phrases. The same principle works with meditation.

This learned response behavior is similar to the Pavlov's dog reflex. In the 1890's, Dr. Ivan Pavlov trained dogs to salivate by ringing a bell. This was because the dogs were trained to associate the bell ring with getting a food treat. Similarly, after some meditation practice, your mantra or sound will elicit the relaxation state in your mind and body. The brain-body connection will associate that mantra, music, or sound you are using for relaxation, and go into that state faster each time. It is like muscle memory in sports. At first, it may take you five to ten minutes just to relax depending, on your stress level and such, but after a little practice you will go into the alpha state very quickly, probably in less than a minute or two.

For the purposes of this book, you'll be meditating primarily for mental programming purposes, but you also can meditate other times simply to relax and expand consciousness. Yogis often meditated for long hours and achieved a transcending state or cosmic consciousness and would awaken afterwards enlightened with gifts of knowledge and wisdom. You might recall from the chapter on *Mind Talents* how hypnotherapist Dolores Cannon also found her patients would access a supreme intelligence source, or cosmic consciousness while in a deep hypnotic trance. There is no reason you cannot get to these states on your own. Spirit channels do this by themselves regularly to connect with spirits, and ESP masters sense these subtle frequencies without effort. It is more a matter of *unlearning* wrongful thinking, than it is learning new thinking.

Remember that we are trying to exit the physical world of senses and enter the inner world of mind-spirit. In 1922, New Thought teacher W. John Murray wrote this:

> *"Man, on the plane of the intellectual, derives his information from two sources, the interior and the exterior. The exterior suggests the finite and the perishable, the interior the infinite and the imperishable, and he is wise who draws more upon the interior than upon the exterior...It is when the intellect begins to materialize everything, and to regard the material world as real as the spiritual universe, that trouble begins. Any attempt to interpret Life from a physical standpoint, instead of from a spiritual one, is bound to produce confusion."*

Murray is saying that the insight you gain from this spiritual meditative state is more trustworthy than what the rational brain produces. When inspecting reality from the standpoint of the senses, the truth may become distorted and biased. Recall the chapter on the *Emotions and the Heart* where we learned how hunches and intuition were received by the heart, bypassing the brains rational filtering. Murray's thinking is along the same lines.

PUTTING A KICKING AND SCREAMING BABY DOWN FOR A NAP

From personal experience, I can tell you that sometimes it's hard to make the commitment or decision to sit down and meditate. It seems like there's a million more pressing things you should be doing instead of "stopping life" for twenty minutes to meditate, especially when you're stressed-out, frustrated, and have no spare time. It's ironic that when you need to meditate the most, it's the last thing you want to do, but actually the best thing you can do.

It's a natural human habit to try to fix things from the outside first, the hard way. But remember the universal law that mind is always the cause and the physical world the effect. Conditions in life always follow an unseen cause. Get the inside fixed and aligned first and you will be amazed how your outer life magically gets simpler and more organized.

For me, it's the same as making the decision to exercise. You never want to do it because you can't get into the mood, but once you start and get a little into it, you end up loving it, and when you're done, you are so thankful that you did it. Whether it's exercise or meditation, I always remind myself of all the wasteful non-productive things I can cut time out of to do this much more rewarding task. Cut out thirty minutes of television, surplus sleeping, social time, Facebook and Internet surfing, or just make your day more efficient in order to justify the time for meditating.

Meditation will take a little patience and practice, but eventually you will develop a need and desire for it. It's like infants that get cranky and irritable. Deep down they desperately want and need a nap, but they don't want to check-out of the world yet. They kick and scream until they drift off to la-la land, and sleep soundly with a smile on their faces, awakening happy and refreshed. The same goes with meditation. You may struggle with having to put yourself down, but will be so very grateful afterwards.

Ideally, you want to practice meditation twice a day, once upon awakening and once in the late afternoon or early evening. When you later incorporate the mental programming, you will strive for about fifteen to twenty minutes at each session. The morning session will get you programmed and positively charged with your new goal self-image to kick off the start of your day. The later session will clear the stress and negative vibes from your system, and reprogram your vibrational state for your goals.

SUMMARY:

Meditation can be a process of relaxation and method to expand consciousness and connect to our source energy. It also is a method of achieving the desired receptive mental state required for programming. In this book, we will deal with meditating primarily for the latter purpose, meditative programming.

When you meditate using Meditative Programming, you will find it paves the path towards your goals, and catapults you towards having a great day. Go ahead and pick out your music and mantras, and get started meditating today.

14

Argumentum...Consciousness

"All that we call Matter (or Substance) and Mind (as we know it) are but aspects of something infinitely higher, and which may be called the 'Cosmic Mind.' He holds that what we call 'Mind' is but a partial manifestation of the Cosmic Mind. And that Substance or Matter is but a cruder or grosser form of that which we call Mind, and which has been manifested in order to give Mind a Body through which to operate."

—WILLIAM ATKINSON, 1906

Although the word "argumentum" means "conclusion" in Latin, we obviously are not at the conclusion of this book. We are, however, at the end of the chapters that cover the science and phenomena behind the origin and essence of mind or consciousness. This chapter therefore, is a wrap-up of the sciences that corroborate the origin and existence of consciousness.

Okay...I am going to repeat the reason why I repeat myself. Why need a conclusion about consciousness? The redundancy is due to the fact mental science is such an elusive and esoteric subject matter. It needs a variety of presentations because each of us are on so many different levels of understanding. I don't know if you, the reader, are a teenager with an opiate addiction, or a senior citizen who's been an alcoholic for fifty years. Do you have a GED education or a PHD? With that range in mind, I'm trying to breakdown and offer these concepts in different contexts, while reinforcing them at the same time.

This is all in an effort to gain your faith in these principles. I'd rather be thorough and redundant, than lacking. So, sorry if it sounds like I'm beating a dead horse. Again, read, reread, or skip at your own pace and level of understanding, so long as it results in your faith and belief in these principles.

Deep down within us all, we possess emotional bodies radiating unique signature frequencies of our self-image. It is this metaphysical entity that governs your life—your present and future behaviors, habits, and accomplishments. Correcting a damaged core self-image is one of our goals because it is this emotional body that manifests the addictive behaviors in us. It is vibrating a negative discordant frequency like a wounded duck flying through the air. In order to correct a bad inner self, we must first understand the mental science basics which entails learning about the mind or spirit-consciousness. In 1922, Charles Haanel wrote:

> "All agree that there is but one Principle or Consciousness pervading the entire Universe, occupying all space, and being essentially the same in kind at every point of its presence. It is all powerful, all wisdom and always present. All thoughts and things are within Itself. It is all in all. There is but one consciousness in the universe able to think; and when it thinks, its thoughts become objective things to it."

Simply stated, not only is everything made of the same thinking mind stuff, but only one entity has the capability to actually think or direct its consciousness, and that is humankind. Mind is always the cause, and matter always the effect, but it is only humankind that has the creative abilities to direct consciousness. When we create with our minds, we objectify unseen mind-thoughts to manifest the seen or physical. In other words, our thoughts truly become things.

MENTAL SCIENCE WRAP-UP

Earlier we learned that consciousness exists in the fundamental particles, the electron and the photon, and that the human mind's thoughts can alter and communicate with them. These fundamental subatomic particles not only possess intelligence, but can receive instructions, process them, and act upon them. They form into atoms, and through the process of chemical affinity, attract or *like* and *dislike* other atoms. They communicate and interact among themselves without any scientific explanation. The manner in which they perform these feats proves that there is an active intelligence or consciousness present that extends to the tiniest subatomic particle humankind can examine. This same mind-stuff, or etheric consciousness, is present in the cosmos where the planetary systems maintain such precise orbits, spins, and cycles. The creation of the atomic world and universe can only be explained by the existence of a conscious intelligence.

The consciousness of the atom continues to display itself in a cumulative effect as the intelligence amasses into successively larger molecules, cells, plants, organs, and bodies. Creation continues to unfold and grow into organizations such as teams, families, groups, and races where we find group consciousness and the *Mastermind* principle at work. Physical matter contains holographic fractals, as the whole exists in every part. However, you subdivide matter or form, you always find mind or consciousness present, even in the empty space or ether. The entire roadmap of the universe is found in the fundamental ethereal substance.

Recall the placebo effect studies that demonstrated how the thoughts of a human can communicate with human cells and organs to mutate, transform, and repair them. We saw how the mind was shown to heal and cure both mental and physical ailments including removing tumors, eliminating pain, and curing depression. We learned how these studies proved that humans can produce opiates, antidepressants, dopamine, serotonin, and other chemicals in the brain and body by pure mind power alone.

The PSI, or parapsychology research, bears witness to the fact that not only do humans have the capability to communicate nonphysical intelligence to one another, they can change physical objects. To bend a spoon, move an object, or cause the roll of a die, the inert object must have the capacity to process intelligence. This proves consciousness is present in sender and receiver—subject and object. Again, we find mind is the cause, and matter the effect.

The cases of spirit channeling and near-death experiences not only prove the fact that spirit or consciousness is eternal, but also validate many founding principles of mental science and spiritual law. Seth's saying of *"You create your own reality...your beliefs form reality"* is a core mental science principle reiterated by many seers and channels. Our consciousness or spirit never dies; we are living in temporary bodies, a grosser form of spirit that is eventually shed like a spiritual skin.

Consciousness extends to all living things, including simple plants, as we learned how they detect predators and emit warning signals, and exhibit signs of intelligence seeking sun and water. Nonphysical intelligence and energies are present in all entities including the plant, animal, and mineral worlds.

Everything in the universe vibrates. On the physical plane, everything is radiating different frequencies... atoms, cells, organs, bodies, animals, trees, buildings, planets, and so forth. There are frequencies that our five senses can detect, and there are those only detectible by equipment such as sound waves, X-rays, radio waves, and the like. Scientists determined that as humans, we see and hear less than one percent of the entire visible and audible, light, and sound spectrums.

In addition to the physical electromagnetic frequencies that science can measure, we also have invisible metaphysical frequencies such as thoughts and emotions. Imagine in your mind what it would look like if every physical and nonphysical vibration could somehow become visible. What if science invented a pair of goggles that would allow you to sense or "see" every frequency that existed—physical, mental, and spiritual, in every frequency range. What would this look like? Try to visualize trillions of living plants, insects, and creatures; millions of television and radio waves; a trillion cell-phone and satellite waves; light waves reflecting off every object; and, voices and thought waves radiating from over seven billion people radiating. It would probably seem like you were in the middle of a television set that had a really bad connection... a solid web of thick static, just like in the movie, *The Matrix*.

OUR FIVE PHYSICAL SENSES

We live in that complex vibrational matrix, with millions of frequencies bombarding us at the same time. Yet we selectively choose to invite only a dozen or so to create our reality. In 1918, Theron Dumont wrote:

"We know that our sensory nerves are capable of transmitting to the brain only a part of the phenomena of the universe. Our senses give us only a section of the world's phenomena. Our senses usher only certain phenomena into the presence of our minds. If we had three or four new senses added, this might appear like a new world to us; we might become conscious of a vast number of phenomena, which at present never have any effect upon our nervous organisms. It is possible to imagine a race of beings whose senses do not resemble ours, inhabiting other worlds."

As Dumont says, it would be intriguing if humankind possessed one or two more senses that could receive another sector of frequencies.... maybe adding the senses, a spider, dolphin, or hawk possesses, or sensitizing our sixth sense so everyone could have ESP.

In a way, we are lucky our five senses each filter only a tiny spectrum of these frequencies. Although we do also receive communication with the heart and through mental telepathy, the majority of the time we are externally focused on the five physical senses. The senses are basically instruments that translate vibrations into signals. These signals are transmitted to the brain which, in turn, converts the signals and turns them into our reality or an internal holographic image of the physical world. The eyes really don't see, the ears really don't hear, and the fingers really don't feel—they are only conduits for vibrational information. Just like the keyboard on your computer doesn't write.

The senses deliver the data which we validate as a reality or truth, and then we associate feelings about these perceptions. It is the resultant emotions or feelings that matter most. The feelings represent the vibrational state of our conscious being. This vibrational frequency is your emotional body containing your core self-image which is governed by the Law of Attraction that dictates the conditions you will experience.

WHEN A TREE FALLS IN A FOREST

Most of us have heard the philosophic question: *"When a tree falls down in a forest and there is no one present, does it make a sound?"* Some people say no, arguing that it takes a human ear to validate a sound. Others say yes, it makes a sound regardless of whether a person is there to hear it or not.

Well, the correct answer (or the one I'm sticking to) is *NO*, because *sound* is the term we define as the instant in which a signal is decoded by the human brain as such. When the tree hits the ground, the impact creates rapid air pulsations emitting from the two opposing molecule masses of the tree and ground. To be classified as a sound, there first must be a human present with functional hearing capabilities. These air vibrations which travel at over 750 mph, then hit the ear drum, which vibrates in resonance, sending signals to the brain. These air pulsations must vibrate within a very specific frequency range in which a human hear can recognize and interpret. At that point, it is perceived as a sound. The signal also contains added information as to the pitch and tones to differentiate the frequency of the tree thump from a crack of thunder or similar-sounding vibrations. Thus, to qualify as a sound, a human observer, with functional hearing, is required and the tree's air pulsations must vibrate within a specific frequency range. The actual air pulsation traveling through the air has no sound itself.

In a manner, this is similar to the double-slit experiment in quantum physics mentioned in the Atomic chapter. The human observer creates a particle form from a wave form, which makes it "solidify" in appearance. The observer is essentially creating the reality of the mass in his mind, which does not exist until he observes it. The same goes with sound—there is no sound until it is observed. With all of the senses, you will find that everything exists purely as energy and vibration, and nothing represents our reality until it is decoded by our brains, which, of course, can be very personal and subjective. People with OCD, obsessive compulsive disorder, are perceiving things is an exceptional way…seeing germs, disorder, and misalignment out of "normal" situations. We all have OCD to some extent, paying particular attention to specific details, having pet peeves, or sometimes the opposite and being ignorant of the senses and internally focused.

Vision and light work in an interesting way. When we are seeing any physical object, light waves are reflected off the object from a light source such as a candle, artificial light, or the sun, which then strike the retina in the back of the eyeball. The retina converts the light waves to an electrical signal. The electrical signal transmits to the back of the brain where it is translated into a vision. There is no light source or photons in the back of the brain, so it is a mystery as to how we actually see such brightness or even an image. It is pitch black dark in the back of the brain. Our eyes do not produce the vision; the image occurs in the back side of the brain. The electrical signals themselves only transmit a code or information about light—not a transfer of light photons. These information-electrons are just energy. It is the magic of consciousness that converts them into a lit holographic image in our mind's eye. In 1919, Swami Vishita wrote:

> "We must never lose sight of the basic fact that all SENSATIONS RESULT FROM CONTACT WITH VIBRATORY MOTION. An eminent scientific authority has said regarding this: 'The only way the external world affects the nervous system is by means of vibratory motion. Light is vibratory motion; Sound is vibratory motion; Heat is vibratory motion; Touch is vibratory motion; Taste and Smell are vibratory motion. The world is known to us simply by virtue of, and in relation to, the vibratory motion of its particles. Those vibratory motions are appreciated and continued by the nervous system, and by it brought at length to the mind's perception.'"

Your vision, like your imagination, is created by the mind or consciousness. This motion-picture screen of the mind is consciousness decoding intelligent information in the form of electrical signals. The brain is the instrument that decodes the outside world to our inner reality, and our interpretation will add feelings to it that create our reality and vibrational state.

If the "mind's eye" is simply a holographic interpretation of external signals, then why cannot we deceive the brain using our imagination? When we place our faith in mental science, we will learn there is no difference, and we can create our own memories, and more so our future reality.

MINDFULNESS: ARE YOU HERE AND NOW?

The outside world is only as accurate as your interpretation of it. Your consciousness, attention, or awareness of the sensory data is what matters. Millions of frequencies flood our senses all the time, but we only perceive what we focus on. Sometimes senses are ignored on the conscious level and we automatically process them on a subconscious level—we sometimes just zone out and go on autopilot. Have you ever driven home from work, daydreaming about something, and found that you didn't remember a thing about the drive? You had just driven fifteen miles without knowing whether you stopped for lights, switched lanes, almost wrecked, or saw anyone you knew. This happens in everyday life, too, when someone is not mindful. Are you mindful of the senses, or are you running films of past events wishing this or that happened differently? Or are you projecting into the future about what may or may not happen?

I know that for the active addict, it's hard to keep much off of your mental plate other than how you're going to get that next buzz—especially if your "jonesing" for a fix. How are you going to process the senses, and hence reality, if your brain is going through contractions thirsting for a hit or a drink?

We alkies are smart when it comes to planning our booze. We are the best at alcohol management—it's relentless and exhausting, but it's our job. We need it to function more than food or water. We do it around the clock throughout the year including holidays, vacation, and even when we're sick—we're professionals at it.

I remember when my dad was quitting drinking, or tried cutting down, he once told me that you know you've licked the alcohol addiction when you stop mentally planning your next drink. He was so right. As an alkie, just about every part of your day is preoccupied with how and when you can get that next drink, and that starts as soon as you wake up in the morning. If we have a planned commitment, work, or an appointment with someone, we get creative and go through the logistics of how and when we'll get alcohol into the picture. We plan our driving route to make sure it has a liquor or beer store on it, or we include a restaurant stop that sells drinks, or a scheme to sneak alcohol into some function. Or maybe it's tucking a couple of miniature of liquor in our socks, or stuffing a couple tall boys under the back seat. We figure the amount of time we'll be without booze and plan accordingly how much we'll need before and after each event. We know exactly how much alcohol is needed, how fast we metabolize it until more is needed.

When I finally got sober, I remember that first day when I actually made it to mid-afternoon and thought to myself, "Wow, I haven't thought about drinking today." What an amazing freedom that was! The physical addiction is one thing, but the mental obsession and preoccupation is the real monkey on our back. It not only saps us of all our time, but sucks all the life energy out of us. It literally collapses our conscious world to the basics of alcohol and survival. When we are actively drinking, we have very little expanded awareness outside of this until we are satisfied with obtaining the booze for the day. If we don't have a drink in our hand, we'll always be thinking about when and where we will.

If we are not jonesing about our next fix, our second favorite thing is to dwell on negative thoughts. When you're an addict, you are usually an unhappy person deep down, and full of hate, whether its towards yourself or another. When we are not being mindful of the here and now, we often allow painful memories or negative situations to seep into our consciousness without realizing it. Bad memories that host strong negative emotions seem to have a life of their own and move about our minds seeking attention and demanding resolution. They usually involve memories associated with feelings of regret, guilt, pain, embarrassment, or sometimes even ego and pride. If these thoughts are allowed to enter the subconscious mind, soon emotions are added to them and they fester and grow into action. They soon alter our moods, metaphysical vibrational state, and our emotional body, resulting in pain and discomfort. Before you know what even happened, the Law of Attraction snowballs these tiny subconscious thoughts into bodily cravings and urges for drugs or booze. Out of nowhere, we suddenly have jolts of nerves starting a fire in the pit of our stomachs craving some booze to put it out, or pills to numb it. With mental science principles, both Meditative Programming and correct thinking practices will stop this chain of events from ever starting or getting this far.

It is easy to see that when we focus our mind on anything, we give it energy, it grows, and we attract more of it. Our goal is to make our desire for health, sobriety, and success at the forefront of our minds and receive most of our attention, and thus mental energy. In 1909, William Atkinson wrote:

> "There is Mind in everything, and everything is in Mind. Consequently, just as Thoughts become Things in the Cosmic Brain, so is it possible for a strongly concentrated and focalized Mind to materialize into objective form things and conditions on the material plane."

THE CONCEPT OF TIME

A single tiny subconscious thought-image can snowball into a full-blown craving in a split second. Mankind cannot come close to building a computer that can process thoughts and images faster than the human mind and brain. The mind-spirit simply is not subject to laws of physical science of space and time—time is not a condition in the metaphysical ethereal world.

Einstein's relativity formula of $E=mc^2$ states that in order to equal the speed of light, matter must be infinite—therefore mass must expand everywhere at the same time—simultaneously and infinitely. This formula corroborates the paradigm that consciousness is infinite and faster than the speed of light. This is why we receive hunches and intuition on things before they happen—because mind is independent of time. This is why the same identical electron in quantum entanglement studies could coexist simultaneously miles apart. Time is one of the cruder creations in nature, and easily surpassed by mind and consciousness in superiority. The ancient Tablet of Thoth was translated as reading:

"Man is in the process of changing, to forms that are not of this world; grows he in time to the formless, a plane on the cycle above. Know ye, ye must become formless before ye are one with the light."

Just as Einstein calculated, to be one with the light you must have infinite mass or be formless. Humankind knew this spiritual truth thousands of years before it was also applied to physical matter with the famous formula of $E=mc^2$.

What that means to mental science is that the mind has no physical limits. Your mind can go to the farthest galaxy and back in a split second, whereas it would take a speeding light particle billions of years. This seems like it's just your imagination, but that's all that there is when you remove matter—ethereal mind substance.

The fact that time is only a mental construct explains for many miracles. The yogis and ancient metaphysicians worked with this concept of mind being infinite and timeless when performing miracles. Proving that there are no space-time limits for the spirit, they would travel as astral beings or a subtle light form and transverse both time and space. They could materialize and dematerialize, resurrect lives, and levitate their bodies at will. When you are faster than light, you are timeless and infinite, just as both Einstein and the yogi taught. Just remember that the faith, knowledge and powers of these miracle workers was exceptionally strong and developed. When you work with mental science, you are working with consciousness, mind, and spirit. You therefore are working in the realm of timelessness. You can change, reverse conditions, transform, and manifest goals as fast as your faith will allow. The "timelessness" of reality is the purpose we visualize with our new self-image "as-if" it was already an existing fact. Recall the psychological fact that the subconscious cannot tell the difference if our imagination is generating pictures from outside the body, or from within when we picture and feel it *as if* it was existing. The future becomes the present in mind, and this is how we visualize our goal self-image to create miracles in our lives. This is how beliefs are converted to faith.

CONSCIOUSNESS SUMMARY

We learned that mind or consciousness exists in everything, and that mankind can use mental science to mold or create from this. In 1904, Erastus Hopkins wrote:

> *"If atoms are not matter because of their electrical reality, neither can man be; and as all that is called matter is made up of Radiant Energy, there can be no matter of itself, which proves and admits all that Mental Science has ever claimed; that the Substance of Matter is Spirit."*

We are vibrational energy beings obedient to our spiritual consciousness. When mind-spirit is directed to an end result using mental science, we create our reality. There is an order of power, and our mind, or conscious spirit, is the strongest—everything else is subordinate. Mind is always the cause, and matter, the effect. This is the metaphysical equivalent of gravity, everything "falls" from mind-spirit to matter.

Using your consciousness and powers of thought, emotion, and faith, you may transmute any goal, wish, or desire into a reality. Sobriety, abundance, health, love, and success are simple goal manifestations that use the laws of creation in mental science. Using this universal law, you will generate a powerful vibrational state that will actualize your wishes. It will literally transform your reality to a healthy, sober, loving, and successful life.... *if* that's what you truly desire.

15

Theosophical Notes

"This Spirit of Infinite Life and Power that is behind all is what I call God. I care not what term you may use, be it Kindly Light, Providence, the Over Soul, Omnipotence, or whatever term may be most convenient. I care not what the term may be as long as we are agreed in regard to the great central fact itself."

—RALPH TRINE, 1897

The great thing about mental science is that it contains the universal naked truth that can be clothed by any religion or deity you choose. After all, most all of the great deities displayed their mastery of mental science and spiritual law in one way or another. However, we are not concerned with deities or religions, but with mental science which is more akin to theosophy. Theosophy, is not a religion, but a type of philosophy that studies the mystery of the universe relating to its divine creation and esoteric nature.

Mind is in everything, everything is alive with a consciousness. I am hoping this underlying message is now established in your belief system— that conscious intelligence is at the origin of all existence. This is not a religious claim—it is a scientific fact based on the evolution of consciousness and intelligence and our studies of the universe. All that is in existence is objectified mind substance, and our consciousness or spirit is sister to the originating thinking substance.

This knowledge of creation and consciousness is an important factor in how we construct our belief systems or paradigms about the world. When we learn mental science, we are forced to acknowledge these truths in order to develop the faith required for our laws to work. If you go on with your life without this wisdom, you will most likely not be using mental science, and will live by the terms and conditions the world hands you. In other words, you either use mental science to get what you want, or the world uses these same laws to create your reality without any direction.

ADDICTS ARE ACTUALLY VERY SPIRITUAL

Alcoholics and addicts are ironically some of the most spirit minded people you will meet. They crave the company of the spirit because they have such desperate needs to fill the emotional-spiritual holes in their souls, to find meaning in life, and feel whole again. They seek the comfort and warmth of that spiritual cocoon in which they can crawl inside, knowing they can hide there without any rejection or criticism. It is when they feel close to the spirit that they feel they are finally getting the sympathy they deserve for their suffering. The spirit gives unconditional love in a way no human being seems capable of providing.

However, by employing drugs and alcohol to access the spirit world, they are left emptyhanded, because their experience is temporary and illusory. They may feel a false spirituality, but it only lasts as long as they are artificially numbed. When they come down off the high, they are that much more depressed because of this loss of a perceived spiritual connection. The harsh, cold world of reality along with the physical pains of addiction are even more reason to find a way to return to that wonderland as soon as possible again. To the addict, it's better to be numb and disillusioned, then to be full of pain and suffer harsh reality.

The addict's desire to fill the hole, and find meaning through a spiritual connection, is a blessing in disguise because it is much more easily obtained when he or she gets clean and sober. They have already established a valid and genuine desire for it, so the attraction has already been established.

Once the addict learns that access to the spirit world is through knowledge, meditation, or prayer, and not with drugs, it is a matter of getting clean, correct thinking and changing his or her inner vibrational state. The addict's exceptionally strong desire for spirit will then act as a powerful force in making a solid connection. Now that the distortion, resistance, and physical burden of the drugs are removed, the addict can freely access the mind-spirit world with perfect clarity.

MENTAL SCIENCE AND SPIRITUAL LAW HAS MANY NAMES

Combining mental science principles with spiritual laws does not constitute a religion of any sort, but a dogma of the core underlying truths of consciousness and creation. In 1883, New Thought and metaphysical writer, A. P. Sinnett, wrote:

> *"The wisdom of the ancient world—science and religion commingled, physics and metaphysics combined—was a reality, and it still survives... it was already a complete system of knowledge that had been cultivated in secret, and handed down to initiates for ages...."*

Many of the ancient alchemists and miracles workers knew of these truths that later were forgotten, lost, or suppressed. Jesus, Elijah, Egyptian priests, seers, yogis, and ancient healers utilized these occult laws every day. The practices of mental science were soon reduced to magicians, psychics, mental healers, and such. These secrets however, are still buried in most ancient religious doctrines using sacred dialect, parables, metaphors, and artifacts. The Bible for one, is full of mental science metaphors and parables, some of which are quoted in this book.

In our studies, we do not conflict with the various religious sects because our laws precede most formal religions. Christianity, Buddhism, and even Vedic and Egyptian religions are just over two thousand years old, whereas humankind has existed for millions of years. The underlying spiritual laws and mental science principles are universal and apply equally to the Jew, the Christian, the sun worshipper, and even the agnostic or evolutionist. Whether adherents to these views agree or not, the laws of mind-spirit are predecessors and thus are commonalities of all religions.

When you study mind, spirit, and consciousness separately from mainstream religious teachings, the subject matter often gets misconstrued. In 1880, Epes Sargent wrote about occult mind science and how they were treated in ancient times:

> "*Certain remarkable psychic phenomena were construed as Satanic and unnatural, and an ancient Hebrew prohibition, founded in ignorance, was made the excuse for punishing with death innocent persons suspected of producing…any inexplicable manifestation of abnormal power.*"

In the past, people showing any occult mental or psychic abilities were treated as outcasts. When the industrial revolution started, the medical and scientific worlds also advanced exponentially. These great scientific and technical advances coincided with several military wars which further suppressed mental-spiritual science practices. Thus, they were eventually forced to go underground, or disappear entirely as the physical sciences dominated the educational systems.

In 1920, Thomas Edison was asked if he believed in an intelligent creator or God to which he replied, "*Certainly. The existence of such a God can, to my mind, be proved from chemistry.*" In Edison's mind, creation was reflected in the atom through its peculiar desires, attractions, and illusive origin. Mental science philosophy follows this same train of thought.

We have given terms for every state of matter that exists in the physical realm, from solids, liquids, plasmas, and gases to the frequencies of radio and x-rays. However, when it comes to the esoteric characteristics or the unseen dimensions of mind-spirit, humankind differs in its explanations and terms. If you call the originating source a God, it implies religion; when you call a human's consciousness a spirit, it implies a soul, again implying God, and thus points to religion again. In 1922, Charles Haanel wrote:

"There is only one Supreme Principle, evading all comprehension of its essential nature. It is the Absolute. Man, can think only in terms of the relative. Therefore, he sometimes defines it as the Universal Intelligence, the Universal substance, as Ether, Life, Mind, spirit, Energy, Truth, Love, etc. His particular definition at any moment is governed by the particular relationship of the phenomena of Being in which he thinks of this Principle at that moment."

Our studies do not have any arguable rules, standards, or codes of living, as do most religions. Mental science does not define morals or ethics, nor dictate rights or wrongs. It does not tell you what is a sin or what is angelic; what is good or what defines bad. It does not have a spearhead entity with a name that we worship. It only has a source or origin that is based on the emergence of intelligence and consciousness with its respective mental-spiritual laws. Spirit is our term for the entity in which our consciousness is gathered, and preceded religion of any kind.

In mental science, we learn and practice the science of mind-body-spirit to achieve our full potential—we do not argue about how these laws are used. Sinners and saints are determined by rules of morality and ethics, which are up to each individual to seek through any politics, dogma, creed, or religion he or she chooses. Mental science plays no favorites as to those with beneficial goals versus those with harmful ones. It does not care if your goals are charitable or selfish. Therefore, proper application requires knowledge, wisdom, morality, and ethics from sources outside of the sciences we study here.

In mental science, we use the knowledge of mind-spirit to better ourselves, to heal ourselves, and to create and grow. It is the goal to remove layers of ignorance and wrong thinking and return our intrinsic powers of consciousness, natural health, and mental abilities.

When you acknowledge the principle that consciousness exists in every creation and that our consciousness is connected to a greater originating source or universal mind, you should sense a change in your belief system and hopefully feel that inner hole beginning to fill. You should have developed the foundation on faith in the mental science principle that lead to a state of excitement or metaphysically high vibratory frequency.

FAITH IN THE UNSEEN

In 1885, Dr. W. F. Evans wrote, *"By faith is not meant the mere belief of a dogma, but the cognition of spiritual realities and verities which are above and beyond the ken of the psychical or unspiritual mind of man."* You must look beyond the senses and trust in powers of the unseen, the nonphysical. To achieve this faith, you must develop a deep understanding, which comes from contemplating concepts of knowledge.

In 1922, New Thought teacher W. John Murray wrote this about learning the subject matter of mental science:

"In order for us to work intelligently with any law we must first understand that law, whether it be that of mechanics, mathematics or metaphysics. One cannot work contrary to any law and accomplish desirable results, and it is for this reason that an intelligent comprehension of law is as necessary in the religious realm as in any other."

The comprehension of law that Murray is referring to is the spirit science that pervades all religions. The golden thread running through all true religions is that the invisible mind-spirit world controls the visible world. To control your external world of conditions you must first take control of your thoughts, images, and feelings. Do not expect outward conditions to change unless you've changed your inner vibrational frequency to harmonize with that what you desire. You must think and believe health and sobriety from within for it to materialize as a reality. *As above, so below.*

To have the tools of mental science at your hands is a gift to living any lifestyle we desire, and obtaining any wish we can imagine. The game of life will change for you when you realize that everything is energy in various vibrational states and that we live in a sea of magnetic consciousness.

FINDING SPIRIT IN A BOTTLE OF "SPIRITS"

"Don't be drunken with wine, in which is dissipation, but be filled with the Spirit." (Ephesians 5:18; WEB)

The desire for the spiritual dimension in life is often felt literally in the heart and solar plexus. Alcoholics and addicts usually suffer from a discordant inner vibrational state that has been created by a variety of underlying emotional issues, and further exacerbated by abuse of drugs and alcohol. This pain causes the inner hole that craves the spirit so desperately to fill it in. That emptiness is both frightening and painful.

In the next chapter, *"Karma and Housecleaning,"* I discuss this emotional discord in more detail, but suffice it to say, for now, that the pain usually stems from an underlying core emotion of fear. The emotion of fear manifests as many emotions such as anger, trauma, jealousy, egotism, disease, and sickness. A misaligned vibrational frequency creates separateness between our spirit and the universal consciousness, and we use drugs or booze to kill this discomfort and pain. The addict is well past using booze and drugs for the euphoric feelings and recreation—they are eventually used solely for medicinal purposes for the cessation of pain, and to fill the emptiness, or hole inside.

The word "spirits" for alcohol originated from the Latin word "Spiritus," which means "from the gods." Drugs and alcohol numb the conscious thinking brain, anesthetize emotional and physical pain, and often provide this illusory feeling of closeness to God. Science has found that alcohol and many other drugs change brain waves to alpha frequencies. When in this literal sense-less state, the addict feels a feeling of warmth and safety, and a loss the physical senses. This is very similar to the brain wave state of a deep meditator who achieves cosmic consciousness. The critical difference is that the drunk or high person is in an illusory state, and not in any control of their mental faculties, whereas the meditator is acutely in control. The addict's temporary mental state of euphoria, often mistaken for a spiritual connection, is very comforting and can often be as addictive and real as its physical counterpart, the chemicals.

The artificially induced spirit is not only temporary, and illusory, but is also destructive. The true spiritual state can be achieved naturally with correct thinking, meditation, and knowledge of the spiritual laws. Enlightenment is an everyday feeling when your paradigm is altered and you have faith in these new concepts of mind-spirit. Once you reach this level of understanding you will see how drugs and booze only retard and distort spiritual illumination and not enhance it.

The negative spiritual effects of alcohol use have been scientifically demonstrated using biofeedback electrical sensing equipment. Eastern researchers discovered that the energy in the chakras, or body's energy centers, was adversely affected by booze. They found that the body is impacted with a decreased electrical activity of the positive chakras, and an increase in the negative or black energy, the "spiritual ignorance or inertia" energy. They contend that all addictions must be treated with a spiritual program, since it has a negative energy build-up or misaligned spirit as a root cause. They insist that treatment of the spirit is the cure, not just of the body.

Do you remember Dr. Emoto's study on how consciousness affected the crystalline structure of water? Thoughts of love and peace resulted in beautifully symmetrical shapes like snowflakes, whereas hate and violence generated jagged, irregular, and chaotic forms. When we ingest drugs and alcohol, this same transmutation is occurring but in reverse order. We are introducing chaotic vibrations to our naturally harmonious core being. We are placing toxic drugs and alcohol to our water system, causing irregular, deranged, discordant frequencies that upset our normally positive vibrational state. The poisons have altered our chemical states, our minds, and our consciousness. The chemical effect seeps deep down to our core and alters our inner vibrational frequency, which, per the law of Attraction, draws more negativity.

The twelve step AA program is very overt about their spiritual steps. They are founded by the principle that a *higher power* is the core to successful sobriety. It is stated in AA literature that alcohol is too powerful to handle by oneself, and that only with the help of a God, that addiction can be overcome. AA's *The Big Book* tells a story of an alcoholic who having had a spiritual revelation had "stood in the Presence of Infinite Power and Love" and put down booze for good, never having a thought of a drink again. This was all that was needed for this man to get and stay sober—a spiritual revelation, a change in belief, a paradigm shift. He didn't even need to go to AA meetings and he was one of the founding characters in the Big Book!

SPIRITUAL EPIPHANIES CAN CURE INSTANTLY

The shift in core belief which is needed to conquer drinking does not always come from study, meditation, or prayer. Many times, people are struck with sudden epiphanies or revelations, which alone are enough to quit the addictive habit. It could be an external traumatic event or sometimes just a change in belief and thinking. Sometimes it's going to jail, surviving a bad car wreck, suffering a family member or friend's death, or something similar. In any case, the psychic change is so startling, it vibrates down to the person's core and alters their inner beliefs and reality. The clarity of life's purpose becomes illuminated, and the drug or alcohol habit is put in proper perspective. Your whole vibrational being is reset; it's like rebooting your computer after cleaning out a virus.

This happened in my life years ago, when my father died. I was at the peak of my emotional pain while he was sick and dying of cancer and also at my bottom, depressed and drinking insanely. His death affected me in such a traumatic way that I quit drinking cold turkey and stayed dry for several years. I did not however, have any program (or desire) to remain that way, so eventually went back.

Many others have quit their addictions by hitting the bottom and experiencing psychic or spiritual illuminations. Again, it could be the loss of a job, a trip to rehab, or a divorce—we each have our own bottoms. Some people just get sick of being sick, or tired of being tired. Some find religion, others find Mother Nature, and others find love. A grand awakening or change in belief has actually been demonstrated through scientific studies using certain drugs. In controlled medical tests, alcoholics were given psychedelic drugs, such as LSD, to see what effect it would have on their addiction. After experiencing the drug, many claimed that they were actually cured of their desire to ever drink again. I'm certainly not advocating using psychedelics, but these results prove how a shift in consciousness and change in belief system will alter one's reality, which includes the views on addiction.

When you change your reality, your inner frequency changes, and thus your outer world reflects this. These LSD tests showed that alcoholism was nothing physical at all, but was purely mental. These psychedelic drugs in no manner affected the subject's DNA, biology or physiology in a manner to cause any psychic change in belief. It was all a result in changing thoughts—an expanded consciousness resulted in a psychic illumination in which drinking was put in its respective place, which was in the trash can. It was ironic that their new-found reality (caused by LSD) now had no place in it for drugs or alcohol.

SUMMARY: WE ARE GODS

We studied how the creation of our physical world was the condensation of ethereal mind substance, how consciousness existed in everything, and how a prime intelligence was the originating source. In the same manner in which the universe was created, mankind has the same creative abilities on his own Earthly scale. In other words, man is similar to a God in creative abilities. In 1902, Richard Ingalese wrote:

> *"As man raises his vibrations and draws the higher Cosmic Forces into his mind and body, his knowledge, force and consciousness expand and he grows more godlike, until at length, in the fruition of time, he becomes a god."*

We use the exact same formula or technique to manifest creation as did "God," simply on our own level or plane of existence. In that sense, we are a microcosm of the original source energy, or, as it is said, we are gods on the earthly plane. Humans create the physical from the nonphysical, matter from spirit, and thus a person's body and circumstances are a result of his or her consciousness.

What they term "God" is the source energy behind the mind-spirit or intelligent consciousness that exists in everything from the atom to the cosmos. The critical difference that exists in humankind that does not exist in other conscious matter is that humans possess a spirit-body consciousness. Humans have will, volition, are self-acting, reflective, self-conscious with powerful imaginative and creative abilities. Other living things do not possess this *soul* or volitional consciousness.

Humankind has the ability to create because we have the discretion to direct the attractive powers of love through our desire and faith and use mental science principles to manifest. Other particles, plants, animals, groupings, and entities at large that are "alive" and living also possess an intelligent consciousness, but are unlike humankind in degree, superiority, and creative power.

We have been given these powers and privileges to have dominion over the Earth "and every creepeth thing" and to create in a like manner as the original source. Once you understand these laws and principles, you can use this creative process deliberately to attain any goal you wish, including curing your addiction, and attaining sobriety, love, health, and success.

16

Karma and Housecleaning

"You will not be punished for your anger, you will be punished by your anger…holding on to anger is like grasping a hot coal with the intent on throwing at someone else; you are the one that gets burned."

—BUDDHA 563 B.C.

CAUSE AND EFFECT

Karma has different meanings to many people. In many Eastern sects, it means the wrongdoings and sins you carry over from past lives by reincarnation. My personal interpretation of karma is the axiom of "what goes around comes around," and the idea that what you do in your life, your actions of good or bad, will return to you in one form or another. In mental science, it relates to cause and effect—mind or spirit always being the cause, and physical manifestations, always the effect.

Swami Vivekananda was an Indian Hindu monk and famous leader of Indian and yogi philosophies. In 1896, he wrote the following:

"Every action generates a force of energy that returns to us in like kind… what we sow is what we reap. And when we choose actions that bring happiness and success to others, the fruit of our karma is happiness and success. Karma is the eternal assertion of human freedom…Our thoughts,

our words, and deeds are the threads of the net which we throw around ourselves."

Karma uses the Law of Attraction by bringing resonance to our thoughts and actions. We do this or that action, or think this or that way, and thus set up a vibrational sequence. We mentally project outwardly, and eventually rendezvous with its repercussion, like a boomerang. The effects we see are always the physical expression of a mental-spiritual precedent.

Some of us may feel that we have legitimate reasons for drinking or drugging, that we were done wrong and our pain is not our fault. It may be true for some of us that it is not our own actions that created our underlying pain. Many of us are victims of combat, abuse, accidents, natural disasters, and other misfortunes that seemed unavoidable. However, many of these "unavoidable" incidents or situations actually do have a traceable origin which actually may have been fateful. The things you do, places you visit, people you associate with, and situations you put yourself in, often are born from a deep metaphysical origin or cause. Karmic action and the Law of Attraction may have been at work in subtle and unsuspecting ways, placing you in situations that appeared out of your control. The past is the past, and should not be regretted, resented, or dwelled upon. These old events, however, are sometimes very emotional and resurface more than we like, causing pain and discomfort. Your past trauma and pain is only as powerful as the focus, attention, and mental energy you apply to those inner voices or thoughts. The thought of a past memory is only an inert film or recording of an event, but is given life by our emotions. Just as we create our goal-image of sobriety and success by mixing thought-images with emotions, we also keep alive past negative memories in the same manner.

When we dwell on past memories with fear, remorse, guilt, shame, or regret, they develop into a negative vibration in our core being. Unfortunately, most addicts have a huge inventory of unfavorable experiences to draw upon, and thus plenty of reasons to host negative feelings. Many of us have been the epitomes of disaster, destroying relationships, finances, and our health. We horde feelings of regret, knowing that we have wasted years of our lives and thus host feelings of self-hate, resentment, disappointment, and self-pity. All of these damaging emotions are poison to our minds and soon crystalize into further conditions of sickness and failure. We need to dig deep and clean the slate, forgive and forget, and restore our vibrational well-being if we are ever to achieve sobriety and reach our other goals.

Your inner vibrational frequency, or emotional body, radiates outwardly, engaging the Law of Attraction to bring you the people, places, and conditions in life that match the frequency you give off. Your vibrations are like the ripples a stone makes when thrown into a calm pond. Say this pond was cluttered with logs every few feet. What would your wave ripples look like then? They would be perfectly symmetrical and uniform until they hit a floating log, and then would be disrupted and disorganized. In a like manner, your negative memories and thoughts are the logs in the pond of the mind, causing a harmonious natural thought frequencies to be disrupted into a discordant pattern. Clean out those emotional logs with right thinking and reprogram for your desires.

EMOTIONAL HOUSEKEEPING

"Emotional housekeeping" is a term I picked up at an AA meeting. In essence, it is the practice of performing a mental and emotional purging of past wrongdoings. In the AA program, several or the twelve steps are dedicated purely to this purpose. During this process, the AA member will expose their innermost private self and divulge their sins and secrets to another person, usually their sponsor. A subsequent step is to then to mend the wounds you caused to others by the actions of your addiction. You might say that it is a confession of sorts.

Following the AA steps works for some people, and the main objective is that we find a means to remove or lessen inner pains. It is difficult to achieve any goals of sobriety or success if we carry around emotional pain, fear, anger, or any other powerful negative feelings that continue to cause a hole in us. You must attempt to rid yourself of any emotional baggage that may be dragging you down or keeping you from moving toward your goals. These burdensome mental obsessions must somehow be released, or substantially lessened, whether it's done professionally with a Doctor or Therapist, with a support group, talking to a friend, or in prayer and meditation with your higher power. On a metaphysical level, the goal is to change a discordant vibrational state into a harmonious, sober, and healthy one.

One of the primary purposes of your new sobriety-success program is to make your new goal image your primary mental preoccupation. If you have a pain or a negative emotion constantly tugging at your mind for attention, then it will be difficult to fully change your vibrational state from negative to positive. Remember that worrying is inverted prayer…we visualize a bad event, mix it with emotions and soon it engages the Law of Attraction to manifest as a reality. If you draw upon a past traumatic event, and bring it back into your life by constantly reliving it in your mind, your vibrational frequency will reflect this Learn your lesson from it and move on, otherwise you will be soliciting the same remedies to come back too, which was drugs and booze.

If you harbor ill feelings, fear, or painful thoughts, this will only weaken your attempts to change for the better. In 1922, New Thought teacher Walter Matthew indirectly wrote about the Law of Attraction as it relates to negative thoughts:

> "If we give hospitality to thoughts which are criminal, wicked, vulgar, angry, selfish, revengeful, fearful and trivial, we will soon find that these thoughts have made a deep impression upon our whole nature and character. Try as we will we cannot conceal the character of our thoughts, for they are revealed by our bodies in sickness or health, displayed in a pleasing or undesirable personality, and reflected in our environment and circumstances. For, conversely, all good, ennobling, positive, constructive thoughts bring us into alignment with all that is uplifting and desirable."

I MET SOME REAL DOOZIES IN REHAB

As you read in my life story, I spent a little time in a couple of rehab centers where I was exposed to hundreds of addicts. You name the addiction, and there was someone there suffering from it…alcoholics, heroin addicts, opiate users, bath salts, LSD, etc. As you might expect, they each had their own mental-emotional issues, drama, and trauma from every standpoint you can imagine. Some of their stories shocked me, some saddened me, and some reminded me of myself.

There were some people you thought shouldn't even be in rehab by first impressions. For example, one lady arrived who was in her mid-forties and appeared quite normal. She was a luxury-home real estate agent that came from wealth and taste (she dressed in her country club tennis outfit every day). She seemed mentally well-adjusted, and was very social. She owned a nice country club house on a golf course, had an advanced college degree, dressed sharp, spoke eloquently, and even looked healthy. She appeared quite normal, but maybe not so when I learned that she drank a quart of vodka every day for the past year, and then slit her wrists attempting suicide in a hotel room two days earlier. She arrived with a 0.44 alcohol level, with 0.08 being legally intoxicated. The intake doctors said another drink or two would have been fatal alcohol poisoning.

There were those who were more overtly problemed too, and people with emotional ramifications of their addictions. I met some that suffered deep emotional trauma that included sexual abuse, rape, childhood molestation, and PTSD from military combat. I met others with legal problems of drug dealing convictions, theft charges, DUIs, bankruptcies, and divorces. Some of those I encountered had medical problems, too—unwanted pregnancies, cirrhosis of the liver, and sexual diseases. I also met those that suffered from physical handicaps, both from accidents and from birth.

Then there were the special upper-class kids. These were the rich, spoiled 18-25-year-old kids that were in rehab mainly because their wealthy parents didn't know how else to deal with them. They didn't seem to have any real underlying problems, they were just excessive partiers that went out of control. In these cases, the addiction cycle worked in reverse. Instead of a traumatic or emotional problem causing the pain that needed numbing, the addiction was the originating source of the pain, with the emotional problems stemming from abuse. Sometimes emotionally balanced, good kids end up a sick and depressed addict just by partying too much with the wrong drugs. The vicious cycle is still created, just reversely. In 1912, Dr. William Sadler wrote:

> *"We desire not only to call attention to the power of the mind over the body, but...the influence of the disordered physical body on the mental state and moral tendencies. The practicing physician is compelled to recognize that in many instances it is the disordered physical health which is to blame for the depressed mental state, and so the vicious circle widens—disorders of either mind and body react the one upon the other, each ever tending to make the other worse..."*

Almost uniformly across the board, a high percentage of the patients suffered with some type of mental issue such as bipolar disorder, depression, anxiety, or insomnia. Just about everyone in rehab was taking a pill for at least one of these problems. Sometimes, our brains have been contorted and poisoned with so much drugs and alcohol, it takes prescription medicine to get our chemical balance corrected. The medications may be temporary or permanent, depending on the damage done.

The primary common thread among all of the patients was that deep down they suffered from a pain that created a spiritual hole, an emptiness. The painful stories I heard about were sometimes tragic and overwhelming, which made me feel fortunate with my own petty problems.

I met a beautiful twenty-year-old girl who used to screw her elder dealer for heroin; a fifty-year-old father of six who lost his job, home, family, and life savings due to drinking; a thirty-five-year-old mother who drank two bottles of wine every morning before taking her kids to elementary school; an eighteen-year-old girl, kicked out of her house because of opiates, who slept in public bathrooms in Chicago for the past year; a twenty-six-year-old man who accidentally killed his 8-year old daughter while driving drunk on a four-wheeler, and was now facing manslaughter charges; a twenty-five-year-old woman who could not stop taking pain pills since she had been fourteen years old because of childhood rape; a forty-year-old man, sexually molested as a youth by an uncle, who deliberately overdosed on prescription pills four times, stopping his heart twice; and the list goes on and on. These underlying pains need to be addressed or they will remain as triggers and perpetuate the addiction cycle. Your emotional house cleaning should be done to clear out any vibrational disharmonies, otherwise they will lurk and resurface.

As I described above, some addicts have fallen victim of an illness, a crime, or an accident while others suffer from guilt or remorse because they committed crimes or caused injury to others. I felt such deep sympathy for the man who killed his daughter while driving drunk. He was genuinely a nice, loving family guy that just could not hold his booze. It would be very difficult to find self-forgiveness for this, but somehow, he must. In some cases, these issues will never go away completely, but they should be treated, dissipated, and put in proper perspective in order to move on, get sober, and start achieving goals.

On a metaphysical plane, any emotional pains and ailments are the cause of a negative vibrational shadow or hole in an otherwise bright and healthy state of being. Drugs or booze work great to mask the pain and fill the hole with an artificial vibrational boost. Eventually, more and more of the artificial boost is needed as this buried emotional pain only festers and gets larger. Soon the vibrational state is so out of balance and discordant that the person cannot operate normally without the drugs or booze.

Clearing out these pains in our lives is critical, and there are many methods for dealing with them. Mental science practices certainly will work for those who have mastered them, but this takes superior mind power along with correct mind-spirit knowledge and faith. Meditative Programming and positive imaging are powerful tools in changing a negative frequency to a positive one, but in some cases outside help is needed to mitigate and remove the psychological traumas.

LAYERS ON THE ONION

Over a period of time, we have developed "layers on the onion," protective shields, and barriers. These manifest as lies and justifications that sometimes only an objective group or professional can help reveal. In cases of serious pain, trauma, and/or medical conditions (both physical and mental), a professional doctor's care should always be sought. Such as the case of the manslaughter dad.

With conditions not requiring professional assistance, there are many other options for "airing out the laundry", and peeling back the onion. Some people just talk out problems with a friend, an AA sponsor, a pastor, spouse, or someone else with a sympathetic ear. Others write journals, pray to their gods, or meditate. This is a huge part of the AA program—confessing your sins and character defects and making restitution to those you have caused harm. The Bible has passages relating to this matter too. In 1 John 1:9 of the World English Bible, it reads, *"If we confess our sins, he is faithful and righteous to forgive us the sins, and to cleanse us from all unrighteousness,"* and in Proverbs 28:13 it follows that, *"He who conceals his sins doesn't prosper, but whoever confesses and renounces them finds mercy."* Again, if outside sources are not needed, desired, or available, some find they can perform their emotional housecleaning alone in prayer and meditation with their higher power.

You must resolve to remove or lessen these emotional pains and use mental science principles to assist you. If there are emotional issues you want to change, use your meditative programming to reinforce new thought habits. Visualize the change in your mind and feel the serenity of resolving past issues. See and feel yourself forgiving or making amends to others. Make it one of your goal desires to rid yourself of guilt, jealousy, anger, and other manifested emotions of fear. If you have ill feelings towards a spouse or employer who has cheated you, see yourself forgiving them for their ignorance. Bury the hatchet in your mind and feel yourself letting go of all negative emotions and being filled with feelings of peace and serenity.

Use right thinking and knowledge to defeat the demons of wrongful thinking. Mental science laws and principles are the most powerful arsenal you have to produce change. Everything begins with spirit-mind and manifests into physical form and outward conditions. Your thoughts create your conditions and do not affect you unless you elect to give them your attention and mental energy. Choose thoughts of your goals, not of past worries—these are history, and cannot be changed.

If we allow old negative emotions to remain buried over a long period, they can often grow into a second-nature, subconscious negativity that you don't even realize you have. You've probably met people like this, the ones who always are in a shitty mood, no fun to be around, or always negative. They are usually harboring an undermining troublesome memory and negative feeling deep within. They may drink or drug for relief of a pain that is subliminal even to themselves. It's like the dog that was beaten as a puppy. You can always tell this dog from the happy ones.

Even long-lasting deep inner pains are sometimes resolved instantly by an illumination or epiphany. It is sometimes as simple as uncovering and acknowledging the cause of an underlying issue to make it disappear completely. The pain will spontaneously release when the core problem is finally unearthed and exposed. Sometimes we harbor painful memories only because of our misunderstanding of the facts, or ill-perceptions. Eugene Del Mar wrote about reaching the truth in your mind and releasing falsehoods as it applies to disease (which is just a manifestation of negative thoughts). In 1922, he wrote:

> *"In order to effectually destroy disease, it is essential that one recognize its mental cause; he should acquire an understanding of the direction of the mind in its false reasoning and erroneous opinion; he should eliminate these through knowledge of the Truth or Principle of Health…Not infrequently, the mere recognition of one's former errors of reason and opinion will suffice to restore normal ease."*

Again, correcting false thinking may require therapy or a support group, but this can also be accomplished with deep introspection, objectivity, and meditation. Curing the underlying problem is as simple as that—get to the core of it, address it, expose it to the light, and watch it wither away. Do not give problems life by feeding them with your feelings, and giving them energy with attention. If you are bringing up a negative memory, it should be to eradicate it not sympathize and support it. Destroy them up with correct thinking.

The main point here is that we must diffuse, dilute, or dismantle our pains and problems. They need to be compartmentalized and put in their respective place—on a mental shelf, and not buried deep inside our psyches to distract us from achieving our goals.

You may be emotionally taxed with going through a bankruptcy or divorce, facing jail time, or even suffering a major illness, but you somehow, with or without help, need to separate these issues from yourself as a spiritual being. You came to this world with nothing but consciousness or spirit, and you will leave with nothing but that, too. In 1910, New Thought Teacher Orison Marden wrote about how negatives affect our life when he wrote:

"Mental discord is fatal to quality in work. The destructive emotions— worry, anxiety, hatred, jealousy, anger, greed, selfishness, are all deadly enemies of efficiency. A man can no more do his best work when possessed by any of these emotions than a watch can keep good time when there is friction in the bearings of its delicate mechanism...A poised, balanced mind unifies all the mental energies of the system, while the mind that flies all to pieces at the least provocation is constantly demoralized... Harmony is the secret of all effectiveness, beauty, happiness; and harmony is simply keeping ourselves in tune with the Infinite."

ALL CHARACTER DEFECTS STEM FROM FEAR

Some of you may not be burdened by any of these major traumas or past pains. Just because you don't have any major "skeletons in the closet", doesn't mean you are free from having mental-emotional hang ups. Many of us addicts also suffer from nontraumatic flaws that keep our metaphysical frequency in a discordant disharmonious state. With a little thought, you can usually trace down most negative emotions or dysfunctional personality traits to a manifestation of fear. Fear of death, personal injury, pain, loneliness, embarrassment, etc. all will eventually grow and manifest into hate, jealousy, self-pity, and on and on.

Addressing one's personality flaws was another important lesson I learned in AA. They call these *character defects*. Ego and pride are often the biggest culprits. Many addicts don't realize their egos are very inflated during active addiction. However, even ego is tied to fear. Ego is essentially the fear of being abandoned, left alone, not loved, and rejected, and booze and drugs are great insulators against this. The man who hides behind a bottle of booze or pills usually has an ego that he cannot sustain sober, and thus introduces his alter-ego.

With addicts, it's always about "me, me, me" because of the demands the addiction lifestyle presents. Drinking or drugs is paramount to the addict, and the ego is enlarged from the invincibility and boisterous effects of being drunk or high. Very little sincere attention is given to others when you are an addict (unless they have something you need like sex, money, booze or drugs).

Deflating the ego by reaching out and helping others in need is one of the best remedies for this common character defect. You won't find many active addicts that are charitable with their time, less merely thoughtful of others. In 1922, Eugene Del Mar wrote:

> *"When one interests himself in altruistic and humanitarian movements or in an endeavor to help, and assist others, to that extent his thought is taken from personal matters, and in his consideration of larger interests his own smaller affairs seem less important and pressing, if they are not forgotten entirely. When one's thought becomes expansive and comprehensive in its scope, petty details of physical life tend to fade away from memory."*

Keep in mind that your five physical senses are tied directly to the ego; thus, the physical brain is an intimate partner. When the brain is disillusioned by chemicals, what does that say about our egos? Maybe this is why guys get whiskey muscles when drunk and are more likely to fight. It's easy to get courageous, boisterous, or lustful since the rational part of the brain is numbed and our primal reptilian brain kicks in.

The ego is also perversely inflated by self-pity. By feeling we are victims of an addictive disease or a depressive disorder, we feel sorry for ourselves. We seek and demand attention, sympathy and comfort from others, which is not seen as an inconvenience to the addict, but a privilege they deserve.

Aside from egotism and excessive pride, there are a host of other character defects that distort our thinking including feelings of resentment, jealousy, guilt, and anger. To reiterate, most negative emotions are associated to the root cause of fear. It is the most destructive force there is. Fear of death or disease, of embarrassment, of failure, of the IRS, of losing your job or house, or of your spouse leaving you, etc. You must re-magnetize your mind with your goal self-image, seeing, feeling, and believing all of your wishes actually coming true. You must bring in the light to that dark room inside you, and positively change your vibrational state. Fear is the great killer.

Resentments, remorse, and guilt of the past and the harm done to others is explained in mental science terms by Ralph Trine in 1897 when he wrote:

"'Do good to those who hate you,' is based on a scientific fact and a natural law. So, to do good is to bring to yourself all the elements in nature of power and good. To do evil is to bring the contrary destructive elements. When our eyes are opened, self-preservation will make us stop all evil thought. Those who live by hate will die of hate: that is, 'those who live by the sword will die by the sword.' Every evil thought is as a sword drawn on the person to whom it is directed. If a sword is drawn in return, so much the worse for both..."

Take the peaceful, serene path when you have the choice. I can personally tell you by experience how the act of forgiveness is amazingly powerful. When you mentally and emotionally forgive someone for doing you harm (even if irrationally accused) it is completely liberating, giving you back your freedom of mind. Orison Marden wrote similarly about releasing negativity in your mind when he wrote:

"What you allow to live in your heart, harbor in your mind, dwell upon in your thoughts, are seeds which will develop in your life and produce things like themselves. Hate seed in the heart cannot produce a love flower

in the life. A sinister thought will produce a sinister harvest. The revenge seed will produce a bloody harvest. Whatever goes from you to others calls out from them the same kind of qualities to meet your own."

Marden likewise is reinforcing both karma and the Law of Attraction principle—what you send out to the world in heartfelt thought-images, will be returned to you.

In one of my rehab stays, we had an elective meditation session that started before regular classes which I enjoyed participating in. At one morning session, one of the group members suggested we try out a new type of mantra that brought serenity and inner peace. It came from a wise Hawaiian therapist named Dr. Len and was called a *ho'oponopono* and had these four simple yet empowering statements that read as follows:

"I love you, I'm sorry, please forgive me, thank you."

Just repeat this phrase or mantra a few times when beginning your meditation. For whatever reason, it really does work. It basically covers all the bases for gratitude, guilt, and resentments.

KARMA SUMMARY

We may possess a biological allergy that perpetuated our addiction, but the original creation of the addiction monster was purely our doing. Now, to change for good, it's just a matter of getting off the chemical addiction and putting mental science principles into practice to achieve sobriety and regain control.

Peel back the onion off your inner pain, whether on your own, with your higher power, with a friend, a sponsor, a therapist, or a doctor. Get to the nucleus of the cause and expose it to the light with correct thinking and mental science practice. Your body and the external conditions in your life are simply an expression of your mental-spiritual state within. Inner pains are causing vibrational discord that mirrors itself to the outer world, causing pain which causes you to seek the anesthesia of chemicals.

What you sow, you will reap, and what you focus on, you attract. If you are preoccupied with negative emotions, these thoughts will generate ill feelings. These ill feelings will alter your vibrational frequency, which will engage the Law of Attraction to bring you more of the same. The little seeds of thought feed off of your focus and grow. Don't feed them the attention and energy of negative emotions. Positive thoughts are vibrationally ten times more powerful than negative thoughts, so purge your inner self with the radiance of a healthy, sober, and happy self-image.

Acknowledge your pains and emotional flaws, expose them, and then dissect and destroy them with right thinking. Cleanse the negative vibrations out of your system and charge yourself with your new, positive, healthy goal images. Realize that you possess the powers of mental science to take control of your future and resolve your past. When you understand mental science and spiritual laws, you will know that any depression, misery, or addiction that possesses you has always been a choice. It's your mind, and no one else can put a thought in it except yourself.

17

Meditative Programming Technique

"First, we assert that there is one original formless stuff, or substance, from which all things are made...and this stuff is thinking stuff; a thought held in it produces the form of the thought. Thought, in thinking substance, produces shapes...if man can communicate his thought to original thinking substance, he can cause the creation, or formation, of the thing he thinks about."

—WALLACE WATTLES, 1910

The two main points being made in this book are: First, is to understand the origin of intelligent-consciousness, and to possess the knowledge and faith of the higher power that underlies it. Second, is to learn the mental science and spiritual law principles, and the techniques for applying the mental science programming. This chapter will show you how to do the latter and apply the mental sciences.

THE THEORY BEHIND THE TECHNIQUE

This technique combines meditation, self-hypnosis, and auto-suggestion into one powerful exercise. It will create for you a positive mid-spirit vortex that employs the Law of Attraction to attain your goals of sobriety, love, health, and success. I like to think of it as *The Secret* on steroids.

This mental-spiritual program will accelerate the manifestation of your and desires. I call this the "Meditative Programming Technique," as it utilizes meditation, plus implements laws of mental science programming. This is an intense method of charging your vibrational state, reprogramming your subconscious mind, and magnetizing yourself to receive your ideals.

The ultimate goal is to permanently transform ourselves vibrationally to match our newly created sober, healthy, and successful self-image. In a nutshell, we do this by getting into a relaxed-receptive state, and then visualizing our goal-images while mixing them with the strong emotions of desire and faith.

The finished end-product, or ideal goal mental state, can be attained the old-fashioned way without this technique, but would take much longer and require much more effort, and is much less likely to succeed. When you try make change on a physical-conscious level, with pure willpower, you deal with many more external conflicts, and it's not even close to the powerful potency of concentrated mental programming. The old way of change is by blood, sweat, tears, and hard work, with wishful hopes that a change will eventually take place. With the mental science technique, you are virtually guaranteed success…you, yourself, are your only enemy. Try changing without it, and you make yourself vulnerable to all of the outside forces and influences, both human and mayic.

I already tried the hard way to get sober—off and on over a couple decades I went to hundreds of AA meetings, got a sponsor, read recovery books, went to detox, rehab and therapy, tried medications, saw addiction specialists, and nothing worked. What works is going directly to the prime source for change, within yourself, using mental science programming. Cut out all the superficial bullshit and remold your core self. With this meditative technique, we communicate directly to the subconscious while connected to our powerful universal energy source. We heal and charge our vibrational state, and reprogram our minds. You create a new reality.

You probably know people who naturally seem to attract health, success, wealth, and love without needing any type of formal exercise like this.

They seem to have an innate knack for being healthy, attracting good circumstances, getting good jobs and relationships, and generally having good luck—you know, the ones with a "golden horseshoe up their ass." These people are not blessed with anything special but simply are employing mental science principles unknowingly. Somewhere along the way, they subconsciously realized that their manners and methods of using positive vibrational states resulted in successful results. From this feedback, it was just a matter of positive reinforcement, and they unconsciously continued to do what worked—it was the path of least resistance. They incorporated the Law of Attraction subconsciously. All successful people engage these laws whether they do so consciously, or unconsciously.

The Meditative Programming Technique is a method to rebuild a new self-image and to accelerate the healing and transformation. It supercharges your vibrations, reformats your mind, and sets you off on the path to reaching your goals. It expedites and amplifies the process of change in a miraculous fashion. It is a concentrated self-change procedure.

This technique has a threefold impact. First, it uses the Law of Attraction for manifesting; second, it uses specialized visualizations and affirmations for subconscious programming; and, third, it uses spiritual laws to positively charge the vibration of your ethereal mind-body. You will transform from a low-frequency, depressed, sick addict into a high-frequency, happy, healthy being.

This technique is similar scientifically to prayer, yet much more powerful. When we pray, we are asking for a higher power to assist in making something happen; sometimes it works, sometimes not. There is an exact science to effective prayer. In order for prayer to work, the mental picture of the desired end result must be clear; the faith that it will manifest must be strong; the powers of mind-spirit behind it must be believed; and, the desire for the wish must be heartfelt and emotional. The prayer must be performed in a metaphysically exact scientific manner. When properly done, prayer follows the same laws of mental science. In essence, prayer is a simplistic variation of the Meditative Programming Technique.

Unfortunately, most people only pray when things go wrong and they are desperate. Their vibrational frequency is usually negative, and they are full of fear and worry. They pray and wish for the best, but subconsciously imagine the worst, and therefore it rarely works, and sometimes even back-fires. The frequency of fear mixed with negative thought-images of the future can only bring bad results. Prayer must be performed in the state of mind of expectancy and faith.

The Meditative Programming Technique is unique, but its fundamentals are not entirely novel, as it simply employs many mental science features of prayer, self-hypnosis, self-affirmation, and of course meditation. In 1922, New Thought teacher Walter Matthew summarized a very similar practice as he explains:

> *"Completely relax, either sitting or lying down, close your eyes and look within, making a clear, mental picture of the thing you desire for yourself or anyone else; work this picture up in all of its details, see it clearly from its conception to the finished product. Like the artist who is working on canvas, do this mental work at least every morning and evening before retiring. The more you persist in visualizing this picture the sooner it will come into objectification."*

Our exercise is similar to the one Matthew described above with several modifications and improvements. Over time, I developed my unique practice by combining transcendental meditation with mental science and spiritual law principles.

Remember the initial goal is to do this Meditative Programming twice a day for approximately fifteen to twenty minutes. I find it best upon awakening, and another time in the late afternoon or early evening.

The process involves the following six steps or levels:

Level-1: Relaxation and Meditation: Relax the physical senses and enter the alpha brain wave state.
Level-2: Gratitude and Love: Affirm universal love and gratitude.

Level-3: Acknowledgement: Recognize and be empowered with the laws of mental science. Confirm faith.

Level-4: Creation and Visualization: Creating your new goal image and vibrational state.

Level-5: Gratitude and Love: Giving thanks for what you are about to receive.

Level-6: Awaken and Receive: Awaken to the new you with *I am* affirmations.

I prefer to call these levels instead of steps since we are descending and ascending into different levels of awareness and relaxation. The deepest level is #4 where you perform your visualizations. The details of each level are as follows:

LEVEL-1: RELAXATION-MEDITATION

You've already learned about meditation, and this is where you put it into practice. The purpose of meditating here is not for deep thought and expanding consciousness, but to get in a relaxed and receptive state so we can do positive image programming. You want to achieve a relaxed state of mind and body, and enter an alpha brain wave state within a few minutes. Once you have practiced pure meditation awhile, you will find that you can enter this state easier and quicker with each session (remember Pavlov's dog).

Whenever there is a conflict or debate between the mind-spirit of a person and his or her conscious brain, the mind-spirit will override and win every time. The occult forces of mind-spirit are simply much more powerful than the crude electrical circuitry of the brain and body. The imaginative powers of the mind-spirit have a higher frequency and are superior in strength than the conscious thinking brain. This is why imagination and feelings are so critical in mental programming.

You are preparing your body to receive and accept instructions through powerful conscious mental visualizations. To do this, you must quiet the brain and body. You should find a comfortable sitting position, take a few deep breaths, and then proceed with repeating your mantra, concentrating on your breathing, or listening to meditation music. Remember to do the visualization of the atoms and universe to stretch out your mind. After a few minutes, you should have the senses quieted, mind and body relaxed, and you should be absorbed in the rhythms of the inner sounds. Your mind should be clear and in a receptive state.

Keep in mind you are to maintain this state throughout this entire process, so it's necessary to passively concentrate on your sounds during the other steps. Sometimes you may be distracted by an erring thought, an outside noise, or an increase in your heart or breathing rate. When this happens, mentally drop back and concentrate on relaxing with your sounds again for a moment until you are back in the correct meditative state of mind.

This step should take a few minutes and will vary with each person's attitude, amount of mind-clutter, stress, and meditation experience. It will get shorter each session as you practice and your "relaxation response" kicks in quicker.

LEVEL 2: GRATITUDE AND LOVE

We now introduce thoughts and feelings of serenity, gratitude, and love. In the world of mental science these feelings are basically a range of frequencies. These frequencies put you in a vibrational state that is conducive to self-transformation and mental programming.

The feeling of gratitude should be felt as an existing fact in the present time and not conditional on something happening to make you feel thankful in the future. You will give gratitude for the things you will be receiving by achieving your new goals, but you must be more thankful for what you have now. Maintain an attitude of gratitude throughout and be thankful in advance of what you are to receive—sobriety, health, love and success. In 1910, Wallace Wattles wrote:

"...the mental attitude of gratitude draws the mind into closer touch with the source from which the blessings come. If it is a new thought to you that gratitude brings your whole mind into closer harmony with

the creative energies of the universe, consider it well, and you will see that it is true. The good things you already have, have come to you along the line of obedience to certain laws. Gratitude will lead your mind out along the ways by which things come; and it will keep you in close harmony with creative thought and prevent you from falling into competitive thought."

Being grateful may be difficult for some who are in bad situations. You may be sitting in a rehab facility right now reading this book and wondering for what you have to be grateful. You may be an addict, be financially broke, have a DUI case pending, have no job, have no significant other, your family hates you, and so on. For starters, you should be grateful that your spiritual vibrations led you to this book. This book will take you on a journey to a new life, renewed health, and literally a new reality. All things from the past can repair themselves in time.

Regrets and resentments are just a waste of your mental-spiritual energy. Now that you know the laws of mental science, you realize that your past vibrational state created your past and changing it will create your future. Give thanks for surviving the dangerous life you lived and for what you have left, what has not been destroyed. Be grateful to have this opportunity to start over having this secret knowledge of mind and spirit to achieve your wishes. In 1908, Prentice Mulford wrote about gratitude with the following:

"Man, may come into full harmony with the Formless Substance by entertaining a lively and sincere gratitude for the blessings it bestows upon him. Gratitude unifies the mind of man with the intelligence of Substance, so that man's thoughts are received by the Formless."

Generate the feeling of love in your heart. Recall that love is also a metaphysical frequency and not just a feeling reserved for family or romantic relationships. Ponder on the feeling of this emotion and its relationship to desire and attraction. It is a core emotion of creation. Love is the feeling that needs to be threaded throughout all of your thoughts. It is the emotion you bring out from the core of the heart.

You are swinging the pendulum to the positive end of the emotional vibration spectrum, so you will need to be free from all aspects of the negative end. It is critical that you eliminate fear, hate, jealousy, and any other low-frequency thoughts. Your vibrational state depends on your thoughts, and you cannot manifest positive goals when you are vibrating negatively. Release all resentments, forgive others, and feel yourself being healed.

Don't forget to repeat Dr. Lens *ho'oponopono* mantra, too: *"I love you, I'm sorry, please forgive me, thank you."* To reprogram your mind, you should have a clear mental slate. Thus, you should make amends, give forgiveness, and cleanse your karma. While in this meditative state, we want to unearth any vibrational discord. Realize the buried pains of the past are simply thoughts mixed with ill-feelings, and most can be removed or lessened with correct thinking. By shielding and protecting pains and fears, we empower them. By exposing them to the light of correct thinking, we dilute and remove them.

This second step should also only take a couple of minutes and will vary from person to person. Everyone will spend different amounts of time on each step, and it's important to get each of these cleared out emotionally and spiritually. So, take your time if you need to resolve certain thoughts.

LEVEL 3: ACKNOWLEDGEMENT-FAITH

You already should be well on your way to developing a strong faith in the mental science presented in this book. The success of this technique is contingent on your faith, belief, and confidence in the knowledge you now possess of consciousness and mental science. After all, *"whatever the mind can conceive and believe it can achieve."* In 1909, Janet Young reaffirmed the requirement of having faith in the mental science dogma when she wrote:

"Knowledge of its governing laws is essential. Persistency in auto suggestion—reiteration of faith and acknowledgment of its powers and self-mastery are necessary to control and command its services...Mind will be the generator, Will the energy, and Spirit the current, producing and manifesting effects—transforming and creating results...Faith is essential in controlling results."

The emotions of love and gratitude gear up your vibrational state, but you must have faith and belief in mental science to get to the frequency which will produce manifestation of desires. Be mindful that you are dealing with spiritual laws that are just as absolute and infallible as physical laws such as gravity. Your desired end result, goals, or ideals come true and objectify into reality when the thought-image is empowered with the emotional energy of faith. You must see, feel, and believe in your mind that you already are this new person and generate that vibrational state. It is law that it will materialize.

Your visualization programming will be wiping clean the mental hard drive that hoards the addiction habit. You will be cleansing and reformatting your brain of these reflexes, habits, and unneeded memories. Your mind's imagining and vibrational powers are not only creating new neural pathways in the brain, they are also paving a new path for your desired reality to unfold on the metaphysical plane.

With these mental science techniques, you are using the powers of mind to accelerate the healing of the body and restoring health. Using the mind, we can expedite the chemical changes in the brain and body, repairing cells and tissues, flushing toxins out of the system, increasing metabolism, and losing weight. You can transmute your physical body as easily as you can create your future reality. Generate this excitement knowing you now possess the knowledge of sacred mind-science principles.

This step also should only take a few minutes. You have learned a wealth of information, so recall what you need to get excited about using your newfound mind powers.

LEVEL 4: CREATION AND VISUALIZATION

At this point, you should be still in a relaxed state and in the background of your mind passively listening to your mantra, breathing, and/or music. The warm feelings of love and gratitude should have washed over you, and the powers of the mind and Law of Attraction have been reaffirmed and strengthened. You should be excited to program your mind and supercharge your inner self with your new goal image.

This mental imaging level is the most import part of the programming, as it is the "meat and potatoes" of the program. This is the process to reprogram your subconscious, change your vibrational state, and to create your future reality. In this step, we visualize the realities we wish for as an existing fact. The future goal become present in mind.

Your addiction has created some strong negative habits causing your brain to develop deep ingrained neural pathways and networks. When you are triggered, these cause biochemical reactions to produce cravings, urges, and mental compulsions to pick up a drink or drug. Your brain senses emotional pain and makes the connection that drugs and booze have fixed it in the past. Remember that these all stem from mind and from what you allow to manifest in your thought-images and beliefs.

Your subconscious accepts whatever your conscious mind passes on as a truth or reality. It is your subconscious that controls your behavior, reactions to life, and your cravings and urges to use. When you mentalize yourself as *already* the sober, clean, and healthy person, your subconscious and inner vibrational state will mold itself to align with this desire.

We want to mentally live in the state of already having achieved sobriety (later you can add other goals). You want to see yourself already sober and doing those things that booze and drugs kept you from in the past. Walter Matthew stated in 1922:

> *"We should endeavor to visualize clearly whatever we want to come into external expression. The mental picture must be impressed deeply upon our subconscious mind, and then the subconscious will immediately go to work to do everything that is necessary to be done to bring our desires into*

manifestation, for it has control over external things and affairs as well as internal."

In addition to feeling deep love and desire for your goal image, your faith must be so strong that you should believe it as existing already. It must feel as though it already exists as a true reality in the mind for it to manifest in the physical world. Your future goal behavior you are seeking must become present in the mind. Even the Bible agrees with this mental principle as it reads, *"Therefore I tell you, all things whatever you pray and ask for, believe that you have received them, and you shall have them."* (Mark 11:24; WEB).

The target of this step is to get into the *feeling* that you are already clean, healthy, happy, and successful. To do this, you will visualize yourself already this way in a variety of your normal life situations as you are achieving your post-sobriety goals. You will generate the feeling of excitement and feel how fantastic it is to be that way right now in your body. Make your future wishes a present reality in your mind.

To kick my alcohol problem, I visualized both the positive and negative aspects in a couple of different ways. Although in mental science it is always better to focus on the positive than to force away the negative, I found it beneficial to have an adverse connotation of alcohol deeply ingrained in my subconscious. Remember that what you focus on is what you attract. You are not attracting drugs; you are assigning a negative association. We want to reinforce the connection between our drug of choice, and the strong feelings of disgust, sickness, pain, and suffering.

You essentially had a love affair with your addiction and now it's time to break up the relationship. You were physically, emotionally, and spiritually committed to your addiction so it's not an easy task. You may even have a broken heart about it. So, what's the best way to get over this in real life relationships? It time to remember the worse things about the relationship…the misery, pain, sickness, embarrassments, and failures. Also, remember who your new love is, or who you would like it to be (health and sobriety). While doing this briefly in the meditative state, this reinforces the negative association at a subconscious level.

LEVEL 4A: NEGATIVE ASSOCIATION— A CLOCKWORK ORANGE

Whatever your drug of choice is, whether it's alcohol or heroin, bring up the worst, most sickening memories and ingrain those in your mind— physical sickness, jail time, fights, financial failures, time in detox or rehab, embarrassments, bankruptcy, accidents and injuries, and so on. I'm sure you have plenty of examples. Your subconscious is recording, memorizing, and reformatting itself based on these images, which are passed on to it as a truth or reality. Make the images real by seeing and feeling them already as an existing fact.

Replay several of these painful episodes in your mind and realize what a toxin your drug really is, how it causes such intense physical and emotional pain. Visualize your bottle or drug sitting on a table alongside an opened box of rat poison, a jug of toxic insecticide, a canister of gasoline, a bottle of ammonia, and an assortment of other lethal and caustic chemicals. Picture how your pills, drink, or drug is the same as all of these other chemicals—lethal and toxic, taking your drug is the same as the rat poison or gasoline. Visualize how a taste of any of them would start your heart racing, your body sweaty, face flushed, and how you'd get violently sick.

Recall how your drug or alcohol use leads you to a trip to the hospital, jail, a rehab clinic, leads you to a DUI arrest, having a fight with your spouse, or a miserable or embarrassing outcome like you've had in the past. For a moment, let yourself feel the depression and misery that monkey on your back creates—that addiction you hate so deeply, the ball and chain.

You are reprogramming your subconscious. As Thomas Hudson wrote in 1893, *"The subjective mind accepts, without hesitation or doubt, every statement that is made to it, no matter how absurd or incongruous or contrary to the objective experience of the individual."* You must program the negatives and reinforce the positives while in this subjective state of mind.

That entire aforementioned negative visualization scene should be rehearsed enough so that it would only take about a minute or so to do in your meditative practice. To repeat, we don't want to dwell or focus on damaging images too long—just enough to see what your poison does to your brain and body. In the end, see yourself putting up your hand, palm out, facing the drug, and saying "NO," and throwing the poison out in the trash or pouring it down the sink or breaking the bottle.

Feel a powerful psychic shield, a white orb or glow surrounding your body that the drugs or alcohol cannot penetrate. This will reprogram and re-magnetize your subconscious to the correct thoughts associated with this poison. This is not unlike the conditioning in Pavlov's dog reflex studies, or those familiar to the theme in the classic movie *A Clockwork Orange*. You will soon develop a subconscious psychosomatic negative knee-jerk reaction to drugs and booze.

At the end of this brief negative-reflex programming, you not only want to see yourself denying the drug into your body, but making a healthy, cleansing choice instead.

Bottled water is such a fantastic commodity. I remember not too long ago that people would laugh if they saw you carrying around and drinking from a plastic bottle of water. What idiot would pay for something that was free? Twenty years ago, people simply did not buy or drink it. Now it's everywhere, which is great for the recovering addict. It's our primary substitute. So, after visualizing the toxic alcohol-drug episode or scene, visualize yourself drinking a glass or bottle of clean, cold water to purify your system. Feel how the water tastes fresh, pure, clean, and natural, and how it quenches your thirst.

See and feel water cleansing toxins out of your brain, liver, and other organs that were previously dark and polluted by drugs or alcohol. Visualize the cleansing of the dark chemical grit wash clean out of them. Your body is being flushed clean and you feel the calming effect it has on you—you feel relaxed and serene. Sense how your body is parched, thirsty, and strongly craves the water. Leave this mental scene knowing you rejected the poison and now crave the water.

Whatever your addiction is—heroin, pills, or booze—keep the image of drinking pure, clean water always in your mind's eye. During the day when you are physically drinking water, make sure you associate these same thoughts—don't just chug it. Take your time to feel the cleansing and purification take place, think of how it reminds you of a calm and serene place, like a waterfall, the beach setting, and so forth.

Recall Dr. Masaru Emoto's study on the mind's power over the crystalline structure of water molecules and transfer that positive healing into your water with your mental energy. Use water as your magic tonic. Emoto's studies proved that the mind can alter the chemical composition of matter, so use your magic water to reverse the damage your addiction caused. Feel it as a source of peace, serenity, positive energy, purification, and healing.

LEVEL 4B: POSITIVE PROGRAMMING—ROLE PLAYING

The bulk of this visualization step is now positive goal imaging. This is about generating the feelings of *already* having achieved your goal of sobriety, health, happiness, and success. Remember in your mind you are *already* sober and are now achieving the goals in life you never could do because of your addiction. In a manner, you will be *acting as if* or role-playing in your mind, but with the knowledge of mental science, you have the faith that you are actually creating a new reality. It should be fun and exciting to role-play in your future healthy, sober, and successful life.

Visualize as if this change has already taken place, and feel your heart swell with happiness about your new lifestyle. You should feel your heart flutter with excitement like when you drive fast in your car. While in your new sober and healthy state, see, feel, and believe yourself doing those sober goals—running that 5K race, having that new career, buying that new car or house, helping your kids in sports, dating that special person, surfing those waves. Whatever your sober desires are, make them real in your mind and feel them as if they are already a part of you.

It's important to visualize your addictive triggers or the people, places, or events that made you anxious, stressed, depressed, or angry to the point you wanted to pick up a drug or drink. In these situations that tempted you to use, visualize yourself positively, declining the drug or drink and moving on with a healthy choice, drinking water, declining using again, being serene and happy

See yourself at a bar, already sober and clean, with coworkers and declining a beer or cocktail by saying one of several reasons such as: *"I'm on a health kick." "I'm going to the gym later." "I'm allergic." "I'm on medication." "Not tonight, I have stuff to do at home." "I'm cutting down." "No, thanks, I quit."* Choose whatever you like and rehearse it in your mind. Whatever your trigger or stress events are, visualize going to these places, or doing these things, drinking clean water and being completely tranquil, serene, and enjoying the experience.

Remember, the most critical key of getting sober and clean is losing the desire for the buzz, or mental pleasure— that good feeling you received from your drink or drug. This is very crucial. Getting detoxed is one thing, but getting truly sober is another. The body is relatively easy to cure of addiction…a few days' detox and you're fine. What is left, however, is the mental obsession, cravings, and urges. You must make it part of your new goal-image to desire, with heartfelt emotions, the mental state of perfect clarity, serenity, and peace. You should have strong negative connotations to the "buzzed" state that is essentially slow, confused, lethargic, mentally foggy, and basically idiotic. Genuinely feel the desire and appreciation for mental clarity and visualize a crisp, clear, witty, fun, and positive brain and mind. You must make this a big part of your new self-image, being mentally aware again, and loving it.

This visualization step should take the bulk (around two-thirds) of the meditation step time. Once you go through this routine a few times, you can start expanding your imagined experiences.

This step is very much like Hollywood acting or role-playing in your mind, except that you are imagining the end result in accordance with your desired self-image—a sober, clean, health, happy, and successful person. Make this a fun and enjoyable experience. This is a mental playground you can live out your wishes and desires, and while doing so reprogram your subconscious and charge your vibrational frequency.

The visualizing should never feel like a chore. If it does, then you need to reevaluate your mental science faith and your desires. When you know for a fact that these mental science principles are indeed infallible laws, you will realize you are the creator of your future, and this exercise should be an illumination and fascination. Why wouldn't it be fun to get anything you wanted? With these laws, you are virtually guaranteed success if they are followed thoroughly. So, make it fun, and fantasize with faith that you are becoming this new person.

Remember that you are creating this new, healthy, sober vibrational state that is a permanent change, not just for this twenty-minute exercise. Remind yourself that you will awaken from this exercise already transforming into that new person.

LEVEL 5: GRATITUDE AND LOVE

We are finished with the meat of the process, the deepest mental level, and now come back up the steps. We come out giving thanks and love again for what we already have and what we are now receiving. When you give gratitude, it is giving thanks for something you have already received (past tense).

Remember that gratitude is a spiritual law of compensation, and you must cultivate this as a habit every time you receive. Fix your attention to your goal self-image and give thanks that you are already this person. Gratitude will strengthen faith.

Wrap up your emotionalized images into a few scenes that summarize your goals. Envision yourself clean, healthy, happy, and serene. Give thanks to the universal intelligence, God, or the creative force for granting you knowledge of this law of mind-spirit. Give deep gratitude for what you are going to receive, knowing that it is law that it will manifest into a reality. In 1919, Ernest Holmes said:

> *"This grateful attitude to the Spirit puts us in very close touch with power and adds much to the reality of the thing that we are dealing with. Without it we can do but little. So, let us cultivate all the gratitude that we can. In gratitude, we will send our thoughts out into the world, and as it comes back it will come laden with the fruits of the Spirit."*

Also, this is a good time to repeat Dr. Len's *ho'oponopono* mantra again: *"I love you, I'm sorry, please forgive me, thank you."* As mentioned before, feel the attitude of gratitude.

LEVEL 6: AWAKEN AND RECEIVE

This is similar to a post-hypnotic stage. As you are coming to your senses, repeat affirmations using *"I am"* statements about the new you with your goals achieved. Using *"I am"* statements is very powerful and direct. For example, you may say one of the following or something similar: *"I am now clean sober, healthy and achieving all my goals." "I now know the powers of mental science and can achieve anything." "I am past my condition of addiction." "I am calm, relaxed, and serene at all times."* You may add other goals here as well such as: *"I am losing weight and looking better every day,"* or, *"I am receiving wealth and abundance."* Put your goals into short *"I am"* summary statements. The scriptures said:

> *"Moses said to God, 'Behold, when I come to the children of Israel, and tell them, The God of your fathers has sent me to you'; and they ask me, what is his name? 'What should I tell them?' God said to Moses, "I AM WHO I AM,"* and he said, *"You shall tell the children of Israel this: I AM has sent me to you" (Exodus 3:13–14).*

Many New-Age thinkers agree that using the words *"I am"* before your goal description of yourself is of divine origin and very powerful. Thomas Troward said in 1917, *"Therefore the Divine Verb reproduces the Divine Substantive by a natural sequence. It is generated by the Divine 'I AM.'"* Charles Fillmore affirms the *"I am"* philosophy, stating that:

> *"Man, should constantly affirm: I AM, and I will manifest, the perfection of the Mind within me. The first part of the statement is abstract Truth; the second part is concrete identification of man with this truth. We must learn the law of expression from the abstract to the concrete- from the formless to the formed."*

After these statements, you can open your eyes, take a deep breath, stretch, and go on with your day or night knowing that you have programmed yourself for sobriety and success.

MEDITATIVE PROGRAMMING SUMMARY

You can summarize the levels as simply:

Relaxation-Gratitude-Visualization-Thanks-Affirmation-Awaken

This exercise may at first seem a little rigid, ordered, or structured but this will change. You will soon find that with a few sessions, and a little practice, you will be performing these steps seamlessly without having to think out each step. As you get more experience at it, you can go "freestyle" and change it up, altering your role-playing and *"as-if"* scenarios, adding new goals as your life's conditions change.

The entire session may at first take twenty minutes or more, but, again, through the power of habit, you will have ingrained networks in your subconscious that make this process smooth and efficient. I personally like to take longer, but if I'm rushed I can jump right into it and do a compressed mini-session in as little as five minutes if needed.

If you simply cannot fit in a Meditative Programming session, then do these steps just before going to sleep, and again upon waking. Before and after sleep, your body will already naturally be in a semi-meditative state, so programming is very effective at that time. It's actually a good habit to do this regardless if you miss a meditative session or not.

It is your choice of thoughts that determine your vibrational state. Never finish a meditation session in a bad mood or low mental frequency—if that happens you merely did not concentrate on what you desired enough, nor did you have the proper faith in mental science. It is purely a choice of thought, and it is all mental science law that follows. You literally can create whatever your heart desires, so your vibrational level should reflect this and be one of positivity and excitement.

18

Enforcing the Law

"NEVER let go of the mental image until it becomes manifested. Daily bring up the clear picture of what is wanted and impress it on the mind as an accomplished fact. This impressing on our own minds the thought of what we wish to realize will cause our own minds to impress the same thought on Universal Mind."

—ERNEST HOLMES, 1919

I thought that this chapter title was a nice touch. No, this is not about jails and cops—it is about supplemental information for using the Meditative Programming Technique, spiritual laws and mental science. So, it is Law *reinforcement*, as much as it is Law *enforcement*.

MAINTAIN YOUR NEW SELF-IMAGE CONSTANTLY

After you have performed your formal Meditative Programming exercise, you cannot just forget about your goal self-image for the rest of the day. You need to refresh your mind with this healthy new self-image throughout the day.

This inner goal self-image is a real 3-D mental hologram that you can refer to when you need support and reinforcement. Just mentally "step into" this image often and feel how good it is being this new person. Pretend or role-play real life situations into this new sober and healthy feeling. Treat the image as an object of strong desire, knowing that with the laws of manifestation, it is already becoming a reality right now. Keep in mind that you are not only carrying around a new self-image, but more importantly, a new feeling, a new vibrational signature, and a new mood. The critical part of the programming and overall transmutation is converting your old, low, negative frequency into a positive one, and *feeling* like this new sober, healthy, successful person now.

Meditative Programming is a powerful technique that boosts your mind-spirit power, but it is not a cure-all. You must also reinforce this practice with positive thoughts throughout the day. You must "ring the bell" to keep the sound chiming. As Charles Hannel said in 1921:

> *"The Law of Attraction will certainly and unerringly bring to you the conditions, environment, and experiences in life, corresponding with your habitual, characteristic, predominant mental attitude. Not what you think once in a while when you are in church, or have just read a good book, BUT your predominant mental attitude is what counts. You cannot entertain weak, harmful, negative thoughts ten hours a day and expect to bring about beautiful, strong and harmonious conditions by ten minutes of strong, positive, creative thought."*

Remember to go one step further in your goal desires. What will you be doing when you are completely free of addiction and have no desire to ever drink or use drugs again? What will you be like at six months sober, then a year, and at year five? It can be anything in the world you desire. Will you be starting a new career, teaching a yoga classes, coaching your kid's sports team, acting in a play, writing a book, competing in an art show, getting a college degree, learning a musical instrument, learning a new trade, running a marathon, or starting on an old shelved project? Live out these sober goals in your mind with faith and excitement. They will never become a reality in the physical world unless they exist in your mind first.

Visualizing beyond your immediate goal to the next successive goal is a metaphysical mental trick of sorts. You change your vibrational state immediately when you do this. Remember, you do not make the battle with alcohol or booze your goal; instead, you make the life of sobriety your goal. You *used* to have an addiction. You do not want to substitute the old addiction for another one, which is the struggle or compulsion with quitting. Recovery should be a milestone and not a career lifestyle. You want a burning desire and love for your new sober life and all it will bring you, and continue to grow from that.

GET OUT YOUR BLOW-UP TOYS

For this analogy, I couldn't resist that subtitle…one that brings up a funny bachelor party…but I hope not too private of a joke for all the readers to get… Well, in any case, this is another reminder on the need to maintain and boost your vibrational state, and make your goal self-image a predominant thought.

Most anything inflatable, whether it's yes, a doll figure, a raft, bike tire, or a hot air balloon, will eventually lose air and begin to wilt over time. It's just physics and gravity. For example, a hot air balloons pressure must be maintained in order to keep the form full so it floats at a certain elevation. Additional air must be pumped in, or the existing air must be (heated) energized, otherwise the balloon will sink or drop in elevation.

Your inner self-image also must be maintained similarly. When your goal self-image is at its peak, it is fully inflated, energized, and vibrating at a high frequency. If left unattended for too long, it will lose energy and start to weaken, and sink low, especially if you are surrounded by negative external conditions always beating at it.

In order to keep your inner image fully inflated and energized, you must boost yourself with confidence, enthusiasm, and faith. We must interject bursts of positive affirmations and visualizations so that this inner self-image remains fully energized and resonating at a high frequency.

One way to do this and keep ourselves moving forward with our goals is performing mini-meditation sessions a couple times during the day. Try it when you have free time to just sit in your car after you park it at work or the store. Lock yourself in the bathroom for five minutes at work. Or put on earphones with meditation music at the office during a break. If you are stuck with a busy travel day, or just can't fit one of these breaks in, then do this when you lie in bed at night and upon awakening. During those brief times, just go mentally to your new self-image and live in that goal-image. Give it more power and life, thereby increasing its vibrations.

These are times you mentally retreat from your everyday activity and give yourself a self-empowering motivational break—visualize with self-affirmations. Get psyched-up like the athlete who jams out to music while visualizing himself winning the game. Instead of daydreaming while you drive or exercise, give yourself "*I am*" self-affirmations while and get excited about your new self. The more focus you place on this image, the more energy you give it and the more powerful your new inner strength gets. Always visualize as if it was already a fact—that you already are sober, healthy, happy, and successful—past tense.

Remember, mental science laws teach that what you vividly imagine in your mind as an existing truth with faith in its fruition, will crystalize into form. The reality we desire is the new self—sober and clean, happy, free, and successful. Your free time should not be spent worrying about the future or regretting the past, but imagining your goals. Make these daydreams productive and make them fun. Imagine and role-play in your mind, and get excited about your new lifestyle. It should not feel forced, but natural.

Try out new experiences when you do your mental programming. At one session, try your new self-image at an upcoming party, then at a work event, maybe at your kid's sports game, or when you run into an old drinking friend. Remember to always include those trigger events that stress your emotions to tempt you to use again, and visualize yourself successfully overcoming the temptation and feeling peaceful, relaxed, and serene. See yourself on the other side of the stressful event or trigger, successfully enduring it. Role-play in your mind with faith in these mental science laws.

MENTALLY LIVE IN YOUR NEW HOUSE, BEFORE YOU EVEN MOVE

In 1919, New Thought teacher Ernest Holmes said, "*This **already-believing** is necessary because all is mind, and until we have provided that full acceptance* *we have not made a mold into which mind could pour itself and through which it could manifest."* Your ideal conditions must exist as already done, as the future will fill the forms you have mentally created.

You are realistically deceiving your subconscious mind into believing an imagined event already occurred by using emotionalized visualizations. This is a fundamental premise of mental programming—when you think and feel that something was done in your mind, then it is so recorded in your subconscious as a fact. There is no such thing as the concept of time in the realm of mind-spirit. By thinking *from* the goal as already achieved, you are not only recording successful experiences in the subconscious, but also changing your vibrational frequency, which then projects to create your future. Always think, feel, and believe yourself as already sober, clean, and healthy with a life of love and success, and that is what will be drawn to you. Another New Thought great, Wallace Wattles, had this to say in 1910:

> *"Live in the new house, mentally, until it takes form around you physically. In the mental realm, enter at once into full enjoyment of the things you want. 'Whatsoever things ye ask for when ye pray, believe that ye receive them, and ye shall have them,' said Jesus."*

To already believe you have received your goal is key, and have faith in the mind-spirit powers that they will manifest.

A simplistic example of visualizing beyond the end result would be if it is your goal is to run your first 5k (3 mile) fun run. To successfully program yourself, you want to visualize the success of finishing the race, not the workouts that got you there. You don't visualize yourself sweating out the two to three miles you struggle with a few times a week training over the past 3 months. You don't keep recalling how you roughed-out the pain on the road, and had to ice down your knees. Instead, you picture yourself already accomplishing the goal—finishing the race with ease, having the great healthy feeling when crossing the line, hearing the cheers of the crowd, sensing the happiness that your family and friends feel, attending the celebration meal afterwards, showing off the cool T-shirt and medal you have earned, and so on. Always go beyond your immediate goal (of *getting* sober) and start visualizing the next successive goal (of *living* sober). Mental science teaches that your subconscious will take for granted that the previous goal has already been accomplished, when you are already mentally living in the future, subsequent goal level.

Our ultimate goal is to achieve a new vibrational frequency such that we *feel* the mood and attitude of our goals as already accomplished—we feel healthy, sober, happy, and successful throughout the day. To do that you must keep "ringing the bell" with reinforcements to your positive vibrational state. This is done by rehearsing and reinforcing your new self-image throughout the day.

WHAT WE RESIST, WILL PERSIST

A craving or urge for a drug or drink means that you have given attention or mental energy to a negative thought, consciously or subconsciously. During the beginning stages of your sobriety, you are on a slippery slope, and your new positive thought habits may not be quite ingrained or solidified. The Meditative Programming is making changes in a powerful, accelerated fashion, but you still have some deeply embedded thinking patterns to override. Once you have developed a strong vibrational state reflecting your healthy, sober inner self-image, it will act as a protective shield preventing the negative thoughts from getting to you. These thoughts no longer harmonize with your new self and will be rejected. Soon they'll disappear completely because they now do not belong in your new reality.

As an addict, metaphysically you were a bundle of negative vibrations that had manifested into a sick physical mind and body. Your body was sick, your mind depressed, and metaphysically you were dark, stagnant, and disharmonic, going against the natural flow in life. This negativity displays itself in some people as always getting sick or maybe even as obesity, bulimia, high blood pressure, and heart disease among others. Mentally it manifests as anger, frustration, anxiety, depression, and even bipolar disorder. It is simply a continuum of the Law of Attraction attracting more disorder to your body. When we use Meditative Programming and mental science, we are bringing light into the darkness, healing the sickness, reviving harmony, and restoring our natural vibrancy and health.

Negative thoughts to a human is like a virus to a computer. Let the virus remain, and it will disrupt normal functions, destroy data, corrupt files, and ruin your projects. Likewise, our underlying negative thoughts and beliefs will consume our health and manifest as pain and disease, and ruin our lives. On our PC, we clean out the virus and install anti-virus software, and, in like fashion, in human life we use mental science to clean and correct the malignant mind. Your spirit consciousness downloads instructions to the physical body which obeys the commands in exact precision. The mind is the software for your matrix world and molds your reality through thoughts, imagination, and faith.

You become what you think about, and thus your current reality is a result of your past thinking. The future will be a result of your present thinking. Have patience—do not be concerned with your present conditions, or be dejected or disappointed if they do not match those that you now desire. The physical world is always transmuting and creating what the underlying metaphysical world is shaping—you must have faith that you are in the process of creating a new reality by changing your inner vibrational frequency.

Remember to live in your mind beyond the stage of addiction and recovery. Do not make beating addiction your goal—make the life after sobriety your goal. Generate the feelings of the sober, healthy, happy, and successful self-image as already being yours. Feel like the winner, not the fighter. Your vibrational state will change, your world will change, and you will achieve your goals in miraculous fashion—this is the law.

19

Addiction Theory and Issues

"This discordant state of vibration throws the physical body into confusion, which causes unhappiness, sickness, and death. In the pure natural animal, the vibrations are perfectly attuned to the astral, the realm which directly affects the physical world. The discordant state of the vibrations in man is caused, we believe, by the constant struggle going on between his higher and lower nature."

— T.A. WILLISTON, 1897

GETTING WASTED

Excuse my French, but when I drank, it was for one purpose only and that was to "get fucked up." There was no such thing as social drinking, having a glass of wine with dinner, enjoying a nice cordial, or any of that bullshit. There was none of that having a couple beers "to relax." If you had a bottle of Jagermeister around, it was coming out, and getting emptied.

In my earlier years, admittedly, I probably tried just about every social drug on the street, but booze was my drug of choice. Nothing else resonated with me like alcohol did. More specifically, I liked beer. It comes in cans or bottles, is premeasured, and therefore predictable. I knew exactly how many would get me to the level I needed to be. Let's see… four beers before a date, six to eight is good for watching football games, three minimum while gardening, if going to the movies...that's at least five, doing laundry is a minimum of six, and after about fifteen, ready for a nap, then a few needed when I woke up. Yes, that's the math I did while driving to the beer store every day...insanity.

If I was at a bar, and the beer wasn't quite doing the trick fast enough, I'd simply add shots of hard liquor. When I started doing shots, things would get crazy. I'd usually buy rounds for my friends, too, just so I wasn't the only one getting wasted. I found out early in my drinking career that you don't stand out as much if everyone else shows their asses along with you. As an addict, you don't stop drinking or drugging when you have a nice buzz—you keep going until you find that "high" you need, but you usually never do. Most times you will only stop when you run out of money, run out of booze or drugs, get sick, pass out, crash your car, or get arrested. Otherwise, there's no excuse not to get severely high or drunk. For an addict, the mental threshold to achieve a satisfactory high is very elusive.

WHERE'S MY "I SURVIVED ALCOHOLISM" T-SHIRT?

I see "I survived..." apparel for all kinds of diseases and illnesses. They have shirts for cancer patients, ribbons for heart disease awareness, and even pink apparel for NFL players during Breast Cancer Month. However, you won't find any recovered alcoholics wearing "I survived alcoholism" T-shirts. That's because of the (legitimate) stigma that goes along with it. Hey you might even die of this disease, just like with cancer, but you got drunk while doing it so it doesn't count.

There are many opinions on what addiction and alcoholism is. Some say it's a disease, some say it's a developed habit, and others say it is just an issue of willpower. I was told that my dad and granddad were both alcoholics and that I probably inherited my alcoholism from them. What I believe I inherited was not a disease, but purely a condition—one with mental tendencies and physical tolerances, an allergy of sorts.

Just as athletes develop "muscle-memory" of movements and routines, I believe the heavy drinker's body and brain develops a tolerance and memory of alcohol abuse, and biologically adapts accordingly. We inherit this high threshold/tolerance both physically and psychically. When booze hits our bodies, we react differently than others, we are allergic in a manner.

In life, we have our struggles, our problems, our stresses, and our pains. We cruise along on life's highway and when we encounter one of these hurdles, it's like a fork in the road. We can either go left, the addictive destructive route, or right, the healthy constructive way. Both involve pain to some extent. When we are born with an addictive tendency, it's like being a left-handed driver, with a left turn toward the unhealthy choice being the natural inclination. Avoid pain by numbing, avoiding it, or burying it. Usually, this tendency is something we learned growing up.

The medical people that insist addiction is a disease acknowledge there are no associated tumors, cancers, malign growths, or even cellular mutations in the addict compared to a normal non-addict. Just about every other disease and ailment has its chemical, cellular, or physical indices and respectfully have therapy or treatment to that same effect. Only the *effects* of addiction can be measured biologically or chemically, but the cause is metaphysical in nature, of mind-spirit, and therefor has no measurable indices

Even if years from now scientists did finally find a molecular DNA mutation was involved, we have already learned in mental science that this is simply a result of action by mind or consciousness as the cause. Any treatment will again be on the effect and not the cause. The physical cellular changes are the ultimate result of mind force and therefore can be reversed in the same manner. After all, we learned how epigenetic studies showed consciousness was an agent in the transmutations of genetic DNA molecules in cells. We've also seen how mind affects the molecular structure of water; how the mind alters subatomic particles; and how the mind acts on the body in placebo effect studies. So, even if the disease theory is proven sometime in the future, it'll be no challenge or threat to the student of mental science—we know that mind-spirit is still at the nucleus of the disharmony which causes the misalignment.

Physically, addiction manifests itself as a chemical imbalance of sorts, an allergy, an innate tolerance, and need for more and more of the drug. For the addict, the euphoric peak recedes much too soon and wears off too quickly. It's like putting air in a car tire that still has a hole in it. So, what do we do when our tire has a slow leak? We keep pumping air in the tire to keep it filled, but air keeps leaking out, so you overinflate it once in a while so it lasts longer between fillings. This is what happens when people relapse and overdose, they overinflate to make sure they have enough air in their *tire*. They OD because they want to be sure they stay high.

ADDICTION: THE MENTAL-SPIRITUAL CONDITION

Addiction is primarily a mental compulsion or obsession to get numb or anesthetized and to blur out reality while in this pain-free pleasure zone. Remember the critical point is that we are addicted to the *feeling* and *effects* more so than the chemical addiction itself. The physical component of addiction is very serious too, but actually more easily handled.

It is the desire for this "buzz" or numbed feeling that must be removed. When we crave booze and drugs, most times it is due to this mental nagging, and is usually triggered by some inner fear or pain we are trying to numb or avoid. We must learn firstly to mitigate and lessen the severity of the underlying pain by using correct rational thinking. Secondly, we wipe out the desire for the drugged or drunk buzz-mind as an alternate to dealing with it, using mental science programming. But behind the mental programming must be the desire for mental clarity, peace of mind, and inner serenity. The desire for mental clarity versus a fogged numbness must come from within. Usually with correct thinking, meditation, mental programming of goals, and studies in the spiritual laws, we can find this desire.

It's truly amazing what pleasure you will find in the subtler things in life when you get sober. Your senses return to full life, and sensitivity to contrast is restored. You find great pleasure again doing simple things once you clear up the fog and numbness the drugs and booze caused. Plus, when you have clarity of mind and a fully functioning brain, you are more receptive to the subtler frequencies associated with extraordinary sensory perception and spirit messages.

The argument whether or not addiction is a true "disease" or not still persists today, but the medical establishment predominantly promotes the disease theory. I'm not alone when I say that I feel addiction was termed a disease for financial, and not medical, reasons. Insurance companies are not required to cover self-induced sicknesses, lack of willpower illnesses, or ill conditions resulting from bad choices or habits. When, however, it is deemed and classified a medical disease, they are forced to cover it, and everybody can then cash in. When people are sick with an insurable disease, the economy flourishes—doctors, nurses, pharmacies, research labs, hospitals, rehab centers, and even schools, colleges, and the government. A huge part of our economy is empowered in these institutions, and they therefore are quasi-political.

If the truth came out that mind was the true cause of our addictive ill conditions, this disease-based economy would be disrupted, and huge companies would lose big money. This is why you can only find the news about alternative healing in obscure media outlets, and that mind cure cases are kept so hush-hush, and suppressed by medical society.

Branding addiction as a disease is a double-edged sword for addicts. On one hand, it is great that addicts can now get insurance to cover costs of doctors, therapists, and rehab, but on the other hand, it provides a scapegoat for their actions and behaviors. When you have a disease, it immediately connotes being a victim of something you have no control over.

I thought Eugene Del Mar understood the truth about disease when, in 1922, he wrote:

> *"One may manifest any physical disease… by visualizing the symptoms that standardize the disease, anticipating the symptoms, and thinking of himself as physically subject to the disease. While this may necessitate considerable effort, no effort seems to be too great when disease is the goal! As long as one accepts the false traditional beliefs that have caused and perpetuated inharmony, he must register physical disease. If one incorporates in his system the cause of disease, inevitably he will manifest its allied result. One who plants the seeds of disease in the prolific soil of false belief, will raise a bounteous crop of physical inharmony."*

Addicts have a choice to pick up a drug to numb their inner pain or to confront their pain in a healthy way. They have a choice to use mental science to correct their negative inner frequency state, or allow it to manifest and grow.

WHO WAS THE FIRST ALKIE IN MY FAMILY TREE?

This inherited alcoholism disease theory is worth exploring a little. Obviously, any inherited behavior must have an origin—there had to be the first heavy drinker, the first alkie or drunk in an alcoholic family tree. Otherwise, how would a nonalcoholic at the base or root of a family tree eventually have a successor, or downstream relative on a branch, turn into an alcoholic? I'm not a Darwinian adept, but it doesn't take much to figure out that if there is no alcoholic trait at the family tree trunk, there can be no trait at the successive branch. Somewhere in between it had to been developed, and nothing manifests in the physical world unless it begins with mind or consciousness. Mind is always the cause, and physical conditions, the resultant effect. Someone is guilty for being the first alkie drunk, and it started with their mind.

The first alcoholic developed when someone down the family lineage suffered with a pain, vibrational misalignment, or sick emotional body and then found and abused alcohol to relieve the pain. Either that, or they deliberately abused alcohol to the point of constant drunkenness. In either case, a physical tolerance built up, and he or she became physically addicted. The next child probably suffered from some pain as well, and was reared knowing booze was not only acceptable behavior, but a great pain reliever, and the chain continued. The child had a faster rate of addiction due to the learned behavior. This repeated a third time perhaps, and, yes, by now physical adaptions took place so that successive generations could tolerate the toxin in higher doses, and the threshold for the effect was raised. The condition or tendency passes on.

The tendency and tolerance for alcohol by the next generation is only triggered upon exposure to the chemical. They are not born with a craving or desire for it. They only seek booze or drugs when they are educated that it cures emotional pain and discomfort, or they somehow are exposed to it. Remove the underlying cause of pain, and you remove the need for the pain killer. It's that simple. Introduce booze into the system, and the allergy is awakened, and this person won't process alcohol nor receive the effects the same as a normal person.

When you have emotional issues and then suppress them with booze or drugs, they burrow deeper, get bigger, and throw off your entire metaphysical vibrational state. The origin is in the kinship to one who suffered a vibrational imbalance, and not in some alcoholic gene or molecule. The cause was mental-spiritual, and so is the remedy. The drinking tolerance component is purely in the physical body, and is not a factor once the underlying cause is corrected.

In my personal situation, I suffered with anxieties and depression which caused a metaphysically disharmonious state. This created an emotional-spiritual hole I carried around and let grow and spread. When any painful emotions tried to surface, I merely numbed it with booze. It was like playing "whack-a-mole" where the moles were my conflicts or problems, and booze was the hammer. More moles? No problem, get more hammers.

Had the issues been resolved in healthy, normal way, I most likely would have passed right through the early drinking stages with no interest, but the glimmer of hope was revealed when I first drank, felt relief, and the allergy started. You find the right combination to unlock the door to normalcy when you find that booze fixes that hole in you. It's a great feeling to feel normal and comfortable in your own skin again.

In my case, the alcohol was not the cause or the problem, it was a symptom of the problem. *I* was the problem, my inner self, and then I used alcohol for so long in a self-medicating manner that it became a physical and emotional dependency. To repeat, the drinking was the symptom and not the problem, but the symptom then became a dependency, and the vicious downward spiral of addiction took its course.

Most people strive to be content, healthy, and vibrationally whole with a balanced mental and emotional life, and a healthy dose of love and self-worth. When something goes off-kilter—such as experiencing a traumatic event, severe stress, or having depression or an emotional problem—a negative frequency is generated. This happens to all of us and is usually healed with love, comfort, and proper rational thinking. For some of us, these healing elements are denied, rejected, or not available, so the negative feeling festers and grows. This vibrational disharmony displays itself as emotional discomfort or pain, which we shield and protect. In many cases, these pains are personal or embarrassing that we keep from others and hide. When we eventually discover drugs or alcohol, the darkness and negative vibration are artificially removed and numbed, and we feel happy, normal, and comfortable again. This hole however, continues to grow inside and get bigger, and we simply find more booze and drugs to keep filling it in.

Drugs and booze can cause addictions inversely from the way pain does. In other words, you can become addicted by abusing drugs or alcohol, and they have the repercussions of pain, as a result, not the cause. If you were born and raised into an emotionally healthy environment and are living in a healthy manner, you most likely are vibrationally fit and you won't have an addiction problem.

How many happy, healthy people do you know that shoot heroin five times a day? How many emotionally balanced, content people do you know that drink a quart of vodka every day? I doubt any. But guess what—if you force one of these happy, healthy, fit people to shoot heroin or drink a quart of vodka every day for a couple weeks straight, then yes, they will become an addict, too. The excessive chemicals will create a vibrational misalignment and a psychic hole will materialize, as will the physical addiction. It's just in reverse order—instead of using drugs to mask the pain, the drugs create the pain and then the pain festers into the addiction cycle.

IS AA A MEDICAL CURE OR A SPIRITUAL PLATFORM?

In my experience, the medical society was contradictory about treating the condition of alcoholism. In my attempts to be cured of this alleged disease, I visited a few different programs and facilities. Each and every time, the medical solution prescribed was to go to Alcoholics Anonymous (AA). The same medical doctors that claim addiction is a clinical disease don't schedule you for surgery, chemotherapy, or medication—they send you to go to AA meetings or therapy. They have no physical treatments available because they know there is no physical basis, or cure for it.

Let me preface that I believe AA has done wonders for millions of people. I personally have learned invaluable lessons there, several of which I've shared in this book. I have several good friends doing great in the program today. However, let's be perfectly clear about the medical-scientific validity of AA, and that there is none. When doctors recommend AA, they are being very contradictory against their scientific training.

When I went to AA, I was told that my alcoholism was a spiritual malady. In order to cure this condition, I had to get a sponsor, confess my sins and wrongdoings, believe in a higher power, and attend meetings (pretty much for the rest of my life). I didn't quite find any medical disease advice in these steps. When in AA, we were told to pray to a higher being; we read from a big book; we confessed our sins; then we held hands in a circle and prayed to God—we even passed around a collection basket. If this doesn't sound exactly like a Christian church, I don't know what does. The only thing missing was the preacher and choir.

I do think AA has many positive attributes, and believe the underlying reason for its success is the fact that it has traces of mental science in their program. As I mentioned earlier, one of the founding spokespersons of AA had endorsed the early works of mental science author Thomas Troward. AA's use of group consciousness (brotherhood and comradery), believing in a higher power, and utilizing prayer parallel some of the fundamental principles of the New Thought doctrine.

The biggest problem I found with AA was unfortunately in the very first step—to admit you are *powerless* over alcohol. This is in direct conflict with the founding mental science principle that we control our own destiny and create our own reality. When you admit you are powerless, you are actually empowering it. In a way, it's a type of inverted worship, feeding the addiction, and keeping it alive with your energy and attention.

In accordance with the Law of Attraction, we want to magnify and focus on what we want, not what we don't want. To proclaim ourselves as powerless is instilling fear and weakness that we are victims. We want to instill strength, desire, and faith in our sobriety. *What you resist persists*. We don't want to fight drinking and make that persist. I don't want to wake up every morning and say I'm powerless about anything.

I felt that going to AA was basically substituting one dependency for another, from alcohol dependency to AA meeting dependency. When I quit, I wanted to be completely free and divorced of the monkey on my back—that monkeys name, its smell, and any thought of it. Why go to a meeting every day to talk about that monkey when with mental science you can erase every memory of it completely? Why endure hearing about people's alcohol struggles, relapses, cravings and such every day? Why not just quit drinking once and for all using mental science principles?

Mental science writer C. H. Mann spoke along these same lines when he wrote:

> "To be continually looking into the ill feelings of your body, always examining your pulse, as it were, forever thinking of this ache or that discomfort, analyzing all the strange or peculiar sensations that may come to you, and discussing such matters with others, —all such conduct gives a basis in your mind for the presence of evil thoughts to aggravate and maintain your ailments."

I agree that by giving addiction our energy and focus we simply exacerbate, aggravate, and give life toward that which we are trying to remove and forget. Let the wound heal.

One thing I have to say, however, is that AA does well in promoting spirituality and prayer, and thus is a creed that uses a couple of the basic mental science and spiritual law principles. If someone is not ready for studying and using the direct principles of mental science and spiritual laws, then I would certainly suggest he or she try AA. If anything, it is a good stepping stone to get started, and full of good-willed people and support.

DETOX IS THE EASY PART

We have been primarily focusing on the mental-spiritual aspects of addiction. But we should also talk a little about the symptoms or physical issues. The physical part of addiction is pretty straightforward—you build an increase in cellular tolerance that matches the increase in chemical abuse, and you biochemically get addicted.

As mentioned earlier, the mental-spiritual addiction to the feeling or effect of the chemicals is at the nucleus of addiction, but our physical bodies get hooked, too. Even if we are mentally ready to quit, we still have a poisoned body that needs to be detoxed properly.

The mental-spiritual "high" threshold is raised very high for the addict and climbs higher each time he or she uses. A normal person who partakes occasionally gets high or drunk with the same amount each time, whereas the addict's tolerance increases. Addicts consume more alcohol or drugs than needed or even anticipated to find this high, and the body's cells and organs soon adapt. Soon the amount ingested to get the required effect is enormous. I've heard it said a hundred times in group therapy sessions how an addict would buy enough booze or drugs to last a few days, only to then consume it all within a few hours. Afterward, he or she would be bewildered and angered by the fact it was all gone.

The requirement for increased quantities for getting a buzz builds both a physical and a psychic tolerance. Continuing this cycle, in a short time you are consuming such huge amounts that the brain, nervous system, and organs simply cannot function properly. The bad consequences then occur: blacking out, driving drunk, uncharacteristic behaviors, and in the worst cases, getting alcohol poisoning or drug overdosing.

When you hit this high consumption level, you have raised your mental threshold which does not go back down but actually continues to rise. The addiction monster you created continues to grow larger even if you quit for a while. When you reacquaint yourself with this monster after a period of sobriety and abstinence, you will not be starting with an infant creature all over again. The monster is not only as big as you left him, but has kept growing while you were away, and now needs more to be satisfied. It's as if you stretched out your drug/alcohol reservoir. This is why many heroin and pill addicts overdose when they relapse. The addiction monster or need for the drug, has grown larger than their bodies can handle, and their bodies will fail before they ever get mentally satisfied.

Making the decision to quit is easy, but doing it one of the hardest things, and we will postpone it as long as possible. It's the body, brain, mind, and spirit all wanting to stay happy and numb. You'll say you'll be ready to quit next week after so and so does this, or after such and such event takes place, or after you finish this or that project or task. You're not ready because of some stressful event still taking place in your life and can't fathom dealing with it sober. Believe me, there will *always* be an excuse and reason why today is not a good day to quit. Even when there is no valid excuse we can find, we say that we just need to "tie one on" one last time, which then goes on forever. If you have a true heartfelt desire to quit, this "drop dead" date should not be a problem at all, and should even be anticipated with excitement.

Quitting the physical component of addiction is what most alkies and addicts fear the most, but is actually the fastest and easiest part. It's a simple black-and-white biological detox ordeal that's over within a few days. If you are actively using drugs or alcohol now, you should get help from a medical professional on how you should quit. It's a dangerous business trying it on your own, dealing with withdrawals and possible seizures. Some addicts and alkies can quit safely on their own. But if it's available, I strongly recommend a medical detox center or some other type of medical supervision. How you quit safely depends on what chemicals you used, how much, and how long; it also depends on your age, condition, health, and so forth. Play it safe and get help with quitting.

No matter how you decide to quit, you should still work on the Meditative Programming every waking and sober moment you have. Read and reread this literature and keep your thoughts magnetized on the positive goal of health and sobriety as often as you can. Remember and ponder on the subjects in this book every chance you have. It will eventually sink in to your mind, your vibrational frequency will change, and you will begin to gravitate to a healthy, sober lifestyle. The cleaner you get, the more mental clarity you have and the stronger your mind powers get in achieving results from these mental science practices. In 1911, James Allen wrote *"To reflect truly, the mirror must be true. A warped glass gives back an exaggerated image. A disturbed mind gives a distorted reflection of the world."* You won't truly understand, nor be able to apply these principles, if your mind is chemically distorted.

If you do go to a detox or rehab center, just don't forget this book! The Meditative Programming Technique should be used as early as possible to start generating the positive momentum for change. By using this technique and applying the powerful knowledge in this book, you will accelerate your healing and recovery and be ready to start realizing the goals of long-term sobriety, health, love, and success in your life. You just need a clear head to fully utilize these tools. These powerful laws of mind-spirit can and will manifest miracles, but you have to give it a fighting chance by providing a functional brain and body with which to work.

If you are struggling with a physical dependence right now, it will be hard to concentrate on much else. Believe me, I know the feeling of having every cell in my body screaming at me thirsting for alcohol and my nerves feeling like high voltage was running through them. When I was in that state of mind, if you asked me to meditate and visualize, I'd tell you to "fuck off and pack sand"—then I'd go get a twelve-pack. You need to be at a certain level place mentally to begin this program, so getting clean, even if its intermittent at first, is important to apply these applications.

WATCH OUT FOR THE EMOTIONAL JACK-IN-THE-BOX

Once you are clean and sober, you'll need to reacquaint yourself with your emotions. Addicts get so used to numbing feelings, they may get ultrasensitive to them when they dry out. At a recovery center, I remember the phrase "get comfortable being uncomfortable." We are so used to not dealing with feelings. This is why it's important to deal with emotional baggage. If the issues cannot be completely resolved and removed (like forgiving an old enemy), they should be addressed therapeutically to dilute their emotional impact. Also, good emotions are often just as much a trigger as are negative emotions. Your birthday or winning a little money at Lotto can set you off just as badly as getting a traffic ticket or bouncing a check. Emotions are sharp as razors and can be strong weapons used for or against you. Take heed of their power.

What's worse for the addict is that when we numbed ourselves and didn't allow ourselves to grow normally, we stopped processing thoughts and emotions needed to resolve inner issues. It's like fast-forwarding past commercials on television. We do the same with booze and drugs and blur the emotional commercials in our lives so we don't feel them. When we do this for enough years, we're frozen emotionally in the past. When you finally do get sober and wake up, it can be pretty scary—enough to start drinking again unless you get ready for a little emotional discomfort.

Some recovered addicts find many excuses to go back to their old ways, including sabotaging good times, isolating themselves, starting arguments, engaging in self-pity, and focusing on remorse and resentments. These people have not let go of their underlying problems and enjoy the game of numbing their pain instead of resolving it. Bear in mind you are different this time as you now possess the knowledge of mental science and spiritual laws. You truly are a different person with this knowledge.

ADDICTION SUMMARY

Remember that drugs and alcohol are the symptoms or effects of addiction and not the cause. Addiction stems from an inner spiritual-emotional pain that is metaphysically displayed as a negative or discordant vibrational state. It manifests as emotional pain, and physically as an increased tolerance, and inability to control.

With addiction, we have no cellular mutations, tumors, or cancers as do legitimate diseases. We may have developed physical allergies and tolerances to chemicals, but these are only effects, and not causes. Our addiction stems from a painful, unbalanced mental-spiritual state. Using mental science and spiritual laws, we correct the misalignment, reprogram the brain and body, and stop the condition from manifesting ever again.

Drug addiction or alcoholism is a temporary condition, not a permanent disease. Recovery should be a milestone, not a lifelong effort. Once we remove the underlying discord and misalignment causing the pain, we are free, completely and permanently.

Addiction follows the fundamental cause and effect principle of mental science and spiritual law. The cause is always mind-spirit, and physical manifestation is always the effect. *As above, so below.* Correct the mind, and you correct the body and conditions.

Addicts and alcoholics have a mental-spiritual condition, a hole in their souls, but it is curable. With the proper help, the active physical addiction can be easily and safely stopped, and the mental-spiritual issues can then be resolved. On a metaphysical level, once the underlying pain or negative vibrational state is corrected, the desire to drink or drug will cease permanently. The innate physical allergy, tolerance, and tendencies may still exist, but will be suppressed and dormant since there is no more need to anesthetize any pain. At that point if the ex-addict picks up again, he or she is simply ignorant, or deliberately numbing another mishandled pain.

20

One for the Road

"Our prevailing thoughts and emotions determine, and with absolute accuracy, the prevailing conditions of our outward, material life, and likewise the prevailing conditions of our bodily life. Would we have any conditions different in the latter we must then make the necessary changes in the former. The silent, subtle forces of mind and spirit, ceaselessly at work, are continually moulding these outward and these bodily conditions."

—Ralph Trine, 1917

Yes, another catchy alkie chapter title I though was applicable. In the past when I would refer to "one for the road," it meant pouring an extra strong drink for the ride home from a bar or party. I always wanted to make sure I never lost my buzz getting home or to the next beer stop. What I'm hoping to give you is not a *drink* for the road, but some *think* for the road—a little knowledge, wisdom, and inspiration for your journey ahead.

The above quote by Trine is a very good summary of the mental science doctrine that states, in essence, the simple fact that *we create our own reality* with our minds, just like the channeled spirit Seth said. The life you now live with its successes and failures, health and sickness, addiction or sobriety, and happiness and despair is a result of the actions of your mind.

227

In accordance with the principles of mental science and spiritual laws, you have consciously or unconsciously created your present bodily and life conditions, which include your habits and addictions. In order to change outer behaviors, you must change your inner self.

MYOB

When you start your new mental science program, you may find that others in your life get more disrupted at your new lifestyle than you do yourself. Your friends, family, and work associates might be too interested in your personal life and prod too much. You know how everyone likes to talk about the drug addict or alcoholic, that elephant in the room? Just subtly get the point across to them to MYOB, "mind your own business."

When addressing your new sobriety and lifestyle program, there's nothing wrong with telling others a white lie that you're on a health kick, trying to lose a few pounds, get in shape, trying a new diet or a new exercise program, and so forth. If you say it's just a two- or three-month health program, they usually won't question it, whereas if you say it is a lifelong change, they may challenge you. By saying you're on a health kick or diet, you can get out of going to happy hour, parties, and other social functions that may be trigger events and that way people don't think you are snubbing them for long.

Once you get a month or so under your belt, others will see the positive change in you and most likely support whatever you've been doing. Plus, after a month or so, you will have developed the strength and confidence to deal with them better. At that point in time, you can just say that you are feeling so good that you want to continue this new health regimen another few months, and so on. People will get used to your new lifestyle, and ones that truly are your friends will support you.

It is sometimes best to keep certain goals and desires a secret, or trust only a few close people. You may weaken the strength of your goals when you talk out loud about them which will dissipate their strength. This is the exact reason why people like to discuss their problems with a therapist or friend, to dissipate the problem's magnitude and strength, making it get smaller or go away entirely. With our goal of sobriety, it's the opposite—we don't want this goal to get weaker or smaller, but grow larger and stronger.

There are some that may want to judge you, or monitor and criticize your progress, thus putting undue pressure and expectations on you. Then there are also those who may be outright jealous about you improving yourself, and beneath the surface would love to see you fail. This probably happens a lot with friends you used to party with, that are still addicts. Deep down they wish they could quit, too. But since they can't, or don't want to, they'd rather drag you down to their level, and see you relapse.

This does not mean you have to do this alone. Share with those who support and reinforce your goals, and can help you when you're feeling down. Remember the power of group consciousness. Especially during the early stages of recovery, supplementing your Meditative Programming practice with a support group is always a good idea. It never hurts to get an extra vibrational boost.

Keep in mind that you will need more alone time, solitude for meditating, time for rereading parts of this book, a chance to study new material, or to exercise, and so on. You need to be doing your Meditative Programming, internalizing these new mental concepts, and building your new self-image. Again, just tell others this is all a part of your new health kick to keep them off your back. Cut out non-productive things in your life, such as social hours and television, and instead do some reading or meditating. Try adding a new, positive habit—go for a walk, a bike ride, join a gym., or go to a yoga class.

Take a mental detour from the Internet for a few weeks—this is a critical stage in your life. You need to focus on your goals and don't need the emotional entanglements and competitive distractions that social networking brings. Do yourself a favor and take a sabbatical from Facebook and Twitter for a month. Just block it, or check-out for a while. In 1911, James Allen talks about distracting social annoyances when he wrote:

"Dwelling upon one's petty troubles and ailments is a manifestation of weakness of character. To so dwell upon them in thought leads to frequent talking about them, and this, in turn, impresses them more vividly upon the mind, which soon becomes demoralized by such petting and pitying. It is as convenient to dwell upon happiness and health as upon misery and disease; as easy to talk about them, and much more pleasant and profitable to do so."

BREAKING UP WITH YOUR LOVER: BOOZE AND DRUGS

Your new mental science program will change your life. You are reformatting your mental hard drive and realigning your vibrational state to the new, sober you. Your excitement level should be through the roof knowing these mental science principles you have learned are virtually guaranteed. Use meditation, music, exercise, and the love of other things in your life to keep your vibrational level energized with your new goal self-image. Recall the mayic rhythms of the universe, and remember to rest and allow the pendulum to swing naturally.

You are breaking up a long love affair with your addiction. The lover that comforted you, shielded you from emotional pain, and physically and mentally pleased you, had also made you sick, depressed, and took away your family, money, job, health, and friends. This lover did nothing positive, only to make you run and hide, until you were a prisoner to it, and in more pain than ever before. It was a liar, and in the end, took everything away from you with nothing to offer in exchange. The pleasure went away, but the bondage remained. But now you are free again. Treat this ex-lover accordingly with disrespect.

DON'T DIG UP YOUR SEED TO SEE IF IT'S GROWING

Do not constantly check to see if external conditions have changed yet and begin worrying about them. You must know that they are changing constantly and at all times, that the universal matrix is transmuting reality to align with your new vibrational frequency. You should disregard all external appearances and conditions that your senses tell you if they conflict with your desired reality, and trust they are changing. Your changed inner image, your feelings, and your faith are the driving force in creating your future.

Keep the attitude that the change into this new self-image is happening right now. Be patient, trust, and believe in your new program and lifestyle. Be prepared to receive that which you ask for—sobriety, health, happiness, love, and success. Remember that impatience is going upstream against the natural flow. You must relax and trust the immutable laws of mind-spirit to work. In 1917, Thomas Troward stated:

> *"But there is one thing we must not forget, and this is the Law of Growth. If the Law which we plant is the seed, then we must allow time for it to grow; we must leave it alone and go about our business as usual...We must not be like children who plant a seed one day, and dig it up the next to see whether it is growing. Our part is to plant the seed, not to make it grow; —the Creative Law of Life will do that."*

Keep your goal self-image constantly in mind, with passionate desire and faith in its actualization. Expect good things to happen, and they will. Do not fret about the physical world if it does not match your desired reality yet; it will change in short time if you maintain faith in these principles.

You keep your mind magnetized on the fact you are now a sober, clean, healthy, and successful person who knows and uses the powerful secrets of mental science. Your desire is for clarity of mind, health, freedom, and serenity. In 1880, Mental Science writer C.H. Mann wrote:

> *"Understand, if you come into the right spiritual state you will get well, but do not bring that faith into such association with your ailments that if they do not immediately remove themselves you are thrown into doubt and confusion. Rather live in your health and turn your back upon your sickness, and be not anxious as to the result. Anxiety and fears open the doors for the admission of disease."*

You are changing subconsciously from the core outward. Little behavioral changes that you don't notice will start to reveal themselves to others first. Expect compliments because they will be coming soon. You'll start hearing how you look better, how you lost weight, look fit, seem much sharper, appear happier, have a healthy glow, and so forth. Your reality is matching your inner self, so you don't see it because it is in perfect alignment—it feels normal.

YOUR FEELINGS ARE YOUR INTERNAL COMPASS

Recognize that your emotions are your compass and guidance system giving you constant feedback on your goal attainment progress and state of vibrational alignment. They comprise your internal GPS, giving you direction and telling you when to make an adjustment in your life travels. In the past, we developed the habit of allowing ourselves to follow our addiction's commands and go down the wrong road. But now we have our internal GPS programmed for sobriety and success.

You will know you're going down the wrong road again by negative feelings and emotions. As soon as you start feeling crappy or get in a bad mood, do a quick audit of your inner thinking and ninety-nine percent of the time, you will find that you were subconsciously dwelling on something fearful or negative. On your mental GPS, where a fork in the road occurred, you simply took the wrong turn—it's as simple as changing directions by correcting your thinking.

Remember that thoughts generate feelings, which in turn generate more thoughts. Per the Law of Attraction, this snowball effect of thought-feelings will manifest into physical conditions, so it is important to cut this cycle off early with right thinking. Sometimes addicts' habitual thought patterns are such that they take the wrong path deliberately or subconsciously in order to succumb to their addiction. This addict, deep down, does not want to quit yet. These addicts will often self-sabotage plans so the events will lead to something negative to give them reason to use again. Some simply start irrational arguments with friends or family, screw up finances, mess up at work, get injured, or even have more elaborate plans. Some addicts find comfort having bad luck and negative conditions in their life. When these bad things happen, they can relapse and blame it on something external.

Underneath all of these external issues, however, was something internal all along. There is still a buried emotional discord, a manifestation of fear—usually feelings of self-pity, remorse, guilt, or resentments. You must keep your emotional "laundry aired out" and your mental house clean. When you crave, or have urges, it usually means you still have an inner voice that you're suppressing which needs to be heard. It manifests as a vibrational discord in your emotional body, which is felt as pain.

TAKE ACTION LIKE ACTOR JIM CARREY

Don't expect miracles to happen from just meditating and visualizing alone— you must also take action. You can't perform Meditative Programming and then go to your old watering hole for dinner. You must supplement your mental programming by taking the first steps. Go ahead and join a gym, start walking after dinner, go to a support group, start a yoga class, stock up at the store on cases of water and healthy foods... whatever makes you feel good in support of your new sober lifestyle and healthy self-image. A little physical activity goes a long way in building faith and confidence.

I watched an interview with comedian actor Jim Carrey on *The Oprah Winfrey Show*. Carrey explained how he used the Law of Attraction to attract his first ten million dollars. When he was just beginning his career, broke, and not getting anywhere, he decided to set a goal of making ten million dollars. He wrote himself a check in this amount, and kept it in his wallet, and would look at it often. He would boost his optimism by visualizing successful times which he would enjoy when he was rich and famous, living in luxury, having TV interviews, being on movie posters, working on commercials, and so on.

Carrey worked hard for well over a year and, although it took some time and a lot of hard work, the next big break for him was a contract for ten million for his first big movie. The Law of Attraction brought him what he had emotionally visualized with faith. What Carrey said next about taking action and visualizing was funny, but true. He said, "You can't visualize and then go make a sandwich and think it's going to happen."

Whether you goal is to get sober or make millions, you must take action too. You need to create your mental ideal, have faith in its outcome, but also take action towards its achievement. As the scriptures, stated, *"Even so faith, if it has no works, is dead in itself,"* James 2:14-26 (WEB)

FORGET ABOUT THE PAST SLIPS

Forget your past failures, remembering that was the *old* you. If you say that you cannot visualize yourself sober because you relapsed five times in the past two years, this is old, false thinking. In 1886 Mental Science writer R.W. Baldwin said:

> *"Practical power resides in ideas, and in the capacity for thinking lies the secret of health and disease. Memory is excellent, but the ability to forget is desirable also. We must learn the ability to forget in disease, the idea of disease, and think only in its stead, health."*

When and if you had any past slips, you did not know the mental-spiritual laws you do now. You didn't practice Meditative Programming or the Law of Attraction. You didn't have knowledge of mental healings and power of consciousness. The *new* you not only possess a new mind-spirit knowledge base, but also knows how to apply these secret powers to work and achieve any goals desired. You have learned the true secret.

Remember, countless super-achievers have already used these mind-spirit principles and the Law of Attraction to heal themselves, perform miraculous mind-power feats, and become great athletes, scholars, artists, and millionaires. You will now use these same immutable laws and principles for achieving sobriety, and attaining any other wishes you desire next.

Forgetting about a slip-up is the same as forgetting about the past. If a slip or a setback of any sort occurs, do not dwell on it. Just learn from it and continue on, knowing your mind-spirit powers are the strongest forces in the universe and will overcome any hurdles. This mental science program takes getting used to and you may have to make some adjustments in your applications. In 1906, William Atkinson wrote:

"The successful man believes in himself and his ultimate success, and, paying no attention to little setbacks, stumbles, tumbles and slips, presses on eagerly to the goal, believing all the time that he will get there...He is not steadily wishing he may get there—he simply feels and believes it, and thereby sets to operation the strongest forces known in the world of thought."

Get back on the horse that threw you, and keep focused on the road ahead. If you dwell on the negative, depressing things in life, you will attract more of it. Acknowledge, manage, and then file these learning lessons and then forget them.

YOUR SCREWED-UP PLEASURE THRESHOLD

One thing is for certain—when you get sober and clean, your ability to feel pleasure will be completely out of whack. Since we basically destroyed our brains and nervous systems with alcohol or drugs, our thresholds are now jacked-up and contorted.

It's like we just got out of a loud rock concert, and someone tries whispering to us on the car ride home. You can't hear a thing! We've blown out our sensitivity thresholds and it will take time and healing for them to return to their normal level again.

This not only applies to sensitivity to emotions, but also to physical feelings too. You're not gonna get snappy and alert with a cup of coffee if you're used to doing meth all day. You won't appreciate a sweet ice cream cone, if you're used to drinking a quart of vodka daily. And your sex life, ability to exercise, reading-memory skills, and so on may be off-kilter for a short while.

We are coming down from a hardcore-chemical lifestyle where we mainlined to hack our brains in getting pleasure. Our brain and senses are completely used to having dopamine, serotonin, endorphins, and adrenalin pumping at super high levels at demand whenever we ingested our drugs.

It will be challenging to make the simple things in life stimulating or attractive until we heal and get our thresholds restored and back to normal. When they are restored, you will be amazed at the abundance of healthy vibrations that give us pleasure. Once again you will enjoy the subtler frequencies of art, music, food, sex, exercise, love, and laughter.

DIAMONDS, FISH TANKS, AND CATCHING A BUZZ

Diamonds are valued at the measure of their purity or clarity. The fewer defects, and the better the clarity, the higher the value. It goes the same for the mind—the clearer it is, the more valuable it is.

Remember, addiction begins in the mind. The physical component of addiction is cleared up simply through a safe detox, but what remains is the monster mental obsession. For our own personal reasons, what we will miss and crave is not ingesting chemicals in our bodies, it's *getting fucked-up*. We will miss catching the *buzz* or high from drugs and booze. We still want the numbing effect, the warm glow, the shield to hide behind, the euphoria—that high that makes boring things fun.

We get addicted to the *feeling* or *effect* more so than the physical chemicals. When I was in full-blown addiction mode, I didn't care if I drank beer, wine, vodka, after-shave cologne, or Listerine. As long as it had alcohol in it, that's all I needed. The compulsion or obsession was to get numb, blur out reality, and enjoy the pain-free high or drunkenness. How I got there didn't matter after a while.

It is crucial to sobriety that we remove the desire for this buzz feeling, and replace it with a strong desire for mental clarity, peace of mind, and inner serenity. We must not only develop a strong dislike for the physical "taste" of the drug or drink, but more so for the effect. Remember, it puts a dampening effect on your ability to enjoy the subtler pleasures in life.

Don't forget that along with the pleasures of the buzz, you also had negative consequences that you should associate. Instead of remembering your high or buzz as pleasurable and numbing, think of the depression, misery, sickness, embarrassment, and bad circumstances it brought. Crave instead the peace and serenity that mental clarity brings with it. Ingrain this new desire deep into your psyche and inner vibrational state by daily affirmations and mental programming. I cannot overstate the importance of this step. Basically, get rid of any desire to be fucked up because you now truly love having clarity of mind. After a little time practicing mental science, this will soon become an ingrained belief.

I was at a large chain pet store not long ago and was browsing in the tropical fish section. There were two large salt water tank displays, both completely set up. Each tank contained an assortment of sea life—sea horses, crabs, bright rainbow-colored fish, neon minnows, baby sharks, brightly colored coral, and beautiful tropical sea plants. One of the tanks was brightly lit and perfectly crystal clear and crisp, and the other one was dark, stagnant, and murky. The fish and sea life in the clear tank were lively and jetting around the sparkling bubbling water in harmony, whereas in the polluted tank, they were lethargic, sickly, and even seemed panicky.

For whatever reason, it made me think of getting drunk or using drugs. The beautiful sober mind representing the crystal clear, colorful tank, brimming with life. The other tank was like a mind on drugs or alcohol—murky, dark, lifeless, chaotic, and sick.

As bizarre as it sounds, whenever I even have the slightest thought of drinking, I think of that clear colorful tank full of beautiful life, and why I would ever want to pollute it with chemicals. It would be like pouring a bucket of nasty crude oil into that clear, crisp lively tank. Mental clarity is my desired state of mind. It is a critical part of getting sober—to truly desire that clarity, harmony, and serenity.

IF ADDICTION ENTERS THE ROOM, DON'T FIGHT IT, SIMPLY LEAVE

Recall the phrase, *"What you resist, persists."* We are moving on from a chapter of our lives when we had an addiction problem to the next chapter, living sober. Keep in mind that this next chapter in life is not about a lifelong battle in recovery. When we quit, we quit. If you think alcohol and drugs have power over you, then they will have power over you. New Thought teacher Ralph Trine talks about right thinking when, in 1897, he wrote:

"If we fear it, or if we antagonize it, the chances are that it will have detrimental or even disastrous effects upon us. If we come into harmony with it by quietly recognizing and inwardly asserting our superiority over it, in the degree that we are able successfully to do this, in that degree will it carry with it no injury for us."

This applies to you drug or alcohol addiction—it's as powerful as you imagine it to be. Once you are physically detoxed, the rest is one hundred percent mental. And what fixes mental obsessions is correct thinking and mental science practices.

A therapist named Rich shared this little anecdote about fighting the addiction demon. Perform the following imaginary exercise: Picture yourself standing on the edge of a large, deep, and dark pit. The pit is lined with deathly spikes. You are holding a rope, and on the other end of the rope across the pit is a big, strong, ugly monster that represents your addiction (for me it was the drinking monster...so Bigfoot with a miller lite T-shirt on). The sight of the monster and pit are dark, gloomy, frightening, cold, and depressing. The monster is pulling at the rope trying to pull you into the pit, and every time he pulls, you pull back with an equal force. The rope is tight with tension, and your muscles are aching and stressed. This fight has been going on for a very long time, and you realize that you must continue this fight to stay alive. So, you fight with the monster with great effort and strain—if you lighten up he will surely pull you into the pit.

Then it dawns on you that you have another choice. Guess what else you can do? You can just let go of the rope, flip him the bird, and walk away in the other direction. Behind you is a beautiful, sunny landscape full of life. Yes, just walk away and go to the healthy life waiting for you. Why make it such a big fight? Just let go, turn away from it and start anew. The bigger you make the problem, the bigger it is. Why fight when you can just leave? It is better to take the creative choice of walking away than to take the competitive choice, which is to stay and fight the addiction. It is always the better choice to go after what you want, and not fight what you do not want. Where your attention goes, your energy goes, and your intention goes.

I myself have chosen to turn around and walk the other way. I will never forget the monster or the pit, and I pray and meditate every day that I never see them again. But my mental science tools will ensure that I will not go down that path to the pit again.

My reality has changed because I have changed my inner vibrational frequency by changing my beliefs, thoughts, and feelings about my inner self-image. There are those people who say that recovery is lifelong, and that addiction is a constant fight. They say they must grit their teeth and fight their demons and cravings every day.

Getting sober is not a fight if your curing and healing is done at the nucleus, your inner core, the mind and spirit. We treat and cure the cause and not the effect, the problem and not the symptom, the inner and not the outer world. When we correct the vibrational discord of our inner core self-image, we can restore harmony and health. The body and your physical conditions are simply physical expressions of the mind-spirit. Walter Matthew put it this way in 1922:

> *"People want health, happiness, power and abundance, but they fail to understand that all of these things are only effects, the cause being within themselves, brought into outward manifestation through the power of prayer, imagination, visualization and mental imagery. Let your mind be hospitable to lofty ideals and noble aspirations. See only the good and beautiful, and there will be no power in the universe that can keep these things from manifesting themselves in your life and experience. Never let your imagination dwell on undesirable things that you do not want to come into your experience."*

BE PREPARED TO RECEIVE YOUR GIFTS

In order for you to receive the manifestation of your wishes, you must be mentally prepared to give gratitude for already having received these things. You should have lived out your sober, healthy goal image mentally many times over with passion and in vivid detail. See and feel how your sober life would be throughout every one of life's conditions, whether you are at work, school, or at parties, or with your family, your friends, or at the gym.

You will never receive anything that you have not already imagined in your mind. It must have already been tuned-in, so that when it manifests, it is in resonance with your vibrational state. If you have not completely changed your inner harmony to that of a sober, healthy, and successful person, then the things which match this frequency will not come to fruition. You must be at the same frequency where you placed your order in order to receive it. It is in this reality you created it and in which it will manifest back to you.

How many times have you heard stories about rock stars who over-dosed on drugs once they acquired fame and fortune, or the successful movie actor who ends up in rehab, or the professional athletes who made millions in their careers and are now bankrupt and broke? These people successfully manifested their goals, but were not prepared to receive their successes. They did not play the mental tape of their goals all the way through. They stopped their goal self-imaging at the point they received fame and fortune, but forgot to also imagine and project how to live that way. As W. John Murray said in 1922:

> "When Solomon asked for wisdom and understanding he got riches in addition, for the one follows the other as the furrow follows the plough. It is where we ask for riches without wisdom or understanding that the Law fails to work, for we require wisdom and understanding to keep riches as well as to get and dispense them properly."

Be mentally prepared for all situations in your mind first. When you desire—picture and feel yourself in your new self-image goal of healthy, sober, and happy—make sure you try to include every event you can antici-pate facing, especially challenging ones involving triggers. Even if you get caught off guard with an unexpected, upsetting experience, you will be so vibrationally fit and strong that you will handle it easily. Play the tape all the way through.

GET HIGH ON THE MOUNTAINTOP

When your frequency level is low, your energy is low, your mood is down, and your consciousness is constricted. When this happens, you cannot see the trees from the forest, you feel confined and stressed, and your consciousness is contracted in lieu of expanded (you probably have not meditated lately!)

When your goal image is in the forefront of your mind, you are generating positive vibrations, and with strong faith, your frequency is high. When you are in this state of being, it is like standing on a mountain versus down in the valley. Being aligned with your goals, you are positively charged, and existing at a high vibrational frequency. You are on the mountaintop seeing the big panoramic view, and you can feel yourself living your goals.

When you are down in the valley, you can only see what's right in front of your nose, and have no true vision, or big picture. Down in the valley, the frequency is low, dense, congested, stressful, and uncomfortable. You want to get back "high" on the mountain top. You used to do this with drugs, but now give yourself a vibrational boost with using correct thought-images and mental science.

When you raise your frequency, your entire perspective changes, and you will perceive what harmonizes with this higher level. You see the glass half full, instead of half empty. It's truly a reality change, since reality is what we perceive. Raise your frequency with faith in the manifestation of your goal self-image.

CONCLUSION

We live in a universe where mind is in everything, from the atom to the cosmos. On a metaphysical level, we, as humans, are simply vibrational energy beings. Our inner self-image vibrational state is our signature frequency which uses the Law of Attraction to create our physical bodies and external conditions in life.

When we harbor and internalize trauma, stress, or negative thoughts, this manifests as a vibrational discord and is felt as pain, or a hole inside. If the pain is not mitigated, lessened, or removed in healthy ways, we find drugs and alcohol to numb and anesthetize it. When we continue and abuse using this method, we get addicted both mentally and spiritually.

To get sober, we must firstly remove the physical attachment to the chemicals, detox our bodies, and then remove the desire for the feeling or effects of these drugs or alcohol. We replace this with the heartfelt love and desire for mental clarity, serenity, and harmony.

Mind or intelligent consciousness is the originating cause of the universe, which creates form, or matter in the image it projects. Humankind has the ability to create in this same manner using mental science and faith. A thought-image, mixed with strong desire and faith in its actualization, will manifest the physical condition. Remember, mind is always the cause, and the physical conditions are always the effect. This is a spiritual law of creation.

We go deep into our inner self and release the control these inner fears and pains have. We give forgiveness and gratitude, release resentments, and change our inner core self-image to a positive healthy and sober vibrational state.

You will achieve your sobriety and health wish when you magnetize yourself with the frequency of already having achieved your goal. Your body, circumstances, conditions, people, and places will all transmute around your new vibrational frequency to manifest this goal as a reality.

You will attract all of the external elements necessary for its attainment, and internally your body will heal and transform itself. Your brain heals, organs repair, and cravings disappear as you think in a natural, healthy manner. Your thought habits, along with your diet and exercise routines, will subconsciously start changing. New healthy options will come about, and sober friends and activities will gather around you. Your new image is attracting exactly what it needs to materialize your goal.

Remember to take your visualizations to the next step and magnetize yourself to be the sober person achieving that next goal in life. See, feel, and believe yourself *after* you are sober, and running that 5k race, losing that weight, starting that new career, starting that great relationship, or buying that house. When you see your sobriety as having already occurred in your mind, then it will become so in reality. Keep in mind, your goal is not the fight for sobriety—it is the life *after* sobriety.

When you hit a troubling fork in the road, and there is a healthy and unhealthy choice, play the tape all the way through on both choices. You will make the right choice.

Recovery is a one-time milestone, not a life-long battle. Other people are welcome to say they are in recovery for the rest of their lives, but not for me. My addiction will never be forgotten, nor disrespected, and I will give gratitude for sobriety daily in meditation. But the battle has ended, it is history; it has no power over me anymore.

You are in now in control of your life. The choice of sobriety, health, happiness, love, and success is simply that—a choice. Create your new self, desire your new self, and use this powerful new mental science knowledge to *be* your new self. Always remember, you create your own reality.

So, you now know what worked for me. I hope it now works for you. Have faith in these principles because they will work! God bless, and Godspeed.

Recommended Websites

www.abraham-hicks.com: Nonphysical entity Abraham channeled by Ester Hicks.

www.bashar.org: Nonphysical entity Bashar channeled by Daryl Anka.

www.Biblehub.com: Translations of all Bible versions.

www.delorescannon.com: Famous regressive hypnotherapist Delores Cannon.

www.ebenalexander.com: Dr. Eben Alexander's story of afterlife experienced during coma.

www.freemeditation.com: Much on meditation basics and varieties.

www.heartmath.com: The Heartmath Organization, studies on the heart and consciousness.

www.newthoughtlibrary.com: Great resource for free New Thought reading material.

www.noetic.org: Institute of Noetic Sciences—mind and consciousness research and testing.

www.sacred-texts.com: Great resource for spiritual, metaphysical, and philosophic books.

www.sethlearningcenter.org: Spirit Seth channeled by Jane Roberts.

www.tm.org: Transcendental meditation information.

www.theconsciouslife.com/meditation: Information on meditation.

www.thelawofattraction com: Just like it says, the LOA with many good articles.

www.yogananda-srf.com: Self-realization fellowship of Paramahansa Yogananda.

www.zero-wise.com: Spiritual health information with Dr. Hew Len

Bibliography

A.F.T.S., *Mind* Magazine, *Theosophy*, Pg. 31, New York, Alliance Pub. Co., Vol. XIII, Feb. 1904

Allen, James, *Man, King of Mind, Body, and Circumstance*, New York, Thomas Crowell & Co., 1911

Atkinson, William, *Mind and Body*, Chicago, The Progress Co., 1910

Atkinson, William, *Dynamic Thought*, California, Segnogram Publishing, 1906

Atkinson, William, *Mind Power the Secret to Mental Magic*, Chicago, Advanced Thought Publishing, 1912

Atkinson, William, *Thought Vibration*, Chicago, New Thought Pub. Co., 1906

Atkinson, William, *The Arcane Formula*, Chicago, The Arcane Book Concern, 1909

Bailey, Alice, *The Consciousness of the Atom*, New York, Lucifer Pub., 1922

Baldwin, R.W., *Ideas Rule, Mental Science Magazine*, Chicago, Mental Science University Pub., Vol II, No. 4, January 1886

Behrend, Genevieve, *Your Invisible Powers*, Html Gutenberg, 1921

Besant, Annie, *The influence of Alcohol Lecture*, Adyar, Madras, India, Theosophical Publishing House, 1898

Besant, Annie, *Thought Power its Control and Culture*, Illinois, Theosophical Publishing House, 1901

Besant, Annie; C.W. Leadbeater, *Thought Forms*," London, Theosophical Publishing House, 1901

Bible, The World English Bible Version (WEB), public domain, HTML, Biblehub.com

Butler, Hiram, *The Esoteric Magazine*, VI, No. 2, *Man and His Capabilities*, Boston, Jul.-Aug. 1887

Davis, Stanton, *Mind* Magazine, *Faith and Healing*, pg. 338, 342, New York, Alliance Pub. Co., Vol IX, 1901–1902;

Del Mar, Eugene, *The Conquest of Disease*, London, L.N. Fowler, 1922

Dumont, Theron, *The Master Mind*, Chicago, Advanced Thought Pub. Co., 1918

Evans, W.F., *Mind-Cure Journal*, *Mental Healing and the Doctrine of Conversion*, New York, A.J. Swarts Pub., Vol. two, N2, 1885

Fillmore, Charles, *Christian Healing*, Kansas City, Unity School of Christianity Pub., 1917

Grumbine, J.C.F., *Psychometry*, Boston, Order of the White Rose, 1910

Grumbine, J.C.F., *Telepathy*, Boston, The Order of the White Rose, 1910

Haanel, Charles, *Mental Chemistry*, St. Louis, Haanel Pub., 1922

Haanel, Charles, *Master Key System*, St. Louis, Inland Printery, 1917

Holmes, Ernest, *Creative mind and Success*, HTML, Sacret-texts.com, 1919

Holmes, Fenwicke, *The Law of Mind in Action*, N.Y., McBride & Co., 1919

Holmes, Fenwicke, *The Faith that Heals*, New York, McBride & Co., 1921

Hopkins, Erastus Whitford., *Science of New Thought*, Conn., The New Thought Book Concern, 1904

Hudson, Thomas, *The Law of Mental Medicine*, Chicago, A.C. Mclurg and Co, 1902

Hudson, Thomas, *Law of Psychic Phenomenon*, Chicago, Mclurg & Co., 1893

Ingalese, Richard, *The History and Power of Mind*, N.Y. The Occult Book Concern, 1902

Mann, C.H., *The Healing of the Body through the Soul, Mental Science Magazine*, Chicago, Mental Science University Pub., Vol II, No. 4, January 1886

Marden, Orison Sweet, *The Miracle of Right Thought*, New York, Crowell & Co. 1910

Marshall, J.H.A. *Mind* Magazine, *Mental Vibrations*, pg. 160, New York, Alliance Pub. Co., Vol XIII Jan. 1904

Matthews, Walter, Human Life from Many Angles, Ohio, Goodwill Publishing, 1922

Mulford, Prentice, *Thoughts are Things*, London, G. Bell & Sons, 1908

Murray, John William, *The Astor Lectures, Realm of Reality*, N.Y. The Divine Science Publishing Co., 1922

Paterson, Charles Brody, *Mind* Magazine, New York, Alliance Pub. Co., Vol IX, *Laws of Health*, 1901–1902

Patterson, Charles *Mind* Magazine, Vol. XIII, Jan. 1904

Sadler, Dr. William, *The Physiology of Faith and Fear*, Chicago, A.C. McClurg & Co., 1912

Sargent, Epes, *The Scientific Basis of Spiritualism*, Boston, Colby and Rich Pub., 1882.

Sinnett, A.P., *The Occult World*, London, Trubner & Co., 1883

Swami Panchadasi, *Clairvoyance and Occult Powers*, N.J., Yogi Pub. Society, 1916

Towne, Elizabeth, *You and Your Forces*, Mass., E. Towne Publishing, 1905

Towne, William, *The Way to Perfect Healing*, Mass., W.E. Towne Pub., 1910

Trine, Ralph Waldo, *Character Building Thought Power*, N.Y., Crowell Co, 1900

Trine, Ralph Waldo, *The Higher Powers of Mind and Spirit*, N.Y., Dodge Pub Co., 1917

Trine, Ralph Waldo, *In Tune with the Infinite*, London, Bell & Sons Pub., 1903

Trine, Ernest, *Creative Mind and Success*, Html Sacret-texts.com, 1919

Troward, Thomas, *The Edinburg Lectures*, NY, R.M. McBride, 1909

The Three Initiates, *The Kybalion*, Chicago, Yogi Publications, 1912

Troward, Thomas, The *Law and the Word*, N.Y., R.M. McBride Co., 1917

Unknown Author, *The Esoteric Magazine*, VI, No. 5, *The Law of Persistent Desire, or Prayer*, Pg. 141, Boston, Oct.-Nov. 1887

Vishita, Swami Bhakta, *The Invisible Powers*, Chicago, Advanced Thought Publishing Company, 1919

Von Wiegand, Karl, *Mind* Magazine, *Absent Treatments in Healing*, New York, Alliance Pub. Co., Vol IX, 1901–1902

Walker, Edward, *Thoughts are Things*, Chicago, The Progress, 1909

Wattles, Wallace, *The Science of Getting Rich*, Mass., E. Towne Pub., 1915

Wattles, Wallace, *The Science of being Well*, Mass., Towne Publishing Co., 1910

Williston, T.A., *The Esoteric Magazine*, VOL X, *Vibration*, California, Esoteric Publishing Co., Apr. 1897

Whipple, Leander, *Manual of Mental science*, N.Y. Metaphysical Publishing, 1911

Young, Janet, *The Subconscious Mind and its Illuminating Light*, San Francisco, Whitaker & Ray, 1909

A great effort was made to verify that certain cited works were pre-1923 Public Domain and thus copyright exempt status. If a copyright infringement is discovered, please contact the author with proper documentation, and the works will be promptly removed and/or corrected. Thank you.

About the Author

Thorne Ivy has a Bachelor's of Science in Business and practices in the field of real estate. Originally from New York, Ivy now resides in central Florida where he enjoys running, sports, and the ocean. This is Ivy's first book. He currently is working on his second book, revolving around sports achievement using these same mental science and spiritual law principles.

If you have any comments, or would like to contact the author, please visit the website:

www.thorneivy.com